MW01659846

# *Biblical* COUNSELING
## QUICK REFERENCE GUIDE

*Personal & Emotional Issues*

DR. TIM CLINTON
AND
DR. RON HAWKINS

Copyright © 2007 by Dr. Tim Clinton and Dr. Ron Hawkins

All rights reserved. No portion of this book may be reproduced, stored in a retrieval system, or transmitted in any form or by any means—electronic, mechanical, photocopy, recording, or any other—except for brief quotation in printed reviews, without the prior permission of the publisher.

Published by Thomas Nelson Publishers, a Division of Thomas Nelson, Inc., P.O. Box 141000, Nashville, Tennessee, 37214.

All Scripture taken from the New King James Version. Copyright © 1979, 1980, 1982 by Thomas Nelson, Inc. Used by permission. All rights reserved.

Produced with the assistance of the Livingstone Corporation (www.LivingstoneCorp.com). Project staff includes:

Linda Taylor

Thomas G. Britton, M.S.

Janine Hess Campbell, MA, LPC

Janyce Dale-Smithley , B.SC. M.Sc.

Albert V. Gernovich, M.S.

Joan Lloyd Guest, MSW, LCSW

Nancy Kane, MS, LCPC

Sally Marcey, LCPC, LMFT

Printed in the United States of America
01 02 03 04 05 — 9 8 7 6 5 4 3 2 1

# Table of Contents

# Introduction

Since the American Association of Christian Counselors began, many people have asked us to catalog the best practices to provide insights and resources at a moment's notice. We're excited to produce the first volume of our *Biblical Counseling Quick Reference Guide,* and we trust that God will use it to equip thousands of believers as we care for hurting people in our churches and our communities.

The promise of modern, mind-boggling advances in every field of science and technology is that life would be simpler, easier, and more fulfilling. Reality, however, is that all of these advances have had the net effect of raising our expectations to unrealistic levels and intensifying stress. Everywhere we look, we find people who desperately need to experience God's care. The Scriptures provide insight into God's compassion and care. David wrote, "The Lord is close to the brokenhearted; he rescues those whose spirits are crushed" (Psalm 34:18). More than ever before, people need God's loving, transforming touch, and amazingly, He has chosen to use people like us as channels of His grace. Our role of caring for hurting people is an unspeakable privilege and an awesome responsibility. We step into others' lives at their critical point of need to "bear one another's burdens" (Galatians 6:2).

One of the primary qualifications for this kind of ministry is authenticity. We can empathize with others because we have walked a difficult path in our own lives and found God to be faithful. Our experience of desperation, turning to God, and finding Him as a loving, strong Father gives us compassion for others who struggle. Paul wrote the Corinthians to explain the source of our authenticity in helping others. He observed, "God is our merciful Father and the source of all comfort. He comforts us in all our troubles so that we can comfort others. When they are troubled, we will be able to give them the same comfort God has given us" (2 Corinthians 1:3-4).

- *If you are a pastor,* virtually every family in your congregation has been affected by addiction, divorce, violence, depression, grief, and other painful evidences of fallen people living in a fallen world. You can use this guide:
    - to give you insights for sermon topics and illustrations,
    - to prepare you to meet with hurting people who come to you for help,
    - to equip you to teach others who want to help hurting people, and
    - to provide resources for staff members and other leaders of the church as you shepherd God's flock together.
- *If you are a professional counselor,* you are already very familiar with the topics in this guide, but it can help you:

- accurately determine the client's problems by using the assessments in each section,
- to see a client's problem and solutions from a biblical perspective,
- give clear guidance to your clients so they can take strong steps forward, and
- be more aware of resources for you client to stimulate right thinking, processing, and action.

- *If you are a lay counselor in your church*, either in a formal care giving ministry or informally, this guide is a valuable resource for you. I recommend that you take time to read through the entire book, marking key points in each section that stand out to you. As you become familiar with the topics, symptoms, approaches, and resources, you will know where to look as you prepare to meet with people who have these problems. Then, the guide will help you:
  - assess the nature and severity of the person's problem,
  - guide your conversation through questions as you give "wise counsel,"
  - remind you that there are limits for a lay-caregiver's role, and
  - assist you in making the proper referral to a professional or agency.

All of us—from the most seasoned professional counselor to the layperson learning to help a hurting friend—need to develop character qualities and skills so that our care reflects the grace and truth of Christ. God has given us abilities and spiritual gifts, and He wants to build into us the qualities of compassion, authenticity, and integrity. No matter how many sharply honed skills we employ, and no matter how much experience we have had, all of us need to depend on God's Spirit to guide us as we care for people, and we depend on Him to touch people's lives with His power and love.

## HOW TO USE THE BIBLICAL COUNSELING QUICK REFERENCE GUIDE

If you have already looked through some of the 40 topics in this guide, you probably noticed that each topic follows an eight-part outline. Before you start using this guide, we want to tell you about the purpose of each of these parts.

### 1) Portraits

The Portraits show how a specific issue (e.g., depression, parenting) surfaces in individual lives and relationships. We provide several portraits for each topic because one issue can present itself in different ways in different individuals' lives.

### 2) Definitions and Key Thoughts

The Definitions and Key Thoughts sections cover some of the most current statistical findings and clinical insights for each issue. This research will help you understand the nuances of the problem and provide direction for your conversations with the person.

**3) Assessment Interview**

The Assessment Interview for each topic provides important, probing questions you can use to assess the person's needs and situation. Often, this section often includes rule-out questions to help you determine if the presenting problem is the actual one, or if a hidden problem is lurking unnoticed.

**4) Wise Counsel**

Wise Counsel provides additional insights into the presenting problem, the biblical perspective, the process of healing and restoration, or another issue related to your care for people. Sometimes the insights in this section are clinical, and sometimes they are pastoral, but in every case, they give added perspective to help you meet the needs of people.

**5) Action Steps**

Action Steps is one of the most important sections in the guide because it helps your conversation move from *assessment* and *problem identification* to creating a *map* and *plan* for healing, recovery and growth. Without an action plan, people are often confused and wander aimlessly without making progress.

**6) Biblical Insights**

In the Biblical Insights section, we provide passages of Scripture that relate to the topic, and we've added several important points for each passage to explain its significance. You may want to explain his content to the person, or you may choose to study it by yourself to enrich your understanding of how God works to change lives.

**7) Prayer Starter**

Many Christians welcome—and even expect—prayer as an integral part of the counseling process, but prayer is not an appropriate intervention with every person you see. If a person isn't a believer or has shown resistance to God, you can pray silently during the session or after the appointment is over and the person has left. We realize individual preferences about prayer and the needs of those we help differ greatly, but we didn't want to overlook prayer as an essential element in biblical counseling. The Prayer Starter sections provide a few simple lines to begin lifting up a prayer out loud or silently; in or out of the appointment.

**8) Recommended Resources**

This guide is not meant to provide you with an exhaustive look at any of the 40 topics. For each one, these pages only give an overview and provide a brief template for addressing the needs. Continuing education is very important, so each Recommended Resources section lists at least a few books or multimedia programs we have found to be useful and trustworthy.

Some of the topics in this guide will seem more relevant to you because you've experienced a particular problem and you've seen God touch your life with His grace and strength. Take time, however, to read through the entire guide so that you develop a working knowledge of each type of problem people face. Then, when you meet with someone with a particular need, you can pull the guide off the shelf to refresh your perspective and counsel the person more effectively.

We hope this guide enriches your ministry and equips you as you care for hurting people.

## RECOMMENDED RESOURCES

The AACC provides training, curricula, books, workshops, and other resources to equip people to care for others. At the end of each topic in this guide, you'll find specific resources for that issue, but we recommend additional materials and online help for those who want broader input on counseling topics and skills. These include:

- *The Bible for Hope: Caring for People God's Way,* by Dr. Tim Clinton, published by Thomas Nelson Publishers
- *Caring for People God's Way: Personal and Emotional Issues, Addictions, Grief, and Trauma,* by Tim Clinton, Archibald Hart, and George Ohlschlager

Other valuable training resources are offered through the AACC's "Light University." Courses include:

- *Caring for Kids God's Way,*
- *Breaking Free,*
- *Extraordinary Women,*
- *Healthy Sexuality,* and
- *Marriage Works.*

In addition, the AACC offers many more resources and training on two web sites:

- www.ecounseling.com, and
- www.aacc.net

Continue to sharpen your skills and deepen your understanding of issues that affect the people God puts in your path. These resources can help.

* * *

The American Association of Christian Counselors has more than 50,000 members throughout the country and around the world. The AACC is dedicated to providing the finest resources to help professional counselors, pastors, and lay counselors care for hurting people. Outstanding training, books, and events augment membership benefits that include the magazine, Christian Counseling Today. For more information about the AACC, go to www.aacc.net.

# Abortion

1

## PORTRAITS

- Kate is in trouble—big time. She's got a scholarship waiting at her chosen college, a handsome boyfriend, a leadership role in her church youth group, and an at-home pregnancy test that just turned positive. She can't give up her dreams for this one mistake. Besides, it's such a simple procedure and no one needs to know.

Almost one million (853,485) legal induced abortions were reported to the cbc for 2001.

- "I have been forgiven, I know it, but why can't I get over this?" Nancy kept repeating the words as she glanced down the pew at church where her two little daughters squirmed beside her, waiting for the chance to be released to go to children's church. She tried to concentrate on the sermon but the Right to Life announcement in the bulletin claimed all of her attention. She frowned and tried to convince herself, "I didn't realize what I was doing."

2

## DEFINITIONS AND KEY THOUGHTS

- People may come to you because they are considering an abortion or because they feel shame for having one years ago.
- The term "abortion" actually refers to any premature expulsion of a human fetus, whether naturally spontaneous, as in a miscarriage, or artificially induced, as in a surgical or chemical abortion. Today, the most common usage of the term applies to abortions that are **artificially induced**. (www.nrlc.org)
- A young woman with an unplanned pregnancy will need to understand that the **"quick and easy" choice is neither quick nor easy** but will carry repercussions for the rest of her life.

In 2001, the ratio of abortions per 1000 live births was 246.

- Often a woman chooses to keep the abortion a secret, especially if she is a part of a Christian community that she perceives might be judgmental or condemning. Her own family members might not know. Therefore, the **grief and loss** surrounding an abortion may remain unprocessed for years.
- An abortion is **not only experienced as a loss but also as a trauma**. Some of the possible side effects are both a tendency to re-experience the trauma with dreams or flashbacks, as well as a tendency to avoid all thoughts or feelings associated with the abortion.
- Other possible **side effects** from the trauma of an abortion are emotional numbing, sleep disorders, difficulty concentrating, hyper vigilance, depression, guilt, and an inability of the woman to forgive herself and others.

- Coping alone with the reality of an abortion is isolating and may reinforce a woman's **sense of shame.** Self-destructive behaviors such as substance abuse may also be present.
- If someone confides in you that she has had an abortion, realize that in sharing this experience, she has decided to trust you. **Be careful to affirm her for being honest, and avoid any verbal or non-verbal behaviors** that might complicate her guilt and shame.

### Myths about Abortion

Many women who are considering an abortion believe these statements are true:

**Myth 1:** "It's a simple procedure; life will resume on Monday."

**Myth 2:** "It's not a baby; it's a blob of tissue."

**Myth 3:** "It's okay; abortion is legal."

**Myth 4:** "My life will be ruined if I have this baby."

**Myth 5:** "It's *my* choice, *my* responsibility, *my* decision."

**Myth 6:** "It's okay to have an abortion; there's something wrong with the baby."

**Myth 7:** "I am alone; no one cares about me."

**Myth 8:** "I don't deserve forgiveness; I knew it was wrong."

**Myth 9:** "I got what I deserved; I did it more than once."

**Myth 10:** "This won't hurt; the pain will subside."

**Myth 11:** "It is my only option; he doesn't want the baby."

**Myth 12:** "It's okay in cases of rape or incest."[2]

(from *A Time to Speak: A Healing Journal for Post-Abortive Women*)

## ASSESSMENT INTERVIEW

**Q1** Show the myths to her. Introduce them and read them, then ask, "Which of these are affecting how you're feeling today?"

### For the woman contemplating abortion

**Q2** How do you know that you are pregnant? Have you had a medical examination? *(These gentle questions about the pregnancy will help the person feel comfortable and take responsibility.)*

**Q3** How far along are you in your pregnancy?

**Q4** What are your current life circumstances?

Consider the findings from a survey of 252 women who joined a post-abortion support group:

- 70% had a prior negative moral view of abortion
- 30-60% wanted to keep their babies
- Over 80% would have carried to term with better circumstances or more support of loved ones
- 53% felt "forced" to have the abortion by people in their lives
- 64% felt "forced" to have the abortion by circumstances in their lives
- Almost 40% were still hoping to learn of some alternative to abortion when they sat down for counseling at the abortion clinic

—David C. Reardon[1]

**Q5** What do you expect will be your family's response to your pregnancy?

**Q6** Do you have adequate social support?

**Q7** Who is the baby's father? What kind of relationship do you have with him?

**Q8** Have you considered any other options besides abortion? Have you thought about carrying the baby to term?

**Q9** What are some possible results in your life if you have this abortion? What might be the results if you make a different choice? *(Often, abortion is chosen because no other option looks even possible. Sometimes the decision to have an abortion is made quickly to "solve the problem." Communicate that she has some time to make her decision, and help her see that her life will not be "ruined" if she carries her baby to term.)*

**Q10** Do you have any questions about pregnancy and abortion? *(Don't assume that she is fully informed about either.)*

> *While an abortion terminates a pregnancy, the resulting problems can linger and even surface years later. Pro-abortion organizations acknowledge that up to 10 percent of women who have had abortions may also have serious psychiatric aftermath.*
>
> —Yvonne Florczak-Seeman

### For the woman who had an abortion in the past

**Q2** What is currently causing distress in your life?

**Q3** Take me back and tell me what happened. *(Listen for any signs of post-traumatic stress, such as disturbing dreams or triggers that bring the event to mind again. By choosing to begin to tell you her story, she is breaking her silence, which is both the beginning of the healing process and potentially disturbing because denial of the event is no longer possible.)*

**Q4** At the time, what were the main reasons for you making the choice that you did?

**Q5** Do you feel depressed, down, or sad most of the time?

**Q6** Do you have difficulty eating or sleeping?

**Q7** Do you have suicidal thoughts?

**Q8** Are you using drugs or alcohol to deal with the pain?

**Q9** How are you managing life now? What triggers your pain?

**Q10** Do you feel that you have been forgiven by God? Why or why not?

**Q11** Do you feel that you can forgive yourself? Why or why not?

## 4 WISE COUNSEL

### Wise words for the woman contemplating abortion

Be sure to provide her with **practical support** to encourage her to carry her baby to term. Have information on hand about agencies that provide medical care and a home to stay in for pregnant women. Emphasize to her that she is making a decision for both her life and her baby's life. Encourage her to see the longer perspective rather than getting to college next semester or keeping her place on a sports team, but avoid any hint of a judgmental attitude.

Address any **behaviors that endanger her safety,** such as suicidal behavior or substance abuse.

## ACTION STEPS 5

### For the woman contemplating abortion

#### 1. Consider the Options

- The woman may feel that her only option is an abortion, but she has other alternatives. Throughout the United States, nearly 3,000 Crisis Pregnancy Centers are staffed by volunteers who want to explain the alternatives and who will lovingly help her.
- Find the nearest CPC in your community. Look in the Yellow Pages under the heading "Abortion Alternatives," or call, toll-free, 1 (800) 848-LOVE.

#### 2. Communicate

- Discuss the need to communicate with other family members about the situation.
- Explore the best approach for talking with family members. You may need to be involved as a third party to facilitate understanding and help explain the reasons for her choice.

*A baby's heart begins to beat around 22 days after conception.*

#### 3. Get Help

If she is a minor, encourage the girl and her parents to contact the Crisis Pregnancy Center together.

#### 4. Follow Up

- Be sure to follow up with her by setting another appointment.
- Emphasize that although she may regret her pregnancy, she can begin immediately to make some wise choices regarding the future of her baby.
- If she decides to have the abortion, continue to be gracious and supportive. She will need a wise friend as she deals with the shame and grief.

### For the woman who had an abortion in the past

#### 1. Tell Her Story

Encourage her to tell more of her story in future discusions with you and through journaling.

There have been more than 40 million abortions in the twenty-six years since the U.S. Supreme Court legalized unrestricted abortion on January 22, 1973.

### 2. Get Help

Several organizations and materials exist to facilitate healing from an abortion. Know which ones exist in your area for a referral. Some organizations to look for include A Time To Speak, Project Rachael, and Victims of Choice.

### 3. Find Support

If there is a confidential grief support group in your area, encourage her to attend.

### 4. Be Reassured

- Be sure to communicate both verbally and non-verbally your acceptance of her and God's forgiveness for her.
- Healing from an abortion is a process and certainly can't be accomplished in one session, however healing is possible. Reassure her that forgiveness, including an ability to accept God's forgiveness and to forgive herself, are possible through God's grace.
- Abortion is not the unforgivable sin.

6

## BIBLICAL INSIGHTS

***If men fight, and hurt a woman with child, so that she gives birth prematurely, yet no harm follows, he shall surely be punished accordingly as the woman's husband imposes on him; and he shall pay as the judges determine. —Exodus 21:22***

- This verse shows God's protection of the most defenseless people on the planet—children in the womb. Even causing a premature but otherwise healthy birth was a punishable offense.
- God is the champion of life and has always protected women, children, and the weakest members of society.

A Los Angeles Times poll found that 74% of women who admitted having had an abortion stated that they believe abortion is morally wrong.[3]

***Your eyes saw my substance, being yet unformed. And in Your book they all were written, the days fashioned for me, when as yet there were none of them. —Psalm 139:16***

- God knows each person from the moment of conception. His eyes see the unformed body in the mother's womb.
- Many claim that a child in the womb is no more than a mass of tissue, but the Bible makes it clear that God sees the tiny embryo as a new life with a future already prepared.
- To abort a child is to end a human life unjustly—in short, to commit murder.

***Before I formed you in the womb I knew you; before you were born I sanctified you; I ordained you a prophet to the nations. —Jeremiah 1:5***

- God is well acquainted with every individual from the time each person is conceived. He has plans for each one.
- God knows everything, and sadly, He knows that some young lives will end all too soon.

***Then Herod, when he saw that he was deceived by the wise men, was exceedingly angry; and he sent forth and put to death all the male children who were in Bethlehem and in all its districts, from two years old and under, according to the time which he had determined from the wise men. —Matthew 2:16***

- Although the arguments over abortion almost always use the language of agonizing choices between two lives, the practice of abortion almost always comes down to the choice between a life and convenience, or between a life and other plans, or between a life and a lifestyle.
- The thinking that makes an unborn child disposable doesn't have to change much in order to consider the elimination of unwanted living children.
- The defenders of the "right of choice" believe they can make any choice they want and that choice is right because they made it. Choice may be a human right, but every choice isn't a right one. The right to life is higher than the right to choose.
- There is an absolute standard in the character and revelation of God. All choices we make will be measured against that standard, and we will be accountable for them.

*The highest percentages of reported abortions were for women unmarried (82%), white (55%), and aged less than 25 years (52%).*[4]

## PRAYER STARTER

Lord, we pray for Your grace and wisdom to overflow into my friend's life. She is worried, scared, and needs a touch from You . . .

## RECOMMENDED RESOURCES

*Aborted Women—Silent No More*, by David C. Reardon

*Forbidden Grief: The Unspoken Pain of Abortion*, by Theresa Burke

*Post-Abortion Kit: Resources for Those Suffering from the Aftermath of Abortion*, by Focus on the Family

*A Season to Heal: Help and Hope for Those Working through Post-Abortion Stress*, by Luci Freed and Penny Yvonne Salazar

*A Time to Speak: A Healing Journal for Post-Abortive Women*, by Yvonne Florczak-Seeman. Published by Love From Above, Inc. Books can be purchased at www.lovefromaboveinc.com.

Web site: www.family.org (Focus on the Family)

Web site: www.jfaweb.org (Justice for All)

# Addictions

## 1 PORTRAITS

- Rachel was very active in the church, along with her husband and young children. Although she was not always reliable, she was eager to help. She attended church regularly—even the evening services. One Sunday evening Rachel came in late and loudly. She was obviously drunk. Her children were in tow, but very embarrassed.
- Tim never seemed to have money for all his bills. He also seemed to be sick a lot with a constantly stuffy nose. A member of the congregation saw him on the street giving money to a man in a passing car. The man handed him a small package. When he asked Tim about it, Tim reacted, "Oh, it's just a prescription I needed."
- Dawn loved Bingo games. No one thought much about it until a neighbor discovered her young children home alone one night while Dawn was playing cards at the Bingo parlor.
- Reggie had always been famous for how many beers he could drink without feeling any effects—but something had changed. He'd been drunk several times recently, according to friends, and last night he was arrested for DUI.

*Therefore, if the Son makes you feel free, you shall be free indeed.*
*-John 8:36.*

## 2 DEFINITIONS AND KEY THOUGHTS

- An addiction is **a dependence on a substance** (alcohol, prescription medicine, marijuana, street drugs, food, or cigarettes) **or activity** (gambling, sex, and shopping).
- An addiction is **a physical** (as in alcohol or most other drugs) **or psychological** (as in gambling or shopping) **compulsion** to use a substance or activity **in order to cope with everyday life.** For example, without alcohol, the alcoholic does not feel "normal" and can't function well.
- Addiction is a behavior that is **habitual and difficult or seemingly impossible to control**. It leads to activity that is designed solely to **obtain the substance or cover up its use**—the housewife hiding bottles all over the house, the drug addict shoplifting to support his habit, or the gambler embezzling to pay off debts.
- Characterized by the **defense mechanism of denial**, the addict blames his or her problems on someone else—the boss is too difficult, the spouse isn't affectionate enough, the kids are disobedient, or the friends are too persuasive. The addict refuses to take responsibility.
- **Drug addiction is the biochemical dependence** on a substance— over time the body needs the substance in ever-increasing amounts to stave off the symptoms of withdrawal.

*50% of child abuse and neglect cases are connected with the alcohol or drug use of a guardian.*[1]

- **Non-drug addictions** include compulsive overeating, gambling, sexual addiction such as that to pornography (see the section on Pornography), and compulsive spending.

### Causes of Addiction

- **Emotional:** Addicts are emotionally wounded. One study of sex addicts found 81% to be sexually abused, 74% physically abused, and 97% emotionally abused. [2]
- **Relational:** Addictive behaviors are related to troublesome early life relationships. For adults, addiction causes stress in interpersonal relationships and leads to social difficulties. [3]
- **Physical:** Addicts become physically dependent on their substances, developing tolerance and needing more to get the same effect, and experiencing withdrawal without them.
- **Cognitive and Behavioral:** Christians who struggle with addictions often have illogical or irrational thoughts that cause them to forget their identity as children of God. Unrealistic expectations about themselves and others are also common.
- **Spiritual:** At its core, addiction is rebellion against God. In addition, the addiction—drugs, alcohol, food, work, sex, or any other substance or behavior—becomes a false idol to the addict.

### Character of Addiction

- **Unmanageability:** For addicts, their dependency on the addiction makes their lives out of control.
- **Neuro-chemical Tolerance:** God designed our bodies to adapt to what is presented. Therefore, addicts experience tolerance—their bodies need increasing amounts of a chemical to procure the same effect.
- **Progression:** Many addicts begin by simply experimenting—trying out a drug, going to a casino, or taking a puff on a cigarette. However, because more of a chemical is needed to achieve an effect, the addict will increase addictive actions in strength or frequency.
- **Feeling Avoidance:** The addiction is used to improve the addict's emotional or psychological state—it is a way of avoiding feelings of loneliness, anxiety, anger, sorrow, etc.
- **Consequences:** Estrangement from God, the manifestation of habitual sin, health issues, and social and interpersonal problems are all consequences common to addiction.

### *Serenity Prayer*

God take and
receive my liberty,
my memory, my
understanding and will,
All that I am and
have He has given me

God grant me the
serenity
to accept the things
I cannot change.
Courage to change
the things I can,
And wisdom to know
the difference

Living one day at a time
Enjoying one
moment at a time
Accepting hardships as
the pathway to peace
Taking, as He did, this
sinful world as it is,
Not as I would have it

Trusting that He will
make all things right
If I surrender to his will
That I may be reasonably happy in this life
and supremely happy
in the next. AMEN.

3

## ASSESSMENT INTERVIEW

Remember that a **key characteristic of addiction is denial**. The substance use is never an issue for the user. Breaking down this denial is part of your job in assessment (if it already seems clear that dependency exists).

When interviewing the user, **focus on asking concrete questions** about circumstances, events, and symptoms. If asked in a non-threatening and nonjudgmental fashion, the person should respond fairly honestly. If speaking with a family member, reframe these questions and ask them about the user. (In many cases, addicts don't get help until they "hit bottom," which often is the threat of a spouse to leave. The spouse, then, may have initiated the appointment and may insist on attending.)

### Rule Outs

**Q1** Has your use of this substance increased or decreased over the years? *(Tolerance, or the need for increasing amounts of the substance, is a key distinguishing factor between a substance abuse problem and dependency.)*

**Q2** *(For substance abuse)* Have you ever experienced a time when you did not remember what you did while drinking or drugging (for instance, a blackout)? Have you ever experienced anxiety, panic attacks, shakes, or hallucinations after not drinking for a while?

*Approximately 40% of all crimes are committed under the influence of alcohol; 40% of people convicted of rape or sexual assault state that they were drinking at the time of the offense; 72% of rapes on college campuses occur while victims are intoxicated to the point that they are unable to consent or refuse sex.[4]*

### General Questions

**Q3** Has anyone ever suggested that your use of (a substance or behavior) is a problem? If so, why do you think the person said that?

**Q4** Have you ever been concerned about your use of (a substance or behavior)? If so, why?

**Q5** How often do you use this substance and how much at each use?

**Q6** Do you ever try to hide your use from family members or friends?

**Q7** At what age did you first use (a substance or behavior)?

**Q8** Have you ever done anything while under the influence of (a substance or behavior) that you later regretted? Have you ever had a conviction or ticket for driving under the influence?

**Q9** Did anyone in your family of origin use a substance in excess while you were growing up? Who was that? How did it affect you?

**Q10** Has your use of (a substance or behavior) ever affected your job or your family? What happened?

**Q11** Have you ever quit or tried to quit using? What happened when you did? How did you feel?

**Q12** Do you want to quit for good? Tell me more about it.

**Q13** How do you see your life improving if you can quit using (a substance or behavior)?

## 4 WISE COUNSEL

Safety is always a key issue. **Try to find out if the user has been driving under the influence or has small children at home who might be endangered.** If so, take immediate steps to protect the user and others.

**Try to speak with other family members** who are old enough about how they handle the user's behaviors. For example, family members need to be taught to say "no" to car rides if the user is under the influence and to call for help if the user is unable to supervise younger children.

**If physical or sexual abuse occurs when the user is under the influence, then encourage family members to leave the home immediately**, going to a relative's home or a shelter for victims of domestic violence.

If **verbal abuse** is an issue when the user is under the influence, encourage family members to seek counseling or groups for family members of addicts.

## 5 ACTION STEPS

### 1. Contract and Accountability

The user should sign a contract with you that he will stop use and get immediate help for his addiction.

### 2. Prevent the User from Driving

- Get rid of the user's car the first time he drives under the influence—that sets a clear boundary regarding substance abuse.
- To protect family members, the user, and innocent bystanders, you need to convince this person to stop driving or doing anything while under the influence.
- The Club® and other antitheft devices prohibit driving, and sophisticated electronic devices can prevent driving unless a breathalyzer test is first passed.
- Point out that these restrictions are for the good of the person and others, and that continued usage will cause repercussions in the rest of his life—in his family relationships, career, and financial security.

### 3. Get a Thorough Medical Checkup

- A medical exam will confirm or rule out any medical problems caused by use of the substance.
- An addiction such as alcoholism is a disease, so treatment from a doctor is certainly recommended.
- People recovering from any addiction are recovering from a disease.

*In the year 2000, approximately 85,000 deaths in the U.S. were attributable to either excessive or hazardous drinking—making alcohol the third actual leading cause of death. In 2001, there were 1.4 million arrests for driving under the influence of alcohol or narcotics: That is 1 out of every 137 licensed drivers.*[5]

In 2001, there were 1.4 million arrests for driving under the influence of alcohol or narcotics: That is 1 out of every 137 licensed drivers.[6]

### 4. Get Professional Help

Encourage the user to allow a professional in chemical dependency to assess whether the substance use is an addiction. These assessments are available at community mental health agencies, some hospitals, and community substance abuse centers (common in urban and suburban areas and through county governments in many rural areas).

### 5. 12-Step Groups

Millions of people have found help through Alcoholics Anonymous and similar organizations. This rigorous program promotes sobriety and restoration of values and relationships through honesty, faith, repentance, and responsibility. They recommend addicts go to "90 meetings in 90 days" and get a sponsor who will help them take steps toward wholeness.

### 6. Encourage Family Members to Seek Support

Your community may have support groups such as Al-Anon, Families Anonymous, or a Christ-centered twelve-step recovery program. You may need to do some research and direct the family to a good program. These programs are based on the "Twelve Steps," the most successful program in the world for treating addiction.

6

## BIBLICAL INSIGHTS

***Woe to those who rise early in the morning, that they may follow intoxicating drink; who continue until night, till wine inflames them! —Isaiah 5:11***

- Many alcoholics are so dependent on alcohol that they begin early in the morning and continue drinking until late at night.
- The tragedy of addiction is that it controls and dominates the desires and choices of the addict.
- The even greater tragedy is addicts' rejection of the Lord's work in their lives. God alone can provide the lasting comfort, joy, and relief that people mistakenly seek in alcohol and other substances and behaviors.

***And I said to her, "You shall stay with me many days; you shall not play the harlot, nor shall you have a man—so, too, will I be toward you." —Hosea 3:3***

- Addictions are powerful enemies to our relationship with God. Whether the addiction is to alcohol, drugs, sex, gambling, Web-surfing, shopping, or whatever, addicted people can attest to their seeming inability to control their desires.
- Addictions usually begin very subtly—an experience, substance, or individual that brings pleasure begins to become an obsession. Eventually, the obsession takes control. Rarely can a person escape the addiction without some form of intervention.

Due to the more than 2 million people per year who drive under the influence, the National Highway Traffic Safety Administration claims that alcoholism statistics indicate 17,000 alcohol-related traffic fatalities in each of the last three years.[7]

- Addicts need to determine to change, replace the addictive substance with something more wholesome, and then finally find a way to meet their need in different, more healthy ways.
- Addictions destroy individuals, families, friendships, reputations, and careers. Addictions make people victims of their own desires. Despite all this, God offers hope. God wants to free people from anything that takes His rightful place in their lives. He wants to show them that He can meet all their needs. With God's help and the compassionate accountability of other believers, addicts can be set free—bought back. Jesus has already paid the price.

*The results of a 2003 poll show that 8.2% of people 12 and older have used illicit drugs in the last month.*[8]

***All things are lawful for me, but all things are not helpful. All things are lawful for me, but I will not be brought under the power of any. —1 Corinthians 6:12***

- God gave people "richly all things to enjoy" (1 Timothy 6:17), but Satan works tirelessly to take God's blessings and twist them into evil.
- Believers are allowed to enjoy many things as long as they are not forbidden by Scripture, but they should never allow themselves to be controlled or "brought under the power of any."

*It was found that 56% of substance abusers admitted for treatment met the DSM IV criteria for borderline disorder, a high percentage of abusers display self-damaging impulsive tendencies.*[9]

***Therefore put to death your members which are on the earth: fornication, uncleanness, passion, evil desire, and covetousness, which is idolatry. Because of these things the wrath of God is coming upon the sons of disobedience. — Colossians 3:5-6***

- These verses describe some of those sinful desires that believers should "put to death." Sexual sins, evil desires, and covetousness (or greed) should have no place in a believer's heart.
- It takes a conscious daily decision to say "no" to these sinful temptations and rely on the Holy Spirit's power to overcome them.

## 7 PRAYER STARTER

Dear Lord, thank You that my friend has come here today to seek help for an addiction. Please help him to be open to considering that this might be a true addiction for which he needs to get practical help. Lead us by Your Holy Spirit to the resources that will be most helpful, and thank You for Your willingness to forgive even addiction . . .

## 8 RECOMMENDED RESOURCES

*Healing Life's Hidden Addictions: Overcoming the Closet Compulsions that Waste Your Time and Control Your Life*, by Archibald D. Hart

*Don't Call It Love*, by Pat Carnes

*Freedom from Addiction: Breaking the Bondage of Addiction and Finding Freedom in Christ*, by Neil T. Anderson

*80% of studies find a positive correlation between drug abuse and personality disorders.*[10]

# Adultery

## 1 PORTRAITS

- Carol wanted to trust Don. She continually reminded herself that Don was a good father and husband. She pushed out of her mind the thoughts that there might be someone else. Then one morning as she was cleaning up his home office, she found a credit card statement that detailed hotels and restaurant charges in New York. She hadn't heard Don talk about traveling there on his frequent business trops.
- Barb enjoyed working with her boss, Carl. Their conversations were stimulating and she always came away feeling affirmed. She was thankful that she had such a good relationship with him . . . until it became more than that. Her eyes filled with tears as she began to recount their affair. "I can't remember exactly when we started having feelings for each other," Barb recounted. "I never imagined it would lead to this!"

## 2 DEFINITIONS AND KEY THOUGHTS

*How common is adultery? There are contrasting statistics. Some say 2 out of 3 married men and 50% of married women have cheated on their spouse.[1] Others believe that only 10% of couples experience adultery.[2]*

- Adultery occurs when a person has a **sexual relationship with someone other than his or her spouse**. This relationship may or may not include an emotional connection.
- Adultery may also involve an emotional affair. Though it is less understood, an **emotional affair can be even more threatening** to a marriage than physical adultery. It occurs when husband or wife turns to someone outside the marriage for primary emotional support. For example, emotional affairs can occur when a couple is experiencing conflict or distance, and the husband or wife turns to a friend for companionship, support, and sharing of personal struggles.
- Tragically, infidelity in marriage is becoming **increasingly common**. Statistics show that Christians are just as likely to be tempted to marital unfaithfulness as non-Christians. Women are as likely to have affairs as men.
- **Poor communication, unresolved conflict, and/or unrealistic expectations** leading to marital dissatisfaction are key reasons for extramarital affairs. If a spouse isn't getting significant needs met at home, he or she may look elsewhere.
- Spouses may unwittingly become involved in affairs because they are exposed to situations for which they are **unprepared** or **have not set wise boundaries**.

- Many affairs begin gradually as **well meaning friendships.** The people involved are unaware of how the relationship is changing until the seemingly impossible becomes possible, and then becomes a reality.
- The roots of infidelity can also be traced from emotional deprivation in childhood. In these cases, a person has a **constant hunger for approval and attention**. For example, if the wife can't fulfill those needs, the husband may feel cheated, let down, and may seek the attention of others outside the marriage relationship.
- Many adulterers think they are looking for love when in fact they are seeking to **feel better about themselves**.
- A person may be unfaithful as an act of **retaliation and anger** against his or her spouse (whether consciously or unconsciously).
- For some, as money and positions of power increase, so does an increasing **sense of entitlement** to life's pleasures, including the expectation of sexual pleasures wherever they can be found.
- Ultimately, adultery is a **self-centered choice**, intentionally ignoring the needs of the person's spouse, family, and the commandments of God in order to satisfy his or her own selfish desires.
- At its root, adultery is a **lifestyle of deception** designed to hide the sin, but also, thriving on lies such as, "I deserve to be happy," "My spouse will never change," or "Nobody is hurt by this.".
- The chase and keeping secrets are often more exhilarating than the act of adultery.

*The best way to ensure your marriage is to maintain your friendship. A lot of times, what men miss most is the time they spend just hanging out with their wives. That's why so many affairs begin as friendships—it's that intimacy a man is looking for.*
—Scott Stanley

## 3 ASSESSMENT INTERVIEW

### For the Faithful Spouse:

Q1 How did you find out about the infidelity?

Q2 How long have you known?

Q3 What do you feel you need right now in light of this information?

Q4 What feelings has this stirred up for you? *(It is not uncommon for the person to feel a variety of emotions from resentment to sadness.)*

Q5 What do you want to do about your relationship with your spouse?

Q6 Are you willing to work with a professional counselor to explore the wounds that have been created and seek reconciliation if your spouse repents?

### For the Unfaithful Spouse:

Q1 Have you told your spouse?

> *By the most conservative estimate . . . in the United States, 1 in every 2.7 couples—some 20 million—is touched by infidelity. That number equals almost 4 out of 10 husbands and 2 out of 10 wives.*
> —Janis Abrahms Spring

**Q2** What prompts you to want to discuss this now?

**Q3** Do you want to restore your marriage? *(It is not uncommon for the offending spouse to feel confused as to what he/she wants to do, especially if the affair was longstanding and/or involved a deep emotional commitment.)*

**If the unfaithful spouse wants to restore the marriage:**

**Q1** Are you willing to completely cut off all ties to the third party? *(This is the most significant question. You will be able to tell a lot by how the person replies. Is there hesitation? Does he/she avoid eye contact?)*

**Q2** Do you want to explore the reasons that perpetuated the affair?

**Q3** Are you aware of the needs you were seeking to have met in this relationship?

**Q4** What are the effects of the affair on your spouse?

**Q5** Whose responsibility is the affair—yours or your spouse's? Explain your answer.

**Q6** Are you committed to being accountable for your time and relationships on a daily basis?

**Q7** Are you willing to pursue professional counseling to seek forgiveness, understanding, and reconciliation?

## 4 WISE COUNSEL

God can restore a marriage shattered by infidelity. Increasing numbers of couples are braving the path of healing and restoration of their marriages. To begin the healing process, both spouses will need to

- *understand what caused the infidelity in the marriage.* This will require a long, thoughtful look at the marital pattern that has developed, as well as what each person has contributed to the marital breakdown. Difficult though it is, each spouse should focus on his or her own issues instead of criticizing and blaming the other person for the problem.
- *rebuild trust in each other* by telling each other the truth and by being accountable to each other. It is vital for each person to keep his or her word. If one spouse promises to do something, he or she needs to follow through and do it. Finally, trust can be rebuilt by using gestures of affection and nonsexual touch to express care and affirmation.
- *take time for restoring and enriching the marriage***.** The restoration process involves identifying and reestablishing what was good about the marriage before the adultery. The enriching process involves learning and implementing new skills and behaviors to strengthen the relationship.

## For the Faithful Spouse:

A normal process of grieving occurs when someone has been deeply wounded.

- *Shock/Denial.* The "No, not me" stage occurs when the wounded spouse is unwilling to accept the reality of the spouse's unfaithfulness. He/she may blatantly deny facts about the spouse's activities.
- *Anger.* The Why me?" stage happens when the person is aware of being violated and may express deep resentment and rage toward the unfaithful spouse.
- *Bargaining.* This stage is characterized by the comment, "If I do this, you'll do that." The person wants to swap conciliatory behavior for a change in the spouse. For example, he or she says, "If you stay, I'll change," rather than addressing the deeper implications of the infidelity.
- *Depression.* In this stage the person faces the reality: "It really happened." The person realizes the full impact of the infidelity on the marriage and mourns the loss of what the relationship once was. The wounded spouse realizes he/she will need to make a decision about the future of the relationship.
- *Acceptance.* In this stage, grief has run its course, and the person realizes, "I still have a lot to live for." The person has come to terms with all of the implications of the unfaithful spouse's actions and is willing to move forward.

*Although the process can often take a long time, healing and recovery are possible through the Holy Spirit's work in our lives, healing, supporting, and helping spouses forgive one another and rebuld their marriage on a solid biblical foundation.*
—David M. Carder

The first three (and perhaps four) stages can be experienced rapidly within a few hours, or across days or months depending on the individual. You need to **evaluate which stage the person is currently experiencing** and gently encourage him/her to work through that stage. (Note: The stages of grieving may be experienced out of order, several at once, and a person may repeat these stages many times.)

Encourage the person to **avoid immediately making any long-term decisions**. It is not uncommon for a hurt spouse to have feelings of wanting to end the marriage because the task of rebuilding the relationship may seem too difficult.

**Separation**, especially if the affair has been going on for a long time, **may allow both parties time** and emotional space to process feelings and clarify the situation. The goal of separation is to have the couple **begin to rebuild a friendship** and reestablish trust.

## For the Unfaithful Spouse:

**Require full disclosure of the steps leading up to the affair**, the details of the relationship, and any information that was kept hidden.

Remind the person that **there will be a "withdrawal" factor** as he/she breaks off any connection with the third party

Inform the person that he/she needs to **re-engage emotionally with his/her spouse** by spending as much time as possible to begin rebuilding trust.

The person will need to **begin to account for all of his/her time** in order to begin to demonstrate trustworthiness.

Inform the person that restoring the relationship **will take time.** Developing new patterns and a commitment to learn about each other on a deeper level are essential parts of the healing process.

Inform the person that **seeking forgiveness also involves restoration** and a deeper commitment to love and honor his/her spouse than has been previously given.

## 5 ACTION STEPS

### 1. Prayer

Each spouse should seek daily time before God in prayer, reading the Scriptures, and asking Him for the ability to grow in Christlike attitudes and actions.

### 2. No Contact

The unfaithful spouse should have no contact whatsoever with the third party. Like an addiction, the only way out is complete abstinence.

### 3. Commitment

The unfaithful spouse needs to be willing to make a radical commitment to regain the trust that has been broken.

### 4. New Lifestyle

The unfaithful spouse should commit to a lifestyle of transparency and honesty. Remind him/her that no area is off limits for inquiry.

### 5. Forgiveness

The faithful spouse should commit to the process of forgiveness. Forgiveness will be a multi-layered journey, and the person will need to make daily decisions to continue to forgive again.

### 6. Reconciliation

Explain to the couple that forgiveness is required but reconciliation is conditional. Reconciliation is based on the other person's true remorse and repentance. While the Bible never commands divorce and many couples stay together and heal, some may never be able to work through the brokenness.

### 7. Wise Counsel

The couple will need to commit to working with a professional counselor who can help them evaluate the communication patterns that may have contributed to the affair.

> He heals the brokenhearted and binds up their wounds.
>
> —Psalm 147:3

## 6 BIBLICAL INSIGHTS

***Drink water from your own cistern, and running water from your own well. —Proverbs 5:15***

- This beautiful metaphor describes the joy of marital fidelity. To "drink water from your own cistern" pictures the marriage partners belonging only to each other, enraptured with each other's love.
- By contrast, to become enraptured by another person and turn to adultery may feel exciting at first, but it will end up being "bitter as wormwood, sharp as a two-edged sword" (Proverbs 5:4).
- God's Word clearly teaches that married people should keep their vows and remain committed to each other.
- Adultery is embracing a false love—it will hurt everyone involved.

> You shall not commit adultery.
>
> —Exodus 20:14

> Whoever commits adultery with a woman lacks understanding; he who does so destroys his own soul.
>
> —Proverbs 6:32

***Let your fountain be blessed, and rejoice with the wife of your youth. As a loving deer and a graceful doe, let her breasts satisfy you at all times; and always be enraptured with her love. —Proverbs 5:18-19***

- The Bible does not speak against sexual fulfillment—in fact, sexual delight and marital love are exalted in the Song of Solomon. Sexual fulfillment is always depicted in the Bible as within the boundaries of marriage.
- Adultery is a great tragedy because it has severe consequences. People risk all that they have built over a lifetime—marriage, family, respect, honor—when they commit adultery. Sexual sin can be very appealing, almost an overwhelming temptation, but it must be resisted.
- The way out is to rejoice in one's marriage and to be satisfied with one's spouse's love (Proverbs 5:18-19). To violate that commitment will lead to pain, grief, and self-destruction.

***"When I passed by you again and looked upon you, indeed your time was the time of love; so I spread My wing over you and covered your nakedness. Yes, I swore an oath to you and entered into a covenant with you, and you became Mine," says the Lord God. —Ezekiel 16:8***

- We can find great comfort in the fact that our heavenly Father can empathize with the pain of someone who has been betrayed by a loved one. Knowing that He understands can help us trust Him in our own hurt and pain.

***You have heard that it was said to those of old, "You shall not commit adultery."* —*Matthew 5:27***

- Quoting from Exodus 20:14, Jesus reminded His listeners of the commandment against adultery. Then He said that looking at another person lustfully is committing adultery in your heart. Jesus explained that thinking about an act is the same as doing it, because actions begin with thoughts and desires.
- Since lust and adultery are first embraced in the mind and heart, believers should try to avoid situations that cause temptation.

7

## PRAYER STARTER

Dear Lord, there is much pain here today. Hurt and betrayal are affecting this marriage. You have promised, Lord, that You are close to the brokenhearted and will bind up their wounds. You are the Healer, the Restorer. We ask for Your guidance in this painful situation . . .

## RECOMMENDED RESOURCES

*After the Affair: Healing the Pain and Rebuilding the Trust When a Partner Has Been Unfaithful*, by Janis Abrahms Spring

*Broken Promises: Healing and Preventing Affairs in Christian Marriages*, by Henry A. Virkler

*Love Must Be Tough*, by James Dobson

*Surviving Betrayal: Counseling an Adulterous Marriage*, by Donald R. Harvey

*Torn Asunder: Recovering from Extramarital Affairs:* by Dave Carder

# Aging

## 1 PORTRAITS

- Will and Marilyn had married late in life and had kids even later. With their kids entering adolescence, they were confronted with the possibility of becoming caregivers for Marilyn's widowed mother after she fell, breaking her hip.
- Sarah has been a frequent volunteer at the church since she retired from the school district. But her health has been failing recently, and she's not sure how much longer she can live alone.
- Edward is a widower and has cancer that has spread to his liver. A church member has expressed concern over his living conditions, fearing that he has not been caring for himself properly.

## 2 DEFINITIONS AND KEY THOUGHTS

*In 2003, over 12% (about 36 million) of the U.S. population was 65 or older, and the elderly are one of the fastest growing people groups in American society.*[1]

- Aging is a natural process. **The rate at which people age varies** according to many factors such as family history, attitude, chronic medical conditions, and lifestyle.
- Although the risk of disability and illness increases with age, **poor health is not an inevitable consequence of aging.** People with healthy lifestyles that include regular exercise, balanced diet, and no tobacco use have half the risk for disability than those with less healthy lifestyles.
- Caring for aging parents can be gratifying, but our ability to care for them depends on a lot of complex issues, such as your own health, whether you are still raising children, financial resources, and emotional resilience. **Even though being a caregiver is laudable, it is not necessarily the wisest decision if there are other options.**
- The "**sandwich years**" is a phrase referring to middle-aged people who are still raising children and are also caring for their parents. They are "sandwiched" between these two generations, which can feel like a vice grip of pressure.
- As people age, their **idiosyncrasies tend to become more pronounced.** Easy-going people may continue to be laid back, but those who were uptight at a younger age may become more anxious as they age.
- People entering their later years **experience many transitions and endure many losses,** such as retirement; moving from parenthood to grandparenthood;

lessened physical abilities, strength, and energy; the deaths of friends and peers; lowered social status; a tighter financial budget, and the loss of a spouse.

3

## ASSESSMENT INTERVIEW

As you talk to the aging person or the family member, remember that **aging and caregiving take many forms**. Try not to project your own values on the person. The older person may value independence far more than you think is healthy, or the family member might be convinced that anyone older than 65 can't be independent. **Listen first**, then gently offer different options if they would be helpful.

### Rule Outs

**Q1** If the elderly person is confused, has he or she been ill? Is there a chance of depression, dehydration, other medical problems, or poor nutrition? *(Several medical conditions and depression can mimic the symptoms of dementia, so always be sure that medical problems and depression have been ruled out by professionals before making any assumptions about a person's ability to live independently.)*

**Q2** Is the older person lonely? *(Loneliness can prompt a person to reach out for help, sometimes acting needier than he or she truly is.)*

### General Questions

**Q3** What level of care do you think you (or your loved one) need?

**Q4** What are your (or your loved one's) financial resources?

**Q5** What medical issues are there? Are these terminal? Chronic? Permanent but not debilitating? Degenerative and progressive? *(Clearly, if a medical condition is temporary, the future plans will be very different than if it is terminal, progressive, or chronic.)*

**Q6** How do you feel emotionally about the possibility of needing to get more care (give care to a loved one)?

**Q7** What family members are available to help?

**Q8** Is the aging person in danger?

Dangerous conditions would include:

- *memory loss* that leads to accidental fires, wandering, or destructive behavior;
- *medical conditions* that require constant supervision or that contribute to sudden loss of stability or consciousness;

> *In God's view, aging is merely the final phase of an upward climb from earth to heaven.*
> —David Seamands

- a *residence* that is deteriorated, unhealthy, or structurally too demanding (e.g., too many stairs);
- an *emotional state* that could lead to extreme despondency or psychosis (distorted thinking, such as paranoia).

4

## WISE COUNSEL

When counseling a caregiver, impress upon the person the complexity of issues related to aging and the wealth of resources for caregivers and for the elderly. Consult with agencies, church-related ministries, and other organizations to identify available resources.

Encourage the person to **gather all the facts** (from doctors, other family members, neighbors, etc.). The goal is to find out how the aging person has been doing and whether there are critical concerns.

About one in every eight, or 12.4 percent, of the population is an older American.[2]

Assess whether there is any possibility of **physical or financial elder abuse or neglect**.

- *Financial abuse* occurs when friends or family members take financial resources from an older person for their own benefit. This is a particular risk when the older person is confused and no longer controlling his or her own finances.
- *Elder neglect* occurs when a spouse or live-in family member deliberately neglects the needs of the older person for food, clothing, shelter, a clean environment, and protection from extremes of temperature. Sometimes, this occurs inadvertently when a previously healthy spouse becomes confused or sick and is no longer able to provide a safe environment for a vulnerable spouse.
- *Elder abuse* is physical violence directed at an older person. This could be a form of domestic violence that has been ongoing for years but the victim is now over 65. Or, it could be abuse of an older person by a caregiver who is a family member or a stranger.

5

## ACTION STEPS

### For older people:

Poor health and the loss of independence are not necessarily the inevitable consequences of growing older. To preserve health and independence, older people should consider the following strategies:

- Early detection of diseases. Screening to detect diseases early, when they are most treatable, saves many lives. Older adults should be encouraged to participate in recommended screenings.

- Healthy lifestyle. A healthy lifestyle is more influential than DNA in helping older people avoid the decline associated with aging.
- Immunizations. Flu shots, pneumonia vaccines, and other important immunizations reduce a person's risk for hospitalization and death from illness.
- Preventing injuries. Falling is the most common cause of injury with older adults. More than one-third of adults 65 and over fall each year, and of those, 20–30 percent suffer moderate to severe injuries that reduce mobility and independence, says the CDC. Remove tripping hazards in the home and install grab bars in key areas, like bathrooms. These simple measures will significantly reduce an older person's chance of falling.
- Programs to help self-management. Consider finding programs to teach older Americans self-management techniques. These programs help older adults cope with and manage the transitions of their later years.

## 1. Rank the Need

- Have the caregiver and the elderly person rank needs in order of importance. Begin to brainstorm with the elderly person how those needs can be met with minimal upheaval. Most of the time, the choice is not between living alone or moving to a nursing home. There are dozens of options in between, including:

- *Non-medical home care* for cleaning, meals, or home maintenance
- *Meals on Wheels* and similar programs for delivery of meals
- *Help at home* during key hours for things like bathing and dressing
- *Adult daycare* during daytime hours for those who have family members with them at other times
- *Seniors housing complexes*—apartment complexes with some extra supports available that are offered at a lower price for needy older people
- *Shared housing* with a younger person who is not a family member
- *Retirement home* living often relieves an older person of loneliness or the need to make meals and maintain a home
- *Catered/sheltered care* or assisted living—situations that provide meals, some medication reminders, transportation to stores, and other support services
- Care in a *private group home* where 2–6 older people might be cared for by a couple who make caregiving their full-time job
- Skilled *nursing care*

Indeed, You have made my days as handbreadths, and my age is as nothing before you.
—Psalm 39:5

Even though our outward man is perishing, yet the inward man is being renewed day by day.
—2 Corinthians 4:16

The silver-haired head is a crown of glory, if it is found in the way of righteousness.
—Proverbs 16:31

*People reaching age 65 have an average life expectancy of an additional 18.2 years (19.5 years for females and 16.6 years for males).*[3]

Half of older women age 75+ live alone.[4]

## 2. Consider the Effects

- Consider the effect of any changes in lifestyle on all family members, not just the older one. A change in location, for example, will not just affect the older person but also any family members who are involved.
- Attempt to keep upheaval to a minimum, especially if family life for caregivers is already tense or demanding. (Adding a family member requiring 24-hour care to a household with teenagers or a special-needs child, for example, might not be the best idea.)

## 3. Consider All Options

- Enumerate all the options and then give all of them prayerful consideration.
- Seek counsel from people who have a lot of experience in helping people find the best solutions.
- Enlist several people—both in and outside the family—to pray about the possibilities.

6

# BIBLICAL INSIGHTS

***You shall rise before the gray headed and honor the presence of an old man, and fear your God: I am the Lord. — Leviticus 19:32***

- God's laws include prohibitions against disrespect for the elderly. The "gray headed" and the "old man" are to be treated with honor and respect.
- The Bible commands respect for our elders who have much to teach from their experience.

***Moses was one hundred and twenty years old when he died. His eyes were not dim nor his natural vigor diminished. — Deuteronomy 34:7***

- Our generation tends to emphasize the importance of youth, but God uses servants of all ages.
- Age does not limit God's ability to work through people. As long as we have breath, we should be serving God.

***And now, behold, the Lord has kept me alive, as He said, these forty-five years, ever since the Lord spoke this word to Moses while Israel wandered in the wilderness; and now, here I am this day, eighty-five years old. — Joshua 14:10***

- The Bible identifies the key to Caleb's lifelong health, vitality, and special favor with God. He "wholly followed the LORD" (Joshua 14:8).
- Caleb is a wonderful model for the proposition that a faithful life—one that perseveres through every trial and hardship—is rewarded with blessings in old age.

Americans are living longer, and the ratio of people 65 or older is growing fast. According to the National Center for Health Statistics (NCHS), there were 35 million Americans ages 65 or older in 2000. By 2030 that number will double to 70 million; one out of every five Americans![5]

*Lord, make me to know my end, and what is the measure of my days, that I may know how frail I am. Indeed, You have made my days as handbreadths, and my age is as nothing before You; certainly every man at his best state is but vapor.* *— Psalm 39:4-5*

- People's lifetimes are short and small in the hand of God, "as nothing" to Him, like a raindrop in the ocean.
- One of the great challenges of aging is to understand that, while time is passing, God is working through us to make a difference in the world.
- No matter what our age, we need to use our time wisely, fully, actively, and selflessly, giving thanks for each new day and seeking how God would have us serve Him.

*Do not cast me off in the time of old age; do not forsake me when my strength fails.* *— Psalm 71:9*

- Older people often feel that because they lack their youthful vigor, they can't effectively serve God. God says, however, that His people "shall still bear fruit in old age" (Psalm 92:14). As they age, their primary role of service may change from active leadership and physical efforts to advising, counseling, and praying.
- Older believers have a lifetime of wisdom and experience that are valuable to younger people. Believers can and should continue to grow spiritually even in their twilight time. They can continue to make a difference for God, helping build His kingdom.
- Young people should not dismiss older people. Instead, they should look to their elders for the godly wisdom.

*According to the Center for Disease Control and Prevention (www.CDC.gov): During 1994 to 1996, 72.2% of US citizens 65 or older reported their health as good, very good, or excellent. 74.0% of non-Hispanic whites reported good to excellent health, as compared to 64.9% of Hispanics/Latinos and 58.4% of non-Hispanic blacks.*

## 7 PRAYER STARTER

Dear Lord, thank You for the life of my friend. Please reveal to us through Your Holy Spirit what should be done next. Give us wisdom and kindness. Help us to see all the options, and lead us in the direction we should go that will be best for all involved . . .

## 8 RECOMMENDED RESOURCES

*Caring for Your Aging Parents: When Love is not Enough*, by Barbara Deane

*Complete Guide to Caring for Aging Loved Ones*, by Walter L. Larimore, Henry Holstege, & Robert Riekse

*Second Wind for the Second Half: Twenty Ideas to Help You Reinvent Yourself for the Rest of the Journey*, by Patrick Morley

# Anger

## 1 PORTRAITS

- David and his wife fight constantly. Last week Dave got so angry that he took a glass vase and smashed it against the wall. It wasn't the first time he's been violent.
- At 16, Sarah feels she is just a burden to her busy mom, so she locks herself in her bedroom with the stereo at maximum volume.
- Brian's new supervisor has been pushing him all day. Wanting to turn off the stress, he goes home and drinks himself into a stupor.
- Only five years old, Timothy hardly understands how he feels, besides pain from the bruises on his back. While other kids draw pictures in class, he can't focus. Scribbling in burgundy crayon, he tears a hole through his paper.

*How much more grievous are the consequences of anger than the causes of it.*
—Marcus Aurelius

## 2 DEFINITIONS AND KEY THOUGHTS

- Anger is a **God-given powerful emotion** (Ephesians 4:26) with intensity that ranges from mild frustration to severe fury. It can last from a few seconds to a lifetime. Anger itself is not a sin. What we *do* in our anger determines whether or not we sin.
- Anger is best understood as a **state of readiness**. It is a natural response to a real or perceived injustice, and it inspires a powerful alertness that allows us to defend good or attack evil. Even Jesus showed anger (Mark 3:5).
- Anger is **mentioned over 500 times in Scripture,** the only emotion in the Bible more common than anger is love. Anger first appears in Genesis 4:5 and last appears in Revelation 19:15.
- Anger can lead to **healthy actions or unhealthy, sinful behavior.** *Careful assertiveness* is a healthy response to anger that involves problem-solving and compassion. *Aggression* is an unhealthy, sinful response to anger that involves hurting or controlling others, revenge, or hatred.
- Anger, when it is an automatic response to a situation, is considered a **primary emotion**. Anger can also be a secondary emotion, meaning it is felt in reaction to another feeling such as fear, hurt, or sadness.

*Men in rage strike those that wish them best.*
—Shakespeare

## Expressions of Anger

Anger always finds an **expression**. People handle anger by:

**Internalization**—Some people *repress* anger and deny anger's presence. This is unhealthy because even though it may not be observable, the anger is still present—turned inward upon the person. Repressed anger can lead to numerous emotional and physical problems including depression, anxiety, hypertension, and ulcers.

Others may *suppress* the anger, meaning they acknowledge anger and then stuff it. In this approach to coping, they redirect anger driven energy into unrelated activity. Their efforts may seem productive, but they neglect to address the root causes of anger. One risk is that people who suppress may become cynical or passive-aggressive—an indirect form of revenge manifesting as sarcasm, lack of cooperation, gossip, etc.

**Ventilation**—*Healthy expression* entails non-aggressive, gently assertive actions that promote the respect of self and others. This addresses problems in a constructive manner.

*Unhealthy/sinful expression* involves acting in an aggressive way that hurts others. Whether you yell, use violence, or withdraw, the motivation is revenge or "payback." People expressing anger this way might say, "At least you know where I'm coming from!" however, they refuse to acknowledge the destructive force of their expression.

**Physical symptoms** include headaches, ulcers, stomach cramps, high blood pressure, colitis, heart conditions, and a host of other stress-related problems.

**Emotional symptoms** include depressioin, criticism, sarcasm, gossip, meanness, impatience, being demanding, withholding love, refusing to forgive, and the compulsion to use anger to control others..

## Levels of Anger

**Irritation**—a feeling of discomfort.

**Indignation**—a feeling that something must be answered; something wrong must be corrected.

**Wrath**—a strong desire to avenge.

**Fury**—the partial loss of emotional control.

**Rage**—a loss of control involving aggression or an act of violence.

**Hostility**—a persistent form of anger; enmity toward others that becomes rooted in the person's personality, affecting the outlook on the world and life.

### *Reasons we get angry*

- **A RESPONSE** to a person, situation, or event, to an imaginary or anticipated event, or to memories of traumatic or enraging situations.
- **A RESPONSE** to a real or perceived injustice or hurt—in the form of frustration, betrayal, deprivation, injustice, exploitation, manipulation, criticism, violence, disapproval, humiliation, intimidation, threats, etc.
- **A RESPONSE** when a boundary in our lives has been crossed.

### Causes of Anger

**External causes**—Anger can be a response to harm someone has inflicted (a physical attack, insult, abandonment) or to a circumstance where there is no person at fault (100-degree days, physical illness, highway traffic). Anger is often a response to a perceived injustice.

**Internal causes**—Anger is sometimes caused exclusively by an individual's misperceptions of reality or destructive thinking about normal life issues ("I should not have to pay taxes!"). Also, memories of traumatic events past can be an example of an internal cause of anger, as can biologically-rooted causes from medication, caffeine or other stimulants, and health issues such as diabetes or dialysis treatments.

## 3 ASSESSMENT INTERVIEW

When people seek help for anger, often **the problem is already out of control**. Also, they may be experiencing shame and fear because they don't understand how to identify and control their angry feelings.

**Resist the urge to give advice**. Instead, **calmly hear the person's story**.

*Depression has often been described as "anger turned inward." Both men and women can express their anger as depression.*

**Q1** If 10 is extreme depression, and 1 is no depression, where are you today on a scale of 1 to 10?

*Substance abuse is often an accompanying issue.*

**Q2** Are you ever under the influence of alcohol or drugs when you experience anger? Do you use alcohol or drugs to avoid feelings of anger?

*If you suspect that either depression or substance abuse is present, you should first deal with that problem. Refer to the sections on Depression or Addictions in this manual. Other underlying issues could include ADD/ADHD, brain trauma, personality disorders, attachment issues, and physical or sexual abuse.*

> *Anyone can become angry. That is easy. But to be angry with the right person, to the right degree, at the right time, for the right purpose and in the right way—that is not easy.*
> —Aristotle

### General Questions

**Q3** What makes you angry?

**Q4** How do you express your anger? Is the way you are expressing your anger working?

**Q5** Have you ever lost control while you were angry? Do you remember the first time?

**Q6** Do you ever take any action to redirect your anger to a non-related activity?

**Q7** Are you ever able to calm your anger? If so, how?

**Q8** Has anger created any health issues?

**Q9** How did you see anger expressed during childhood?

**Q10** Could there be anger from your past that is affecting you now?

**Q11** What was it like to be on the receiving end of someone else's anger?

**Q12** How is the way you express your anger harming you and your relationships?

**Q13** How often do fights get physical?

**Q14** When you get angry, how safe do you feel? How safe do those around you feel?

**Q15** Do others see anger in you that you do not?

**Q16** Do you have anyone with whom to talk about your anger?

**Q17** Will you consider forgiving the people with whom you are angry?

**Q18** Do you pray about your anger?

**Q19** Do you ever allow your anger to escalate? If you do, describe it.

*Men are like steel: when they lose their temper, they lose their worth.*
—Chuck Norris

## WISE COUNSEL 4

**Share some information about anger** with the person. In your own words, be sure to convey that the feeling of aner isn't sin (Ephesians 4:26), but anger needs to be expressed in constructive ways.

**Offer encouragement** that the person is willing to address the problem and stress the importance of beginning immediately because unhealthy expressions of anger can be so destructive. The Bible says that we should be "looking carefully lest anyone fall short of the grace of God; lest any root of bitterness springing up cause trouble, and by this many become defiled" (Hebrews 12:15).

**Explain the importance of following the Action Steps** because those who repress their anger are often depressed, anxious, hostile, or have other psychological and physical problems. Those who express their anger in unhelpful ways devastate their relationships with others. Anger leads to resentment (resentment is "anger with a history"), which then turns to hostility and bitterness.

Evaluate the **history of anger** expressed in the person's life. It is possible that the anger he feels today is not due to a current "trigger," but is instead rooted in anger from his past. For example, someone who is angry at his boss for being demanding might be thinking, "This man is heartless—the same as my father was." This anger is misdirected at the boss.

*According to the National Insitute of Health, 7.3% (or 11.5-16 million Americans) experience "intermittent explosive disorder" in their lifetimes. This disorder is marked by episodes of unwarranted anger.*[1]

5

## ACTION STEPS

The goal is not to be "anger free." Instead, it is to teach the person how to control his response to present feelings of anger, both the emotional and biological arousals that anger may cause.

### 1. See It

- Focus on the source of the anger. List the triggers (in your conversation with the person and as homework). Until the person can control anger, avoid the triggers as much as possible.
- Learn to identify anger before it is out of control. Have the person identify how he feels physically when experiencing anger.
  - Identify angry feelings while they are still minor. State out loud, "I'm feeling angry right now."
  - Be aware of the first warning signs of anger, which may be changes in the body. Anger promotes a sympathetic nervous system response (a physical state of readiness) and biological changes, such as rising heart rate and blood pressure, amplified alertness, tensed muscles, dilated pupils, lowered digestion, clenched fists, flared nostrils, bulged veins.
  - Identify the injustice the person feels has occurred. This is an important step to determine the source and legitimacy of the anger.

> *Consider how much more you often suffer from your anger and grief, than from those very things for which you are angry and grieved.*
> —Marcus Antonius

### 2. Delay It (Proverbs 16:32; 29:11)

- Brainstorm ways to delay the expression of anger:
  - Take a "time out"—if possible, temporarily disengage from the situation (20-minute minimum).
  - Perform light exercise until the intensity of anger is manageable.
  - "Write, don't fight"—jot down troubling thoughts. This exercise is personal and writings should be kept private, and possibly destroyed, not sent.
- Talk with a trusted friend who is unrelated to the anger-provoking situation: Don't just vent—ask for constructive advice.
- Pray about the anger, asking God to give you insight.
- Learn the value of calming. *(A person in a state of fury is not equipped to deal with an anger-provoking situation in a healthy way. Calming will help him let some of his angry feelings subside before expressing anger. Note: Ruminating is the opposite of calming, and makes anger worse by repeating destructive thoughts about an anger-producing event.)*

### 3. Control It

- Brainstorm some ways for the person to express his anger in a healthy way:
  - *Respond* (rational action), don't react (emotional reaction)
  - *Maintain* a healthy distance until you can speak constructively (James 1:19)
  - *Confront* to restore, not to destroy
  - *Empathize* (yelling is a failure to empathize). Speak slowly and quietly (makes yelling difficult)
  - *Surrender* the right for revenge by putting people in God's hands (Romans 12:19)
- If anger begins to escalate to wrath or fury, it is not the time to engage in interactions with others. Instead, the person should temporarily redirect his energy to solo activities to re-establish calm before confronting others.

*A fool gives full vent to anger, but a wise person quietly holds it back.*
—Proverbs 29:11

### 4. Settle It

- A plan should be made for follow up, perhaps:
  - Finding an accountability partner
  - Obtaining individual counseling
  - Joining an anger management group
  - Considering medication
- The person should actively continue spiritual growth to effectively manage anger. The Bible says, "The fruit of the Spirit is love, joy, peace, longsuffering, kindness, goodness, faithfulness, gentleness, self-control" (Galatians 5:22-23).
- Remember to:
  - *Surrender*—to the Holy Spirit (Galatians 5:16)
  - *Reflect*—on the mercy and love God provides (Ephesians 2:4)
  - *Pray*—admit to God feelings and regrets (Matthew 5:43-45)
  - *Forgive*—choose to let go of resentment and bitterness (Ephesians 4:31-32)
  - *Avoid*—ruminating and revenge (1 Corinthians 10:13; 1 Peter 1:13)
  - *Give and receive*—mutual respect with those close to you (Ephesians 5:31-32)
  - *Love*—even those who anger you (1 Corinthians 13)

*It is better to be patient than powerful; it is better to have self-control than to conquer a city.*
—Proverbs 16:32

- *Remember*—what it was like to be on the receiving end of someone else's anger (1 Samuel 19:9-10)
- *Resolve*—the anger issues (Ephesians 4:26)

- Underlying issues, such as deep emotional wounds that have been identified in counseling, need to be considered. Make plans to work on these issues through additional counseling and support groups.
- Focus on the grace and forgiveness of God. Ephesians 4:31-32 says, "Let all bitterness, wrath, anger, clamor, and evil speaking be put away from you, with all malice. And be kind to one another, tenderhearted, forgiving one another, just as God in Christ forgave you."

## 6 BIBLICAL INSIGHTS

***If you do well, will you not be accepted? And if you do not do well, sin lies at the door. And its desire is for you, but you should rule over it. —Genesis 4:7***

- Cain's problem wasn't the reeling of anger. It was how he reacted in his anger.
- At first, Cain's anger was a positive response, but it missed the mark. Instead of Cain becoming disappointed with himself for falling short of God's standard, his anger turned to deadly jealousy.
- Anger needs to be ruled or it will rule. Uncontrolled anger quickly becomes destructive. When you invite God to help you identify your anger and take positive action, anger becomes a servant rather than a master.

***And I became very angry when I heard their outcry and these words. —Nehemiah 5:6***

- Nehemiah's anger was righteous indignation because many Jews were suffering at the hands of rich countrymen who had lent them money.
- Expressing his anger in a healthy way, Nehemiah called a meeting of the money-lenders, who agreed to his firm requests.
- When you feel anger burning beneath the surface, ask God to guide you to a productive way of resolving the conflict.

*Anger is usually at the core of many of our most violent and prevalent social problems like rape, domestic violence, substance abuse, and suicide.*

***Make no friendship with an angry man, and with a furious man do not go, lest you learn his ways and set a snare for your soul. —Proverbs 22:24-25***

- People may not be able to change the anger others express, but they can avoid close ties with "furious" people who are ready to explode. Anyone near them will either catch the brunt of that fury or become similarly furious.
- Carefully choose those who will be your closest friends, business partners, and spouse.

***Then God said to Jonah, "Is it right for you to be angry about the plant?" And he said, "It is right for me to be angry, even to death!" —Jonah 4:9***

- When Jonah learned that God would spare the Ninevites, instead of rejoicing in their repentance, Jonah became angry. His anger at Nineveh's sinfulness was justified, though his selfish anger at God's mercy was not.
- Perhaps, with selfish motivation, Jonah was concerned that his reputation had been ruined with the false forecast of the city's destruction: Or he may have desired a front-row seat at Nineveh's demise—after all, Assyria was Israel's enemy.
- We need to honestly consider the inspiration of our anger.

***"Be angry, and do not sin": do not let the sun go down on your wrath, nor give place to the devil. —Ephesians 4:26-27***

- Note that this does not say, "Never be angry." Anger is a God-given emotion and, if handled well, will promote positive change.
- Do not allow anger to cause you to act in ways that you will later regret.
- Do not turn anger upon yourself or pretend you are never angry.
- Deal with anger as quickly (and responsibly) as possible—before the sun goes down—so that you do not "give place to the devil."
- Seek to resolve differences with others respectfully. Then continue together in the Lord's work. Remember, Satan loves to use anger to divide believers.

## 7 PRAYER STARTER

Lord, we all get angry. Anger is a powerful emotion that You have given us, and Your Word teaches us clearly about the constructive and destructive force that anger is. Help us to follow Your Word, Lord, by teaching us to control our anger when we have been threatened and wronged. Bless us, God, that we might see clearly, and not hurt others in our anger . . .

## 8 RECOMMENDED RESOURCES

*The Anger Workbook* (Minirth-Meier Clinic Series), by Les Carter and Frank Minirth

*Making Anger Your Ally*, by Neil Clark Warren

*When Anger Hits Home: Taking Care of Your Family Without Taking It Out on Your Family*, by Gary Oliver and H. Norman Wright

See www.AACC.net and search keyword "Anger" for the latest and best in audio, video, and print resources on anger.

# Bitterness

## 1 PORTRAITS

- David's father was killed by a drunk driver when David was a teenager. Life was difficult for David's family after that. The drunk driver was given only a light sentence. David is bitter toward the man, the judge, the jury—and at his father for leaving him alone.
- Adam's parents constantly belittled him as he was growing up. Now an adult, he suffers from depression and anxiety and can't figure out why he can't "get over it."
- Laura's husband doesn't seem interested in meeting any of her emotional needs. When she tries to talk to him about it, he is distant and cold. Over time, she has given up hope that he will ever change, and she sees no reason to continue in the marriage.
- Claire's boss is demanding and extremely critical. He humiliated Claire in front of her coworkers by judging her work unfairly, and mocking her efforts. Claire can't seem to let it go and fantasizes about plots for revenge.

*If we could read the secret history of our enemies, we should find in each person's life sorrow and suffering enough to disarm all hostility*
—Henry Wadsworth Longfellow

## 2 DEFINITIONS AND KEY THOUGHTS

- Bitterness is an attitude of **extended and intense anger and hostility**. It is often accompanied by resentment and a desire to "get even." It is a result of not forgiving an offender and letting hurt and anger grow until the pain and resentment sour the person's view of life.
- Bitterness is a sin that **destroys life**. Hebrews 12:15 warns that bitterness corrupts by its poison. Romans 12:17 commands us not to seek revenge, but rather to let God avenge.
- Bitterness can **only be conquered by forgiveness and faith** that God will cause justice to prevail someday. Ephesians 4:31-32 says to get rid of bitterness by replacing it with forgiveness.

### Key Elements of Bitterness

*Unresolved anger*—Ephesians 4:26 says that we can be angry without sinning. But when anger is unresolved and allowed to ruminate, it turns into bitterness.

*Inability to grieve*—Experiences of trauma and loss, and relationships that don't live up to expectations and fail to meet legitimate needs can result in feelings of sadness and loss.

Anger is a normal part of the stages of grief, but when we fail to grieve, this anger turns to bitterness.

When people are unable (or unwilling) to face the reality that their needs are never going to be met by a certain relationship, the result can be bitterness. Taking time to grieve the loss is an important prerequisite to becoming free from bitterness.

When people refuse to admit that the relationship will never become what they had hoped, that refusal causes bitterness. "Hope deferred makes the heart sick" (Proverbs 13:12).

*Lack of control*—When other people don't meet a person's needs, he or she can become obsessed with thoughts of, "If they would just do this . . ."

Give it up! People may never do what someone else desires or expects, and they can't be made to. We can only control ourselves. Much bitterness could be avoided if people accepted this truth.

He will repay my enemies for their evil.

—Psalm 54:5

Whatever you do, do it heartily, as to the Lord and not to men.

—Colossians 3:23

### Key Characteristics of Bitterness

*Resentment*—despising the offender

*Obsessive thoughts of revenge*—daydreams about ways to make the person pay

*Sarcasm*—seemingly innocent humor that bites

*Critical or unkind comments*—open, negative remarks

*Self-righteousness*—the perception that "I'd never do to anyone what you did to me."

*Conflicts with others*—with the offender or with others who get in the way of free-flowing anger

*Hostility*—action designed to punish

*Aggressiveness in relationships*—using demands, outbursts, and violence to cause others to cower

*Controlling behavior*—determination not to ever let anyone hurt us again

## ASSESSMENT INTERVIEW 3

Listen to the person's story. **Show empathy by listening closely** with appropriate feedback, and restate emotions to make sure you understand what the person is saying.

Bitterness may not be the presenting problem a person brings to counseling, but **it is often the real problem** underneath. Gently lead the person through the following questions to help him or her come to this realization.

If any of the questions hit a nerve, bring back a memory, or upset the person, **stop the questions and explore that issue**. Let the person talk about it further. Show compassion for the pain he is feeling. Don't feel compelled to ask all the questions. If a few of them uncover the issues, you've achieved your goal.

*I imagine one of the reasons people cling to their hates so stubbornly is because they sense, once hate is gone, they will be forced to deal with the pain.*
—James Baldwin

## General Questions

**Q1** Tell me what brought you to counseling today.

**Q2** What things have you already tried to help you with this problem?

**Q3** What do you hope will happen as an outcome of counseling?

**Q4** Let's start by getting some background information that will help me get to know you better:

Tell me about the family you grew up in, about your mother, father, sisters, brothers and anyone else who lived in your home or was an important part of your life. *(Attitudes toward life are molded in the family of origin, so it's important to see who and what shaped your person into the person he is today. This will help you understand him and his reactions, and help him understand himself.)*

Tell me about your adult life, your job, your marriage, your children, your church. *(Ask these questions one at a time, but the general idea is to get him talking about his life and how this problem has affected it.)*

**Q5** On a scale of 1 to 10 with 10 being contentment and joy and 1 being total despair, where are you today?

**Q6** Do you use alcohol or drugs to escape your hurt and bitterness?

**Q7** Do you feel you might hurt yourself or others? *(If you suspect that depression or substance abuse is present, you should deal with that along with the bitterness. Refer to the chapters on "Addiction" and "Depression.")*

**Q8** It sounds like you have been hurt a lot in your life. Do you feel bitter about that?

**Q9** When did you first notice feelings of bitterness?

**Q10** What events led to those feelings?

**Q11** How has this bitterness affected your quality of life?

**Q12** Can you remember anyone else in your life being bitter?

**Q13** How did it affect that person?

**Q14** What effect did that person's bitterness have on you?

**Q15** What feelings did you have when this person/this event first caused offense or made you bitter?

**Q16** Tell me why you were angry and what hurt your feelings. *(Often people feel anger when first offended because they are hurt, but underneath the hurt are expectations, and underneath the expectations are needs.)*

**Q17** What expectations did you have from the person who hurt you?

**Q18** What need did you have that the person failed to meet?

**Q19** Do you think that person will ever meet that need? Why or why not?

**Q20** Can you accept that?

**Q21** Can you forgive the person for that? *(If forgiveness is a tough sticking point, refer to the topic of Forgiveness and work through it in a separate session.)*

**Q22** What would forgiveness look like?

**Q23** Where else could you get that need met?

> *Revenge has no more quenching effect on emotions than salt water has on thirst.*
> —Walter Weckler

## WISE COUNSEL

4

**Share some information about what bitterness is.** If the person doesn't realize that the root of his problem is bitterness, this information will help him see what is going on in his life. Share the results of bitterness and the destruction it causes.

**Empathize with the person.** Help him acknowledge his legitimate needs that were not met (usually by a parent or spouse).

Validate the loneliness and sadness of not having needs met. **Rephrase what he is saying** so he knows you're hearing what he means and that you care about his pain.

Explain the importance of following the Action Steps to get rid of bitterness. Bitterness is a poison that will destroy his relationships with others and hurt his relationship with God. When people are bitter, they can't experience a full and healthy relationship with God. Forgiveness is the only way to get rid of bitterness and restore relationships with God and others.

## 5 ACTION STEPS

### 1. Acceptance

- Make a list of the people who have hurt you.
- Next to each name, write what you needed from that person.
- Next to that, write how it made you feel when that person didn't meet your need.
- In the last column write whether you think that person will ever be able to meet your need. Be honest.
- Accept and grieve your loss.

*The mantra in real estate is "location, location, location." Similarly, there are three things you cannot control in your life: other people, other people, other people.*

### 2. Forgive

- Ask God to help you forgive. Forgiveness is letting go of anger and your quest for revenge. Realize that you are powerless to forgive through your own strength, but God doesn't ask you to do something without giving you His strength and power to do it. *(Refer to the chapter on Forgiveness.)*
- Ask God to help you feel compassion for your offender. Psalm 78:38 says that God is full of compassion. As an act of your will, choose to pray that God will bless the person who hurt you.

### 3. Break the Chain

- Bitterness often runs through families: When a parent doesn't meet a child's needs, that child can become bitter and is then unable to meet his or her own child's needs. The chain can continue through several generations.
- Help the person ask God to help him break the chain.
- If the person has a bitter parent, help him see the parent as an emotional cripple. Just as you would not expect a person in a wheelchair to run a marathon, we don't expect an emotional cripple to meet our needs—he can't. We need to ask God to help us show love to that person.

### 4. Look for Support

- Find a community of support. If you move, pray that God will provide people to give you love, encouragement and support.
- Be proactive and look for those whom God has provided to be a part of your life. Strengthen any healthy relationships you have.
- Join a women's or men's group, or look for a prayer partner.

6

## BIBLICAL INSIGHTS

***Then Saul was very angry, and the saying displeased him; and he said, "They have ascribed to David ten thousands, and to me they have ascribed only thousands. Now what more can he have but the kingdom?" So Saul eyed David from that day forward. —1 Samuel 18:8-9***

- King Saul wasted his last years in hatred and anger. Fears, jealousies, murderous thoughts, and violent rage consumed him without relief. His soul was hardened, and he was unresponsive to any message from God. His bitterness finally turned into self-destruction.
- People who are bitter, angry, divisive, and dark in thought and deed need to be treated with mercy and respect, but they also must be lovingly called to repentance. The church can speak truth to them while taking care not to join them on their bitter journey.

***Can anyone teach God knowledge, since He judges those on high? One dies in his full strength, being wholly at ease and secure; his pails are full of milk, and the marrow of his bones is moist. Another man dies in the bitterness of his soul, never having eaten with pleasure. —Job 21:22–25***

- Job didn't understand why he was suffering so terribly. His words here reveal the depth of his pain and the bitterness rising in his heart. Job maintained his trust in God.
- How we respond to struggles defines our attitude toward God. We can become bitter, or we can press on in faith. God is faithful and will see us through any crisis.

*God wants you to forgive so you can be free from the destructive power of bitterness.*

***But I say to you who hear: Love your enemies, do good to those who hate you, bless those who curse you, and pray for those who spitefully use you. — Luke 6:27-28***

- Loving our enemies doesn't mean having affectionate feelings for them. Instead, it requires a decision to *act* in love toward them no matter how we *feel.*
- We need to deeply experience God's grace and forgiveness for our own sins. Then we'll be able to forgive those who hurt us.

***Repent therefore of this your wickedness, and pray God if perhaps the thought of your heart may be forgiven you. For I see that you are poisoned by bitterness and bound by iniquity. —Acts 8:22-23***

- Bitterness is like a poison eating away at a person's soft heart and turning it into stone—hard and unyielding.

- People poisoned by bitterness, whatever the cause, can be touched by God's grace.

***Pursue peace with all people, and holiness, without which no one will see the Lord: looking carefully lest anyone fall short of the grace of God; lest any root of bitterness springing up cause trouble, and by this many become defiled. —Hebrews 12:14-15***

*When my father and my mother forsake me, then the Lord will take care of me.*
—Psalm 27:10

- Believers need to look out for each other—helping those who are feeling weak and guiding those who are heading in the wrong direction. This will guard against "any root of bitterness" that might spring up.
- Bitterness that is allowed to take root in our lives will spring up into actions and words that can't be taken back. Believers can avoid the root of bitterness by dealing with their feelings immediately.
- When hurt or doubt is allowed to remain in our lives, they provide hospitable soil for the root of bitterness. With God's help, we can keep that root from having a place to grow, and if bitterness has already taken root, weed it out.

7

## PRAYER STARTER

Lord, I thank You that my friend has come in today to talk about this painful situation. I thank You, Lord, that while people often disappoint us, You never do. You have promised to meet all of our needs . . .

## RECOMMENDED RESOURCES 8

*Becoming a Contagious Christian*, by Bill Hybels

*Changes That Heal: How to Understand Your Past to Ensure A Healthier Future*, by Henry Cloud

*Tender Mercy for a Mother's Soul*, by Angela Thomas Guffey

# Burnout

> *Six days you shall do your work, and on the seventh day you shall rest.*
> —Exodus 23:12

## 1 PORTRAITS

- Jane hung up the phone. The nursing home had called again. Her mother was refusing to eat, and they wanted Jane to come immediately. When Jane got into the car, she was surprised by the wave of anger she felt. She felt it was all up to her to take care of everything. Lately she moved in a blur from caring from her children and her husband to her mother. It seemed like everyone always needed something, and lately, she was beginning not to care.
- Tom was barely ever home. The new job had him on the road much of the week. Travel was exhausting, so even when he was home, he barely had the energy to keep up with his two-year-old.
- Sandy is a good student—maybe too good. She's involved in a dozen activities, and she's taking advanced classes. She's starting to have difficulty sleeping, she can't relax, and at times, she can't even focus. She's starting to think that nothing she does is good enough, and so she may not even apply to college.

## 2 DEFINITIONS AND KEY THOUGHTS

- Western culture continues to push the limits, and has become increasingly obsessed with the "pursuit of excellence." Burnout has reached **epidemic proportions**, even within the church.
- Burnout is a stressful state characterized by **physical, emotional, and mental exhaustion, chronic fatigue, and lethargy**.
- Someone experiencing burnout may

  -feel cynical toward life

  -have a strong desire to escape

  -experience a false sense of failure

  -display emotional distancing, numbing, or apathy

  -become hypercritical

  -experience negative feelings toward others

  -show inappropriate anger or sadness

-succumb to depression

-suffer from a resulting physical illness

-abuse alcohol or drugs to numb the pain and reduce the stress

- Burnout is often experienced by those in the **helping professions** such as clergy, doctors, teachers, police officers, social workers, and others who work extensively with people. It is thought to result from the excessive demands that others place on their energy, time, and resources.
- Burnout can also be felt by **caregivers of the chronically ill** or by overburdened parents. These people often feel trapped by the demands of others, isolated, and unable to find sufficient time for rest and relief.
- Burnout is common for people in any role when the demands surpass their capacity for an extended period of time.

## 3 ASSESSMENT INTERVIEW

**Q1** How are you feeling physically? *(If the person is experiencing burnout, chances are he hasn't been caring for himself physically. If he hasn't had a recent physical, recommend that he have one.)*

**Q2** How are you feeling emotionally?

**Q3** When did these feelings start?

**Q4** What prompted you to currently seek help?

**Q5** What are the stressors in your life?

**Q6** How large a part does each stressor play in your stress level?

**Q7** What kind of support do you get—both with your responsibilities and for yourself personally?

**Q8** How well are you meeting the demands you face? *(Someone who feels that he must meet all the needs of an aging parent to be a "good" child is setting himself up for failure.)*

**Q9** What do you do for fun?

**Q10** Are you able to relax?

**Q11** What do you do when you relax?

**Q12** What are the activities you're currently involved in?

**Q13** How would you prioritize these activities?

**Q14** What can be taken out of your schedule?

> *Jesus didn't minister to everybody in Israel, even though He could have. Remember that it is not necessary to have more compassion than the Almighty.*
> —H. B. London

**Q15** What can be put into your schedule to help you have down time and family time?

**Q16** What would keep you from doing that?

**Q17** What is the worst thing that will happen if you say no or pull out of certain responsibilities?

**Q18** What will happen if you don'thing?

## 4 WISE COUNSEL

Any **physical concerns** and issues should be addressed medically.

Try to help the person gain some immediate **short-term relief** from his responsibilities.

Try to help him **mobilize family members and friends** to begin sharing more of the load. Ironically, someone who is overburdened needs this help the most and is often least willing to ask others to provide it.

There is both a **short-term crisis component** to helping someone who is burned out and a **longer-term component** of beginning to live life in such a way that burnout doesn't reoccur. When someone is burned out and overstressed, immediate relief is essential—helping him begin to get adequate sleep, relaxation, and exercise. Then as he begins to recover, help him look at some lifestyle issues that caused burnout, and replace them with healthy choices.

## 5 ACTION STEPS

### 1. Take Control

- Don't relinquish control of your schedule to the whims or demands of everyone else.
- Put a concrete plan in place to relieve yourself of some of your responsibilities. Enlist the aide of family members and friends. Call this a crisis, and help the person see his need for others' help and care.
- For students, help them find the balance between what is essential and what is merely "extra."
- Schedule days more sanely, humanely, and relationally to create a buffer zone of time to enjoy life, reduce stress, and make good decisions about life's demands.

*Rest in the LORD, and wait patiently for Him . . . Don't fret—it only causes harm.*
—PSALM 37:7-8

### 2. Say "No"

- This is a very helpful word—and those who are overworked don't know how to say it.
- While some things can't be dropped (the student has to do the homework, the businessman has to travel), there may be creative ways to schedule to allow for less stress and more rest.

### 3. Understand God's Will

- God never guides you into an intolerable scramble of overwork—after all, Jesus didn't live that way.
- Before you say yes to any new activity, pray about it. Even if it's a good activity, now may not be the time. Realize that there will be other phases in your life when the time will be better.

### 4. Slow Down

- Consciously slow the pace of life.
- Take the time you need to replenish your own resources.

### 5. Set Priorities

- When you set priorities, you may get less done, but you'll be doing the right things.
- When you think about what really matters, much of your frenzied activity will be seen as empty busyness.

*Let the peace of God rule in your hearts, to which also you were called in one body; and be thankful.*
—Colossians 3:15

## 6 BIBLICAL INSIGHTS

***Then God blessed the seventh day and sanctified it, because in it He rested from all His work which God had created and made. —Genesis 2:3***

- From the very beginning, rest has had a special significance for God.
- God rested, and He made the seventh day a day of rest for us as well (Exodus 20:8-11).

***So the Lord said to Moses: "Gather to Me seventy men of the elders of Israel, whom you know to be the elders of the people and officers over them; bring them to the tabernacle of meeting, that they may stand there with you. Then I will come down and talk with you there. I will take of the Spirit that is upon you and will put the***

***same upon them; and they shall bear the burden of the people with you, that you may not bear it yourself alone." —Numbers 11:16-17***

- Pushing hard with many hours and demands can become counterproductive. We need to set boundaries around our time and energy to protect ourselves.
- God is aware of our limitations and encourages us to lighten the load by delegating responsibility to others who can help us be more productive and effective.
- We should consider how we can delegate some responsibilites to others in order to get the job done.

***But those who wait on the Lord shall renew their strength; they shall mount up with wings like eagles, they shall run and not be weary, they shall walk and not faint. —Isaiah 40:31***

- Isaiah reminded God's people of the value of waiting upon the Lord. "Waiting" doesn't mean inactivity; rather, it is patient service that is not overcommitted and overextended.
- Many people desire to "mount up with wings like eagles," but they assume that the harder they run the more likely they will fly. In reality, the harder people run the more likely they will fall. Instead, "those who wait on the LORD shall renew their strength." "Waiting" is the antidote for spiritual burnout.

*Take rest; a field that has rested gives a bountiful crop.*

—OVID

***Come to Me, all you who labor and are heavy laden, and I will give you rest. Take My yoke upon you and learn from Me, for I am gentle and lowly in heart, and you will find rest for your souls. For My yoke is easy and My burden is light. —Matthew 11:28-30***

- Jesus says that He will take from our shoulders the heavy burdens that are burning us out, and replace them with an easy yoke, a light burden.
- Jesus is in touch with the burdens of life that we carry and how much they hurt and exhaust us. When we give our troubled hearts to Him, He gives us rest for our souls. That kind of rest will cure our burnout and renew our enthusiasm for Him and the work He has given us to do.

***And He said to them, "Come aside by yourselves to a deserted place and rest a while." For there were many coming and going, and they didn't even have time to eat. So they departed to a deserted place in the boat by themselves. —Mark 6:31-32***

- Even our Savior was aware of His human limitations. He never seemed to be in a hurry, and He didn't work 24-hour days. Even as more and more people crowded to Him to hear His words and be healed, He would often withdraw into the wilderness and pray (Luke 5:15-17).

- After an exhausting time of ministry, Jesus invited His disciples to take a break in order to refresh themselves.
- A hectic schedule takes a physical, emotional, and spiritual toll on us. God knows that we need to come aside and rest a while so that we don't burn out. He will refresh us so that we can continue to serve Him. Rest and refreshment is not wasted time.

## PRAYER STARTER

7

Dear Lord, Your child is tired—exhausted. He wants to do so much and feels so much responsibility, yet we know that You never call us to burn out. We pray today that You'll help ____ determine what You would have him do to fulfill Your priorities and Your will. Help him discern what can be discarded and what should be added so that life is in balance . . .

## RECOMMENDED RESOURCES

8

*Before Burnout: Balanced Living for Busy People*, by Frank B. Minirth & Paul D. Meier

*How to Beat Burnout I-II:* Broadcast Cassette/CD, by Focus on the Family

*Refresh, Renew, Revive: How to Encourage your Spirit, Strengthen Your Family, and Energize Your Ministry*, by H. B. London

*You have created us for yourself, and our heart cannot be stilled until it finds rest in you.*
—Augustine of Hippo

# Death

## 1 PORTRAITS

- Dave was 46 and enjoying life when he was hit by a car and killed while jogging. His wife came home from work to a mysteriously empty house—and then a police car pulled into the driveway.
- Millie was recovering from a heart attack in the hospital when another massive attack stopped her heart instantly. Her son found her dead on the floor of her hospital room.
- Lilly had a terminal illness and was expected to die. Her parents cared for her after she left the hospital, but a lengthy power outage stopped the respirator that kept her breathing.

## 2 DEFINITIONS AND KEY THOUGHTS

- **Death was not God's original desire** for humanity. God created human beings for life, not death. Adam had received the breath of life (Genesis 2:7). It was not until Adam and Eve sinned that death arrived.
- Death is difficult because it is **loss**—real and painful because a loved one is gone; symbolic because it reminds us of lost innocence, sin, and punishment.
- Death is distasteful and dreaded by humans, though God describes it as a gateway to a glorious new day. **Humans see death as an end** of a journey; God sees it as the beginning of a journey to a better life.
- Responses to death are as **different** as are individuals.
- The bereaved may **ask questions** like, "Why did God take him away?"; "Why did I get mad at her before she left the house?"; "What was I thinking when I let him go without me?"; "What if . . . why . . . ?"
- Sudden death can lead to a **complicated grieving process** because the suddenness often leaves feelings of anger, guilt, and abandonment.
- We now know that there are "stages" of grief as described by various theorists. Upon hearing of a death, most people experience **shock and denial**.

  *Shock* is an emotional and physical response to the news of a sudden death. The bereaved person may experience a racing heartbeat, shortness of breath, and feelings of unreality.

> *I must not think it strange if God takes in youth those whom I would have kept on earth until they were older. God is peopling eternity, and I must not restrict him to old men and women.*
> —Jim Elliot

*Denial* may follow quickly. The person may start doing ordinary things like washing the dishes or balancing a checkbook in an attempt to re-establish normalcy. Denial is usually broken when the bereaved person must face up to the many decisions that follow a death.

### What the Grieving Person Needs

David K. Switzer has described eight needs that must be fulfilled for effective resolution of the grieving process:

To *accept the reality* and finality of the physical death.

To become aware of and express all the *feelings* they have about the loss or toward the deceased. Sometimes this concerns the way the deceased died.

To *break the emotional ties* with the deceased; that is, not act as though the deceased is still physically present.

To *break habitual patterns* of speech and other behaviors that assume the deceased is physically present.

To affirm that *they themselves are worthwhile* apart from interaction and connection with the deceased.

To *reaffirm* and therefore allow to come back to life those characteristics and behaviors that contribute to the ongoing and growing life of the grieving person.

To *cultivate* both old and new relationships.

To *rediscover meaning* in their own lives.[1]

> *For to me, to live is Christ, and to die is gain.*
> —Philippians 1:21

## 3 ASSESSMENT INTERVIEW

Don't be surprised by the variety of responses people have to the death of a loved one. People may do bizarre things in the moments after hearing of a death. It is common for a person to say things like, "Why not me instead?" or "I think I caused it." These are not necessarily true confessions; they are the **cries of a breaking heart**.

**Don't rush** the grieving process. The anguish is a necessary part of the recovery process.

**Don't tell the person how to feel**. Your presence as a loving and attentive listener is your greatest gift to the person who is overwhelmed by grief.

### Rule Outs

**Q1** Are you having any physical symptoms as a result of grieving this death? *(Be aware of signs of physical distress; the bereaved person may need medical attention.)*

**Q2** Are you feeling increasingly depressed and suicidal? Is the grief beginning to subside? *(After a certain amount of time, the grief should be lessening. There will always be pain, but if the person is not improving over the course of several weeks, other intervention may be needed.)*

### Questions Immediately After a Death

*Be very sensitive to the person at this moment. It may be best to avoid asking any questions at all. Just be there.*

**Q3** Who has died and how? Were you present? *(Ask the bereaved to share with you what happened. Talking about the experience is cathartic and will help the bereaved person come to terms with the situation.)*

**Q4** Where are other family members? *(What kind of a support system exists for helping the person through the experience of loss?)*

**Q5** If the deceased had children, where are they? *(Are there any other individuals who will need help dealing with the loss of the deceased?)*

**Q6** Besides the obvious shock and pain, what else are you feeling right now? *(Look for feelings like guilt, anger, and fear. Try to identify the source of the feelings—and then make a mental note to talk further about it at a later time.)*

*"I am the resurrection and the life. He who believes in Me, though he may die, he shall live. And whoever lives and believes in Me shall never die."*
—John 11:25-26

### Questions to Help the Grieving Person

*These questions may be helpful in he weeks and months following the funeral.*

**Q7** Tell me your favorite memories about this person.

**Q8** What did you like best about the person?

**Q9** What were his or her best qualities? What were some things that bothered or irritated you? *(This helps the person realize that the deceased person was not perfect.)*

**Q10** When do you miss this person the most—morning or evening?

**Q11** To whom do you talk when you think about this person?

**Q12** Do you still cry when you think of this person?

**Q13** In what ways is your life better for having known this person?

**Q14** In what positive ways can you keep alive the good memories and the joy of having known this person?

## WISE COUNSEL 4

Some bereaved people may feel overwhelmed by the decisions required after a death. Others will argue with family members over decisions such as cremation or burial, or an open or closed casket. Your first job may be to **help family and friends come to consensus**. Remind people that the wishes of the deceased, if known, are not as important after death as the desires of the survivors. If that means canceling a cremation, then encourage family members to do it.

**Provide reassurance of hope, heaven, and resurrection**, but **avoid being glib** or superficial. When a loved one dies, the loss is acute, and knowing that the person is in heaven is not always an immediate comfort to those who are left behind—because they *are* left behind.

When dealing with a sudden death, **identify a family friend or other volunteer who can help with some of the practical tasks** that must be done for the funeral. Help the bereaved person prioritize what needs to be done. Aid in identifying a funeral home, writing an obituary, calling other family members and friends, etc.

It should be noted that the process of grief and bereavement will **not be resolved by things returning to "normal"** as the person understands it. A death always drastically changes the identity, roles, and responsibilities of the person closest to the deceased. Recovery will come as the bereaved person learns to **cope with and take on the new dynamics and tasks of daily life**.

## ACTION STEPS 5

### 1. Basic Needs

- Encourage family members to focus on basic needs—food, shelter, and safety. If these needs are not met, the critical emotional issues will be even harder to handle.
- People who are experiencing shock may neglect hygiene, forget to take necessary medications, or skip meals.

### 2. Ways of Coping

- Assess the level of emotions present by using some of the suggested questions.
- Some people process emotions better by being busy, while others need to be alone. Help the former to find something simple to do, and help the latter to find a quiet place to be alone.

### 3. Social Interaction

- Urge the grieving person to not withdraw, but to find support in his or her friendships.
- Some friendships will be different (for example, if a spouse has died), but encourage the person to appreciate friends who still want his/her company, even without the other person.

### 4. Helping Children

- If children are involved, counsel the family on strategies for helping them. Children often feel responsible for a sudden death, and teens can react in particularly complicated ways if a relationship to the deceased was tense.
- Children need, first of all, to feel secure. *Reassure them* that their family will be secure and stable.
- If a parent is in acute distress, try to *ensure that the children are cared for* by a familiar person who is calm.
- *Avoid statements* that indicate to a child that God caused the death because He "wanted Mom/Dad/Grandma/Johnny in heaven with Him."
- *Demystify death* for children. Good funeral directors often answer a child's curious questions.
- Help children begin to *process feelings* of anger, guilt, and abandonment. They need to know that such feelings are normal.

### 5. Allowing Time

- Help the grieving person to understand that the pain will take time to subside.
- Encourage him/her to truly grieve. Assure the person that the grieving process is healthy and eventually productive.
- Remind the person, when appropriate, of the stages of grief (see Death for a review of these stages).

*Human see death as something to be avoided as long as possible; God views it as something to be anticipated. Humans see death as a gloomy, dark night; God describes it as a glorious new day. Humans see death as the end of the journey; God sees it as the beginning of the best journey of all.*[5]

## BIBLICAL INSIGHTS

6

***But now he is dead; why should I fast? Can I bring him back again? I shall go to him, but he shall not return to me. —2 Samuel 12:23***

- After the death of David and Bathsheba's first son, David's only consolation was that eventually he would "go to him." While the child was alive, David had begged God to spare his life. When the child died, however, David was confident that the boy was with God and he would see him again.
- Christian parents who have faced the devastation of the death of a young child can take hope in David's faith that God will bring the little ones to Himself.

***Precious in the sight of the Lord is the death of His saints. —Psalm 116:15***

- We feel sad when loved ones die, and it is natural to grieve.
- God says that the death of a believer is "precious in the sight of the LORD." For believers, death is a gateway into the home in heaven where they ultimately belong.

*He whose head is in heaven need not fear to put his feet into the grave.*
—MATTHEW HENRY

***But now Christ is risen from the dead, and has become the firstfruits of those who have fallen asleep. For since by man came death, by Man also came the resurrection of the dead. For as in Adam all die, even so in Christ all shall be made alive. —1 Corinthians 15:20–22***

- Jesus gave us the promise of resurrection from the dead. He accomplished this by becoming human, dying, and then rising again.
- Someday in God's new creation, death itself will be destroyed: "The last enemy that will be destroyed is death" (1 Corinthians 15:26).
- We must always be ready to die, ready to stand before God, and ready to thank Him for all He has done in giving us salvation.

***So we are always confident, knowing that while we are at home in the body we are absent from the Lord. For we walk by faith, not by sight. We are confident, yes, well pleased rather to be absent from the body and to be present with the Lord. —2 Corinthians 5:6–8***

- Exactly what happens after someone dies? The Bible doesn't go into much detail, but it does say that believers who die—that is, are "absent from the body"—will be "present with the Lord" (see also Philippians 1:23). They will experience joy in the presence of God.

> *Some day you will read in the papers that D.L. Moody of East Northfield, is dead. Don't you believe a word of it! At that moment I shall be more alive than I am now; I shall have gone up higher, that is all, out of this old clay tenement into a house that is immortal—a body that death cannot touch, that sin cannot taint; a body fashioned like unto His glorious body.*
> —D. L. Moody

- When Christ returns, believers who have died will be raised and the living believers will be changed. All will receive glorified, eternal bodies (1 Thessalonians 4:16–18).
- God has promised that His people will be with Him forever. We can take hope in God's sure promise.

***I have fought the good fight, I have finished the race, I have kept the faith. Finally, there is laid up for me the crown of righteousness, which the Lord, the righteous Judge, will give to me on that Day, and not to me only but also to all who have loved His appearing. —2 Timothy 4:7-8***

- Believers can face death with confidence, knowing that God is waiting for them.
- On the day we meet Christ face to face, we want to be able to say, "I have fought the good fight, I have finished the race, I have kept the faith."

***Blessed are the dead who die in the Lord from now on . . . that they may rest from their labors, and their works follow them. —Revelation 14:13***

- This chapter in Revelation paints a picture of stark contrasts—eternal life with God or eternal life without God.
- Where will you be for eternity? We can be certain of forgiveness and eternal life by trusting in Christ to cleanse us, make us children of God, and give us the gift of eternal life with Him.

## 7 PRAYER STARTER

Dear Lord, thank You for the life of (the deceased person). Our hearts are very heavy that she/he is no longer here. Although this death may make no sense to us now, give us Your Holy Spirit as a Comforter in the hours and days to come, and help us to understand each other's needs at this time. In Jesus' name, Amen.

8

## RECOMMENDED RESOURCES

*Beyond Death: Exploring the Evidence for Immortality*, by Gary R. Habermas and J. P. Moreland

*Death and the Life After*, by Billy Graham

*The Undertaking: Life Studies from the Dismal Trade*, by Thomas Lynch

*When Your Father Dies*, by Bruce Barton and Dave Veerman

# Decision-Making and Knowing the Will of God

1

## PORTRAITS

- Gracie has always been a bright student in high school. She has been accepted by a number of universities. For the first time in her life, she feels as though she doesn't have the answer. Which school should she attend?
- Casey has been dating Madison for over two years. He is thinking of proposing to her, but with a life-long decision like this, he wants to make sure that this is what God would have him do.
- At 45, Paul isn't sure if he can handle another career change. A great opportunity has just surfaced, but he wonders if his family is up for the challenge. He wonders if this is God's plan to bless him.
- Mary wants to get a divorce. She met another man and wants you to tell her that it's okay for her to make that decision. She believes the grass is greener on the other side of the fence.

2

## DEFINITIONS AND KEY THOUGHTS

- **Don't tell the person what he should do**, even if it seems obvious to you. The person is seeking God's will, not yours.
- Encourage the person to ***wait* on God's answer**. He will reveal His will to those who earnestly seek Him—and God is much more patient than we are.
- Don't allow **superstitions** to enter into the decision-making process (such as blindly opening to a passage in the Bible or following a dream or odd coincidence). God uses His Word, not luck or superstition.
- God is most interested in a **relationship** in which we lean on Him daily for our strength and guidance. He will not show a person his entire life's journey. He wants us to rely on Him all throughout our lives.

*I will instruct you and teach you in the way you should go; I will guide you with My eye.*
—Psalm 32:8

- Decision-making can be **fearful** for some people. They speak of past decisions that ended disastrously, but this, of course, doesn't mean that God wasn't in those earlier decisions.
- Be careful not to put too much credence in a person's feelings. **Emotions can be misleading**—and sometimes cause a person to sin. Some people quote Psalm 37:4 and say that God wants to give them the desires of their heart. This is true only after the first half of that verse is fulfilled, which is that they should be delighting themselves in the Lord.

## ASSESSMENT INTERVIEW 3

Most Christians **want to know and follow the will of God**. They just want to know without a doubt that they are doing it.

First, explain to the person you are counseling that there is a difference between God's "directive" and His "permissive" will.

**Directive Will:** This is God's specific, absolute, unchangeable, unconditional directions for us to follow. Examples of God's directive will are as follows:

-Assemble with others in worship (Hebrews 10:25)

-Only marry another Christian (2 Corinthians 6:14)

-Raise children by God's standards (Ephesians 6:4)

-Obey and honor parents (Ephesians 6:1-2)

-Support one's own family (1 Timothy 5:8)

-Proclaim Christ (Acts 1:8)

-Meditate on the Scriptures (Psalm 1:2)

-Show love to others (1 Corinthians 13)

*If any of you lacks wisdom, let him ask of God, who gives to all liberally and without reproach, and it will be given to him. But let him ask in faith, with no doubting, for he who doubts is like a wave of the sea driven and tossed by the wind.*
—James 1:5-6

**Permissive Will:** God's permissive will is what He allows to happen. God has given us directives, but He permits us to choose to follow or not. For example, we can choose to be faithful to our spouse or commit adultery, to speak the truth or lie, and forgive those who hurt us or let anger fester into bitterness.

Ask questions that will help the person understand that **God does have a plan and will reveal it**. Discovering God's will is a process that occurs slowly. Often God is honored by any number of possibilities, providing they glorify Him. Remember, it's much easier to see God in the rearview mirror than through the windshield. That means that as we look back on our lives, we can usually see how God was working and how He was actively involved. It's much harder to look forward and see how our choices will work out.

**Q1** Tell me about your relationship with the Lord.

**Q2** What major decisions have you made in the past that turned out well or poorly?

**Q3** Do you believe that God guided you when you made those decisions?

**Q4** If so, how could you tell?

**Q5** What might happen in this current situation if you make the "wrong" decision?

**Q6** How do you think God will respond if you make the wrong decision?

**Q7** If you make the wrong decision, do you think God could accommodate that wrong decision and turn it into good?

**Q8** How might God direct you toward His will or plan in this decision?

**Q9** How will you know if you have made the right decision?

**Q10** Will any or all of the options you are considering bring glory to God?

**Q11** You are searching for the unrevealed will of the Lord. Do you currently follow what you already know is the revealed will of God as described in His Word?

## 4 WISE COUNSEL

**Faith and action** go hand in hand. It is not necessary to make a final decision hurriedly, but we must not become complacent and do nothing. We should search the Scriptures and seek counsel from mature believers.

God's peace is often—but not always—**His confirmation.** This peace is a knowing, a revelation, a confirmation that God is with us and we are walking in His will. Sometimes, however, we may know that we need to do something that is very difficult. In these times, we can be confident in God's leading even if our hearts feel anxious.

## ACTION STEPS 5

### 1. God Will Show His Will

Remind the person of James 1:5-6. Assure the person that God wants to reveal His will to him even more than he wants to know it. God will speak through His Word, His people, and through prayer. Be patient and pray through the decision at hand. Occasionally, God leads His children into darkness to test us and strengthen our faith. These times are part of God's plan to deepen our relationship with Him.

*The Christian life is not merely a matter of getting from here to there . . . from point A to point B. Instead, God's will for us in this life is more about the journey itself.*
—Charles R. Swindoll

### 2. Be Patient

At times, it may be necessary to make the decision to not make a decision. In other words allow yourself the luxury of purposely not deciding until a later time. Often, God's will becomes evident after a period of time, and we will have to backtrack if we rushed into a decision. During the waiting period, keep seeking God's will.

### 3. Be Proactive

Have the person list the major decisions that he has made in the past. Also have him list the results of those decisions. Then have him mark the decisions that he believes God directed.

### 4. List Options

Have the person list as many options as he can think of regarding the current issue.

### 5. What's Obvious?

Are any of those options automatically outside the will of God? For example, are any illegal or immoral?

### 6. Keep Praying

Have the person commit to pray over his options for a specified length of time, reading Scripture and looking to God for direction.

### 7. Get Wise Counsel

Have the person solicit advice regarding this decision from a trusted Christian friend or family member.

6

### 8. Make the Decision

After the specified amount of time has passed, encourage the person to make a decision and accept that decision as God's will.

## BIBLICAL INSIGHTS

***Yet there shall be a space between you and it, about two thousand cubits by measure. Don't come near it, that you may know the way by which you must go, for you have not passed this way before. —Joshua 3:4***

- Every day brings new experiences and new challenges that stretch our faith in God. Without God, people are left to wonder what direction to take. With God, believers can know that every new day is in His hands and He will guide according to His eternal plan.
- As the Israelites followed the ark in order to "know the way," so we can look to God and His Word in order to know the way He wants us to go.

> *In each action we must look beyond the action at our past, present and future state, and at others whom it affects, and see the relation of all those things. And then we shall be very cautious.*
> —Blaise Pascal

***But [Rehoboam] rejected the advice which the elders had given him, and consulted the young men who had grown up with him, who stood before him. —1 Kings 12:8***

- Rehoboam's unwillingness to listen to the older and wiser men ultimately led to the division of his kingdom.
- It is wise to seek counsel, and then we can compare a person's advice to God's Word. God knows the way we should go.

***I beseech you therefore, brethren, by the mercies of God, that you present your bodies a living sacrifice, holy, acceptable to God, which is your reasonable service. And don't be conformed to this world, but be transformed by the renewing of your mind, that you may prove what is that good and acceptable and perfect will of God. —Romans 12:1-2***

- Paul used a sacrifice as a picture to describe how believers should live, offering *themselves* to God as living sacrifices. In this way, they could be transformed by the Holy Spirit and have renewed minds.
- This transformation and renewal helps God's people know His good, acceptable, and perfect will.
- We are promised that we can know God's will for us when making tough decisions. We need to humbly pray and seek His guidance, knowing that He will answer in His timing and in His way. He probably won't, however, answer every question before we take action.

***If any of you lacks wisdom, let him ask of God, who gives to all liberally and without reproach, and it will be given to him. —James 1:5***

- Sometimes we must choose between two good options. Whatever the choice, we need God's wisdom to see life from His perspective and make good decisions.

- When we ask, we need to be willing to do what He says!

***Now this is the confidence that we have in Him, that if we ask anything according to His will, He hears us. —1 John 5:14***

- How can believers know God's will as they make decisions? First, they should consider whether they truly want to know what God wants and if they truly want to follow His leadership. Then they should pray and study God's words for guidance.

- The Holy Spirit will help them interpret and apply principles from His Word, but He won't give us full insight into the infinite, deep wisdom of God to know why He does certain things.

- Believers learn how to seek God's will, asking not what they want, but what He wants for them. When the answer comes, believers realize it and can act upon it.

## 7 PRAYER STARTER

Thank You, Lord, that You promise to give wisdom to those who ask. My friend needs wisdom today in order to make the right decision. He wants to know Your will and wants to do what You would have him do, but it's just not clear to him right now . . .

## 8 RECOMMENDED RESOURCES

*Decision-making and the Will Of God: A Biblical Alternative to the Traditional View,* by Garry Friesen and J. Robin Maxson

*The Journey of Desire: Searching for the Life We've Only Dreamed Of,* by John Eldredge

*Using Your Spiritual Gifts,* American Association of Christian Counselors Life Enrich Video Series, by Ed Hinson

*The Weathering Grace of God: The Beauty God Brings from Life's Upheavals,* by Ken Gire

> *We must make the choices that enable us to fulfill the deepest capacities of our real selves.*
> —Thomas Merton

# Depression

1

## PORTRAITS

- Tyler is 12 years old, and he is having trouble in school. Since his father walked out, Tyler has become increasingly violent around the house and argumentative with his teachers. He has lost most of his friends, too.
- Each morning Angela struggles to find the energy to get out of bed. She feels listless and down. Her kids need her, but she can't summon the energy to even interact with them—much less prepare meals or clean the house.
- George is having a hard time thinking clearly. He lost his job and just can't seem to crawl out of the hole he feels like he's fallen into. He doesn't interview because he's so down, so he sits around at home and plays on the computer. And he just keeps spiraling downward.
- Martha's husband died a year ago. She has struggled to find herself since he died. Recently, her friends report that she is talking more and more about death—and her desire to go ahead and die soon.

2

## DEFINITIONS AND KEY THOUGHTS

*Besides the obvious impairments in mood and relationships, untreated depression affects multiple areas of a person's life. It is one of the top three causes of disability and diminished work productivity.*

- Depression is **on the rise**—people born after 1950 are ten times more likely to experience depression than their predecessors. Those between ages 25 and 45 have the highest incidence of depression, though adolescent groups possess the fastest rate of depression growth.[1]
- **Women are twice as likely** to experience depression as men.
- Depression causes inestimable pain for both those enduring the disorder and people closest to them. It is said that depression destroys the lives of the victims and of their family members unnecessarily. Most sufferers **don't seek treatment** or believe their depression to be a treatable illness.[2]
- Depression differs from sadness, which is a God-given reaction to loss that serves to slow people down so that they may process grief. When one is sad, self-respect remains intact, intrinsic hope is maintained, and relief comes after crying and receiving support.

### Types of Depression

- *Clinical/Major Depression* is distinct in that symptoms are so severe that they disrupt one's daily routine.
- *Dysthymic Disorder* is a chronic, low-grade depression.

- *Bipolar Disorder*, previously known as "manic depression," is a type of mood disorder with severe changes in affect. A person may have periods of euphoric elatedness contrasted with periods of severe major depression. These cycles may occur rapidly or over several months.

- *Seasonal Affective Disorder (SAD)* is a severe onset of "winter blues" in which a person experiences depression due to, studies show, lack of sunlight (or Vitamin D).

*Depression is not something you can just "snap out of." It's caused by an imbalance of brain chemicals, along with other factors. Like any serious medical condition, depression needs to be treated.*[7]

## Causes of Depression

- Depression can be caused by **many life issues** including: unresolved anger, failure, rejection, divorce, abuse, fear, feelings of futility, lack of control, grief and loss, guilt or shame, loneliness or isolation, negative thinking, destructive misbeliefs, and other sources of intense stress. This is sometimes referred to as **"reactive depression."** In this type of depression symptoms may be lowest in the morning and increase throughout the day.

- **Medical and biological factors** can also facilitate depression: inherited predisposition to depression: thyroid abnormalities, female hormone fluctuations, serotonin or norepinephrine irregularities, diabetes; B-12 or Iron deficiencies, lack of sunlight or Vitamin D, a recent stroke or heart attack, mitral valve prolapse, exposure to black mold, prescription drugs (anti-hypertensives, oral contraceptives), or recreational drugs (such as alcohol, marijuana, cocaine). When rooted in biological causes, it is sometimes referred to as **"endogenous depression."** With this, sufferers often feel worst in the mornings. Note: Persistent reactive depression will change a person's brain chemistry and may lead to endogenous depression.

## Symptoms of Depression

- Symptoms include decreased energy, fluctuating body weight, depleted concentration, irritability, bouts of crying, hopelessness, despair, a disinterest in pleasurable activities, social withdrawal, and thoughts of suicide.

- The Bible is replete with examples of depression for a variety of reasons and results:

  David wrote that his depression was caused by unconfessed sin (Psalms 38; 51).

  God used depression to get Nehemiah's attention (Nehemiah 1–2).

  Job's devastating losses led his wife to advise him to "curse God and die" (Job 1–3).

  Elijah was so depressed over the situation with Israel's leaders that he wished to die (1 Kings 19).

## 3 ASSESSMENT INTERVIEW

### Rule Outs

**Q1** If 10 is extreme sadness, and 1 is feeling well, where are you today on a scale of 1 to 10? *(If the person is on the low side, find out what is causing the sadness. The issue to address may not be depression, but other concerns.)*

**Q2** Are you using drugs or alcohol?

**Q3** Are you currently taking any medications?

**Q4** When was the last time you had a thorough physical examination? *(If the person hasn't seen his doctor recently, give a medical referral.)*

**Q5** Do you have significant mood swings? *(Ask about the existence of mania or hypomania, and if they exist, give a psychiatric referral.)*

> *Anxiety in the heart of man causes depression, but a good word makes it glad.*
> —Proverbs 12:25

### General Questions

**Q6** How long have you felt depressed?

**Q7** What was happening in your life when you first became depressed? *(Someone who is depressed needs acceptance and gentleness. He may already be feeling as if he has failed in some way. Begin by listening to his story without judgment.)*

**Q8** Have you been depressed before?

**Q9** Do you have a family history of depression?

**Q10** Do you have difficulty concentrating?

**Q11** Have you lost interest in pleasurable activities?

**Q12** Have you noticed changes in your eating or sleeping patterns?

**Q13** Are you dealing with guilt or fear about anything? *(Fear is prevalent in many kinds of depression—anxiety is present in 70% of those diagnosed with depression.)*

**Q14** What do you see in your future?

**Q15** Have you had any thoughts about injuring yourself, or suicide? *(Sometimes the thoughts are vague, such as "It would be better if I were not here." Pay particular attention to the means for carrying out these thoughts. Someone who is suicidal and imagines having an automobile accident has both a plan and a means to carry it out.)*

## 4 WISE COUNSEL

A dangerous symptom of depression is **suicidal ideation**. If, as a result of your questions, you discover that the person intends to hurt himself, don't hesitate to involve other family members or a mental health professional. (See also the section on "Suicide.")

If you recommend that your person see a physician, **make sure he understands that it is OK for him to take medications** if needed to get depression under control. Communicate that using medication doesn't mean that he is weak or lacks faith.

## ACTION STEPS 5

### 1. Watch Physical Health

- Research shows that thirty minutes of moderate daily exercise is very helpful in elevating mood. If there would be no health risks, encourage the person to exercise, such as taking a brisk walk. Tell him you'll be checking up. Have him get a partner to walk with—it makes it harder to avoid the activity if someone is waiting.
- The person should have a medical checkup and should work with a doctor on a diet program. Better eating habits (for example, less sugar and more vitamins) can be a big help.

### 2. Get Behind the Scenes

- Help the person deal with whatever situation might be behind the depression.
- If he has recently suffered a significant loss, acknowledge that loss and begin to help him grieve. Give him permission to feel upset, but also draw him back to the light, emphasizing both the pain of the loss and the opportunity for future happiness in Christ.
- Encourage honest thinking about what might be other deep sources of the depression.
- Encourage him to keep a journal and write down thoughts that occur over the next couple of weeks regarding what is behind the depression.
- Have him carry a "daily mood log" and record times when he feels most depressed, what is happening, and what he is thinking at those times.

### 3. Begin Clear Thinking

- Challenge the person's negative statements and beliefs about hopelessness, helplessness, and worthlessness.
- For example, your person may say, "I'm no good. I have nothing to give to anyone." Ask pointed questions about strengths to draw out the fact that this person does indeed have value.
- Ask the person to prepare a list of ten things he likes about himself over the next week—and three of them have to be physical characteristics. Tell him you will ask him to tell you those ten things.
- Explain that very few things are really hopeless, and very few situations are "all bad."

- 35 million Americans (more than 16 percent of the population) suffer from depression severe enough to warrant treatment at some time in their lives.
- In one given period, 13 to 14 million people experience the disorder.[4]

### 4. Get Social Support

- Who are his friends? How can they help him counter the depression?
- What social groups is he currently involved in? *(Social isolation only deepens depression.)*
- What is the person's level of church involvement? Who at church could be of help and support?

### 5. Pay Attention to Spiritual Issues

- Does he have any unconfessed sin that is the source or is contributing to the depression?
- Does he need to forgive someone who hurt him?
- Is he motivated to pursue God's truth, forgiveness, and healing?
- Does he believe that God can remove his depression and provide a fresh sense of joy?

## 6 BIBLICAL INSIGHTS

***But [Elijah] went a day's journey into the wilderness, and came and sat down under a broom tree. And he prayed that he might die, and said, "It is enough! Now, Lord, take my life, for I am no better than my fathers!" —1 Kings 19:4***

- Life has highs and lows, and as in a mountain range, the lows often come right after the highs. Like Elijah, we may scale the heights of spiritual victory only to soon find ourselves in the dark valley of depression.
- While certain forms of clinical depression should be professionally treated, some depressed feelings are part of life's ups and downs.
- Like Elijah, we should listen for God's "still small voice" (1 Kings 19:12) to comfort us.

***Then as [Elijah] lay and slept under a broom tree, suddenly an angel touched him, and said to him, "Arise and eat." Then he looked, and there by his head was a cake baked on coals, and a jar of water. So he ate and drank, and lay down again. — 1 Kings 19:5-6***

- Depression can drain energy, twist values, and assault one's faith.
- Depression can affect anyone.
- God provided care to Elijah on many levels. He provided food so that Elijah regained his physical and emotional strength. An angel touched Elijah, confirming to Elijah that he was not alone. Also, God twice encouraged Elijah to rest.

*Depressed Christians certainly should continue praying, reading the Bible, confessing sin and pursuing holiness, but unless God or a professional Christian counselor says otherwise, don't assume the depression is caused by a spiritual problem. That type of thinking can keep a depressed Christian from seeking professional help.*[5]

***Why are you cast down, O my soul? And why are you disquieted within me? Hope in God, for I shall yet praise Him for the help of His countenance. — Psalm 42:5***

- Depressed feelings sometimes cause some people to turn away from God. Others, like David, allow those disquieted, depressed feelings to make them "hope in God," remembering His goodness.
- During these times of discouragement, living by faith takes on new meaning.
- Depressed people need to learn to trust what they can't feel or see. They need to understand that happiness comes from communion with God, and being thankful for all of His gifts to us..

***To console those who mourn in Zion, to give them beauty for ashes, the oil of joy for mourning, the garment of praise for the spirit of heaviness; that they may be called trees of righteousness, the planting of the Lord, that He may be glorified. — Isaiah 61:3***

- The Bible recognizes the heaviness of depression. God's love and understanding reach out to those who are depressed and discouraged.
- God promises to give consolation, beauty in place of ashes, oil of joy in place of mourning, and a garment of praise instead of a spirit of heaviness.

*Out of the depths*
*I have cried to*
*You, O Lord;*
*Lord, hear my*
*voice!*
*Let Your ears be*
*attentive*
*To the voice of my*
*supplications.*
*. . .*
*I wait for the Lord,*
*my soul waits,*
*And in His word*
*I do*
*hope.*
—Psalm 130:1-2, 5

## 7 PRAYER STARTER

Lord, at times we all feel downhearted. Today, my friend feels like he is walking in darkness with no way out. I pray, Lord, that You will provide healing and help us discern what is going on deep in his heart. If there is deep pain or loss, guilt or shame, help us to have the discernment to bring it into the light and confess it by Your grace . . .

## 8 RECOMMENDED RESOURCES

*The Feeling Good Handbook*, by David D. Burns

*Happiness is a Choice: The Symptoms, Causes, and Cures of Depression*, by Frank Minirth and Paul Meier

*Unveiling Depression in Women: A Practical Guide to Understanding and Overcoming Depression*, by Archibald D. Hart and Catherine Hart Weber

# Discouragement

## 1 PORTRAITS

- Mark has worked two jobs most of his adult life just to make ends meet. He has three children and a wife who works in the home and has a part time job outside the home. Recently, Mark lost the higher paying of his two jobs. If that weren't enough, their older son was suspended from school that same week for drug possession. Mark blames himself for not being at home enough.
- Lila is a young woman who has been out of college and in the work force for almost five years. All her college buddies are married, and she longs for a husband and family. This is all she has ever dreamed of. She had a longterm relationship for almost seven years with a Christian high school sweetheart. She blames herself for the breakup, and wonders "what if?" She sits at home alone most nights in her tiny apartment. A married friend is worried sick about her and doesn't know how to help her.
- Phil is 60 years old, and he realizes he doesn't have enough money saved for retirement. He's tired of working, and a lot of top jobs in his company are going to younger men. He doesn't see any way to make enough money so he can ever retire. He feels trapped in his work.

## 2 DEFINITIONS AND KEY THOUGHTS

> *There are three stages in the work of God: Impossible; Difficult; Done.*
> —Hudson Taylor

- Discouragement is a **feeling** of despair, sadness, or lack of confidence. A discouraged person is disheartened. Three underlying causes contribute to discouragement:

  Lack of confidence in ourselves

  Lack of confidence in God

  Lack of hope for the future
- Because discouragement is a feeling or emotion, it can **play games** with our minds. We need to learn how to control our minds, and replace discouragement with thankfulness, faith and hope, and lean on God for strength.
- Joshua was challenged with discouragement as he led the people of Israel into the Promised Land. God told Joshua, "Be strong and of good courage" (Joshua 1:6).
- God also reminded Joshua that the key to overcoming discouragement was a personal relationship with Him and letting God's truth give us perspective. The

Lord told Joshua, "This Book of the Law shall not depart from your mouth, but you shall meditate in it day and night, that you may observe to do according to all that is written in it. For then you will make your way prosperous, and then you will have good success" (Joshua 1:8).

- Discouraged people often blame themselves or God and ask, **"What if . . ?"** This is Satan's trap, his way of trying to have us think, "I blew it," "God doesn't care," or "God isn't capable."
- God has a much bigger picture for our lives than we could ever imagine. Challenges are God's way of refining us, preparing us for a bigger role in His kingdom.
- If not dealt with, discouragement **can lead to depression**, which can stop people in their tracks. People should be taught how to deal with their discouragement before it becomes depression.
- Discouragement reveals an **unwillingness to trust God**. It can be dealt a death blow when people consistently cast all their cares upon God.

*The answer to discouragement is getting our focus off ourelves and our limited resources and focusing on the unlimited power of God. He can do for us what we cannot do for ourselves. Even in the face of life's greatest challenges, His grace is sufficient.*
—John R. Cheydleur

## Causes of Discouragement

Shouldering our own worries, cares, and fears, then collapsing under the weight.

Events that are out of control.

Events that were in our control, but were handled poorly.

Past or current failure, or the potential for future failure.

Inability to handle family or personal stress.

## ASSESSMENT INTERVIEW

3

**Q1** What are some things, events, or people that make you discouraged?

**Q2** Do you have control over these things or are they out of your control?

**Q3** Describe yourself using three adjectives.

**Q4** Describe what you think someone else would say about you (a friend, a parent, a coach).

*(Note about questions 3 and 4: Sometimes there is an underlying problem of lack of self-confidence which leads to discouragement. If you suspect this, it needs to be addressed.)*

**Q5** When you feel discouraged, what do you do?

**Q6** Do you have a direction or plan for your life?

**Q7** What do you see yourself doing three years from now? Five years from now?

**Q8** Is failure an option for you? What does God think about failure?

**Q9** Envision yourself failing at something. How does that make you feel?

**Q10** Envision yourself succeeding at something. How does that make you feel?

4

## WISE COUNSEL

Feelings of discouragement signal that **it is time to pray.** Too often people neglect prayer when they become overwhelmed (ironically, this is when they need to be relying on God more).

Help the person understand that God uses our trials to shape our personal and spiritual lives for the better, and for His glory. Paul tells us, "Not only so, but w] also rejoice in our sufferings, because we know that suffering produces perseverance; perseverance, character; and character, hope. And hope doesn't disappoint us, because God has poured out his love into our hearts by the Holy Spirit, whom he has given us" (Romans 5:3-5).

*Look, the Lord your God has set the land before you; go up and possess it, as the Lord God of your fathers has spoken to you; do not fear or be discouraged.*
—Deuteronomy 1:21

Many times **events that are out of control** lead to discouragement. This is where faith in Gods steps in. Realizing that God sees the events in our lives before we do should help us not feel so overwhelmed.

There are times when discouragement is a result of **something the person could have controlled** (such as flunking college or being late to work). These events should be seen as wake-up calls and opportunities to improve, not hopeless or disastrous events.

Often the discouraged person needs someone to be **accountable** to—especially if this has been a lifelong struggle.

The person needs to see discouragement as an **opportunity to grow in Christ** and rediscover purpose and direction. Help the person to see discouragement as a time to **step back and look at life** and perhaps change some goals or behaviors (consider whether the unachieved goals are in keeping with God's plan for the person's life).

Feelings of discouragement can **creep into our lives from time to time.** They are normal because of our human nature. Share with the person that even when we have confidence in the greatness of God and a grip on handling challenges, discouragement can still occur in our lives from time to time.

## 5 ACTION STEPS

### 1. Be Realistic

Understand that discouragement is a part of life and often is a result of situations that are out of our control. *Failing* doesn't mean that we are *failures.*

### 2. Give Discouragement to God

When we have confidence in God, we gain confidence in His ability to use difficult situations for good in our lives. Prayer connects us with God's heart so our faith is strengthened.

### 3. Rethink Goals

Ask God for a fresh direction, and make plans for an optimistic future.

### 4. No "What Ifs"

Stop considering what might have been because that type of thinking only brings comparison, self pity, and despair.

### 5. Don't Focus on Feelings

Stop using feelings to determine how to handle discouragement. Feelings can change drastically with our mood. We need to grasp God's truth about His wisdom, sovereignty, love, and power.

### 6. Keep a Journal

Call it "Discouragements that Become Encouragements." Document each discouragement and what was done to turn it around.

### 7. Be Ready

Encourage the person to be ready for what God may have in mind. Help the person see that with confidence in God, he will gain confidence in himself. This will be a huge step toward overcoming discouragement.

*Be strong and of good courage, for to this people you shall divide as an inheritance the land which I swore to their fathers to give them. Only be strong and very courageous . . . This Book of the Law shall not depart from your mouth, but you shall meditate in it day and night, that you may observe to do according to all that is written in it. For then you will make your way prosperous, and then you will have good success.*
—Joshua 1:6-8

## 6 BIBLICAL INSIGHTS

***The steps of a good man are ordered by the Lord, and He delights in his way. Though he fall, he shall not be utterly cast down; for the Lord upholds him with His hand. —Psalm 37:23-24***

- Following God, having our steps "ordered by the Lord," doesn't guarantee success in every endeavor. In fact, some lessons that God wants to teach can only come through failure.
- When God's people fall, however, He doesn't allow them to be "utterly cast down." Instead, He helps them back up so that they can learn what He wants to teach them and move on with joy and hope.

- The only real failures are those who give up on God, wallow in self pity, and refuse to get up and go on.

***For a righteous man may fall seven times and rise again, but the wicked shall fall by calamity. —Proverbs 24:16***

- Trial and error are part of the road to success. As a person continues to try, "failure" is really no more than a setback, a possibility to learn from mistakes and try again.
- Failure can be our greatest teacher, even when it is painful and embarrassing. God's definition of success doesn't preclude failure, but it includes a willingness to refuse to quit, to learn from our mistakes, and to try again.

***And let us not grow weary while doing good, for in due season we shall reap if we do not lose heart. —Galatians 6:9***

- Paul encourages believers to "not grow weary while doing good."
- We should never allow discouragement to make us become idle. Our good works are valuable to God.

***Being confident of this very thing, that He who has begun a good work in you will complete it until the day of Jesus Christ. —Philippians 1:6***

- We won't be perfect until we are with Christ.
- In the meantime, when we feel discouraged by our failures, we should remember that God won't give up on us. He began His good work in us and will complete it when we meet Him face to face.

*Casting all your care upon Him, for He cares for you. —1 Peter 5:7*

- Casting our cares on God takes a great amount of trust and humility. We need to give Him all of our cares—not just the ones we think are big enough or important enough. God will even shoulder the troubles that we have brought upon ourselves—we can give them *all* to Him.
- His shoulders are big enough to carry all of our fears, worries, and troubles. When we give our cares to God, we can brush off our discouragement and get back to work. We have much to do for God!

*Why are you cast down, O my soul?*

*And why are you disquieted within me?*

*Hope in God, for I shall yet praise Him*

*For the help of His countenance.*
—Psalm 42:5

7

## PRAYER STARTER

Dear Lord, Your child is discouraged today. He feels that he can't get past this, and he can't do better. He feels that he has disappointed You and doesn't know where to turn. Help him to see that You are the God of second chances. Show him the path You want him to go, and the changes You want him to make as a result of this discouraging time . . .

8

## RECOMMENDED RESOURCES

*Moving On Disappointment with God & Life and the Recovery of the Heart*, American Association of Christian Counselors Life Enrich Video Series, by Tim Clinton

*Brokenness: How God Redeems Pain and Suffering*, by Lon Solomon

*The Dream Giver*, by Bruce Wilkinson

# Divorce

## 1 PORTRAITS

- Jennifer's husband filed for divorce the day after she found out about his affair with a coworker. She was devastated and begged him to attend counseling, but he has no interest in saving the marriage.
- Doug's wife walked out two years ago, leaving him to care for their three-year old son alone. "She didn't want to be a mother anymore," he says. He wonders if he should file for divorce and move on with his life.
- Emily's husband began beating her a couple of months after they were married five years ago. He always apologizes, and she always takes him back, but then it happens again and the cycle is repeated. "As a Christian, I feel I have to stay with him," she explains, "but I'm terrified of him."
- Luke and Cathryn constantly fight over everything. "I'm worried our fighting is hurting the children," Cathryn sighs. "I think they'd be better off if we'd divorce. At least they would have a peaceful home."

35% of people who become married suffer a divorce.[78]

## 2 DEFINITIONS AND KEY THOUGHTS

- Divorce is more prevalent in our generation than any other time in history.

According to the 2000 census, for some U.S. ethnic populations, single-parent households outnumber homes with a married-couple family.[1]

Research by The Barna Group shows that 35 percent of people who marry get divorced, and 18 percent of people are divorced multiple times.[2] Multiple divorces are extraordinarily common among born-again Christians, and 23 percent are divorced two or more times.[3]

Almost half (46 percent) from the Baby Boomer generation have undergone a marital split, and millions more are expected to divorce in the next ten years. Younger generations are likely to reach similar heights.[4] Between 40-50 percent of marriages that begin this year will end in divorce.[5]

For marriages with children, Wallerstein and Blakeslee (in their book, *The Good Marriage*) state from clinical experience that many children continue to battle with unhappiness even up to ten to fifteen years after the divorce of their parents.[6]

Almost 46% of Baby Boomers have been divorced, and millions more are expected to split in the next few years.[8]

Although Christian churches try to dissuade congregants from divorce, the rate of divorce among Christians is identical to the non-Christian population (35 percent). Alarmingly, the data shows that these divorces rarely occur before the married people have accepted Christ as their Savior.[9]

- **Divorce is a death** in every sense of the word: the death of a marriage, a family, and a dream. No one, especially a Christian, enters marriage expecting the marriage to end in divorce.

## Scriptural View of Divorce

- Malachi 2:16 says that the **Lord hates divorce**. The rest of the verse reveals that Malachi was speaking to men who were disloyal to their wives. God's compassion toward the injured party is clear.
- Romans 12:15 says that we should "weep with those who weep." People recovering from the trauma of a broken marriage **need the church** to:
  - Share in their sorrow
  - Offer compassion
  - Give reassurance that their church family will not reject them
  - Impart hope that God will somehow bring good out of this
  - Offer opportunities to serve in the church

## Biblical Exceptions for Divorce

- **Sexual activity outside the marital covenant** breaks the marriage vow. In Matthew 19:9, Jesus said that if a spouse has committed this type of sin, the other spouse is free to divorce and remarry. This does not mean divorce is required in instances where sexual sin has been committed, but it is permitted.
- Some maintain that **the abandonment** of a believer by a non-believing spouse leaves the believing spouse free to divorce the deserter (1 Corinthians 7:15).
- Current studies about divorce among Christian scholars and pastors offers several views of divorce and remarriage. Take time to read articles and books to determine which view most closely matches God's design.

> It is unrealistic and unfair to think that regardless of sure danger and possible loss of life, a godly mate and helpless children should subject themselves to brutality and other forms of extreme mistreatment. At that point, commitment to Christ supersedes all other principles in a home. I am not advocating divorce . . . but I do suggest restraint and safety via separation.
>
> – Chuck Swindoll

## Reasons for Separation

- **Physical abuse** is not addressed in the Bible as a reason for divorce, but nowhere does Scripture command a woman to stay in a home where she or her children are being physically abused. Separation (not divorce) is necessary for physical safety. Restoration should be predicated on **true repentance and by a significant change** in the abuser's behavior that lasts for an extended period of time. The church can serve as a protector of the abused by providing them with a safe place to stay, counseling, economic assistance, and using church discipline to hold the abusive spouse accountable.

> *Children feel that their childhood has been lost forever. Divorce is a price they pay as forfeiture to their parents' failures, jeopardizing their future lives.*
> —Dr. Judith Wallerstein

- **Mental or verbal abuse** are not biblical reasons for divorce, although in some cases, such as severe belittling and demeaning behavior, abuse can be cause for separation. Restoration of the relationship should be an ultimate goal.
- **Chemical addictions** to drugs or alcohol that result in harmful behavior to the spouse or children can be a reason for separation.
- **Physical neglect**, such as not providing appropriate food, clothing, shelter, or supervision for the children, can result in life-threatening situations. The spouse should remove the children if necessary to provide a safe environment. Restoration should again be the ultimate goal.

### Consequences of Divorce

- Divorce creates **new problems** in exchange for the old ones (see under Wise Counsel below).
- Divorce **devastates children**. That pain follows them into adulthood and affects their personalities and life choices.

## 3 ASSESSMENT INTERVIEW

### For Individuals or Couples Contemplating Divorce

When an individual or couple goes to counseling with divorce as an option, **it is usually the last stop before a lawyer**.

### Rule Outs

**Q1** Do either of you have reason to believe that you are in physical danger from the other?

**Q2** Has there been any type of abuse (physical, verbal, or sexual) to either of you or your children? *(If there has been physical or sexual abuse, the first step is to get the abused spouse and children away from the abuser and to a safe place. Counseling can't begin until this takes place. After the abused person is safe, the couple can meet for counseling. It is good for both spouses to be present during counseling times.)*

### General Questions

**Q3** What do you hope the outcome of counseling will be?

**Q4** Tell me about your marriage. How long have you been married?

**Q5** Do you have any children?

**Q6** How did you meet each other?

**Q7** What first attracted you to each other?

**Q8** How did you know this was the person you wanted to marry?

**Q9** What was your first fight about?

**Q10** When did the problems that bring you here today first arise?

**Q11** What have you tried already to solve these problems?

**Q12** Do you feel there is any hope for reconciliation?

**Q13** Do you both want a divorce? Why or why not?

**Q14** Have you asked God's permission to get a divorce?

**Q15** What would you need for you to want to reconcile?

**Q16** Do either of you think you have biblical grounds for divorce?

**Q17** What are they?

**Q18** How is your walk with the Lord?

**Q19** Tell me about your background, your parents and your siblings. What was growing up like for you?

**Q20** Are there any divorces in your family or among your friends?

**Q21** What do you think divorce will accomplish for you?

**Q22** How do think the divorce will affect your children?

**Q23** Would you like to see what the Bible says about divorce?

### For a Victim of Divorce (A Person Divorced Against His/Her Will)

When a victim of divorce comes for counseling, it is a positive sign that he or she feels worthy of help. The person's **self-worth, however, probably has been eroded or shattered** by the divorce.

Reinforce his or her decision by reminding the person that the Bible says **the wise seek counsel** (Proverbs 12:15).

### Rule Outs

**Q1** On a scale of 1 to 10, with 10 being joy and 1 being hopelessness, where would you put yourself? *(You will want to rule out the presence of clinical depression.)*

**Q2** Do you feel down much of the day on most days?

### General Questions

**Q3** Tell me what brought you here today.

**Q4** What do you hope the outcome of counseling will be?

**Q5** Tell me about your marriage. How did you meet your spouse?

**Q6** Did you notice any character qualities that gave you concern?

**Q7** Did your feelings change during the marriage? How?

**Q8** How did your parents feel about your spouse?

**Q9** When did you first realize there were problems?

**Q10** How did your spouse tell you he or she wanted to end the marriage?

**Q11** What were your feelings?

**Q12** What did you say and do?

**Q13** Who did you go to for help?

**Q14** Were they helpful?

**Q15** What was the reaction of your family? Your spouse's family?

**Q16** Do you have any children? How old are they?

**Q17** How did they react when they heard?

**Q18** How are they doing now?

**Q19** What are your plans for getting on with your life?.

**Q20** How has this experience made you stronger?

**Q21** Do you go to a support group?

**Q22** What support do you have around you?

**Q23** How are you and your children doing financially?

**Q24** What is your relationship with the Lord like?

**Q25** Do you feel the Lord has rejected you or forgotten about you?

4

## WISE COUNSEL

### For Couples Contemplating Divorce

Share what God says about divorce. Explain that **God hates divorce** because of the hurt and devastation it brings to people.

Make clear that the only biblical reasons for divorce **are sexual sin (by one or both of the partners in violation of the marital covenant) and abandonment**. Make it clear that people are not commanded to divorce in these situations but are allowed to. **Forgiveness and restoration** are also an option when true repentance is demonstrated by the partner who has violated the marital covenant.

**Empathize** with the pain and hurt both spouses are going through, but share with them the new problems divorce will bring:

Financial difficulty of providing for two households

Probability of custody battles

Stress of single parenthood, with no one to help

Guilt from seeing their children's world torn apart

Dealing with sending children back and forth between them

The possibility of anger, grief, loneliness, or even hopelessness

*Divorce does not eliminate problems; it just substitutes a new set of problems.*

### For Victims of Divorce

Share that **God sees the person's troubles, but it grieves Him** to see the person hurt like this (Isaiah 40:27-28).

Using *Biblical Insights*, let the person know that God loves him or her with total acceptance. He **understands the feelings of betrayal and rejection** because He was also betrayed and rejected.

Explain the importance of grieving and the time it takes.

Grieving usually takes **two to five years and consists of five stages**: Denial, Anger, Bargaining, Depression, and Acceptance. A person may go through these stages many times in different order before complete healing occurs.

**Validate the evil** done against the person. Though the person is a victim, he can **become a survivor**.

Give hope that **God can bring good** out of this (Romans 8:28).

Share with the person that other people may judge him unjustly, and he will be tempted to feel guilt and shame because of the divorce. It is important that he **not accept that shame and guilt**.

*God does not hate divorced people—He hates the cruelty of divorce.*

Express that the person will never be truly healed and released until he **forgives himself and the spouse**. As long as he feels anger and resentment, he is not free from them. (For more, see the section on Forgiveness.)

5

## ACTION STEPS

### For Couples Contemplating Divorce

#### 1. Put the Divorce on Hold

- They should delay the divorce settlement and attend marriage counseling if they have not yet done so.
- They should also begin to meet with a trained marriage mentoring couple who can encourage and instruct them.
- Ask: "Considering the devastation a divorce causes for all involved, isn't it worth your best efforts to save this marriage if you can?" At the end of the marriage mentoring and counseling, they can revisit their decision and see if there is any reason to be hopeful.

#### 2. Go to Marriage Mentoring and Counseling

- Have on file the names of several good Christian marriage mentors and counselors.
- These people should have a record of success in helping couples restore their marriages.

#### 3. Read Books

- See the suggested list at the end of this section.
- Explain that many couples were once where they are and now have healthy and fulfilling marriages. It is helpful to read books that helped others.

### For Divorced People

#### 1. Recovery Group

- Counsel the person to begin attending a divorce recovery group. Many larger churches have these groups. Research and recommend ones in your community.
- Some groups last a specific number of weeks; others are using twelve-step programs.

## 2. Go to Counseling

- Start individual counseling on a weekly basis. The person needs someone to whom he can be accountable for taking steps toward healing.
- The person may want to make a commitment to meet with a counselor once a week for several months, and then monthly for awhile.

## 3. No Major Decisions

- The person should not make any major life decisions for at least a year without consulting his counselor or pastor.
- This caution guards against making poor decisions while he is still emotionally vulnerable.

## 4. No New Relationships

- The person should not rush into any new dating relationships.
- The person should focus on letting God fill the emptiness inside him. He needs to heal before entering another relationship.

## 5. Church Involvement

- Encourage the person to get involved in church and join a Sunday school class.
- Encourage the person to seek out friends of the same sex to whom he can talk and with whom he can do fun and meaningful activities.
- When he feels up to it, encourage him to serve and help others.

# BIBLICAL INSIGHTS 6

***They said to Him, "Why then did Moses command to give a certificate of divorce, and to put her away?" He said to them, "Moses, because of the hardness of your hearts, permitted you to divorce your wives, but from the beginning it was not so."* —Matthew 19:7-8**

- God has always intended each married couple, one man and one woman, to remain married for life (Genesis 2:24). Moses had indeed permitted divorce (Deuteronomy 24:1), but only because of the "hardness" of human hearts.
- Divorce is permissible, but marriage vows should not be taken lightly.

- God would have couples do their best—with His help—to keep their marriage intact. If a divorce occurs, God's compassionate love can heal even the deepest wounds.

***When a man takes a wife and marries her, and it happens that she finds no favor in his eyes because he has found some uncleanness in her, and he writes her a certificate of divorce, puts it in her hand, and sends her out of his house. —Deuteronomy 24:1***

- God desires marriages to stay together. Because sin has infected all relationships, however, some marriages don't survive.
- Moses' commands regarding divorce were given in a culture where a man could divorce his wife verbally and leave her with no property or rights. These commandments regulating divorce in Israel protected those left most helpless—the woman and her children.
- The Bible does not give people an easy way out of their commitments. People are expected to honor their commitments.

***The woman answered and said, "I have no husband." Jesus said to her, "You have well said, 'I have no husband,' for you have had five husbands, and the one whom you now have is not your husband; in that you spoke truly." —John 4:17-18***

- Divorce is not an unforgivable sin. As painful as divorce is for all involved, and as heartbreaking as divorce is for those who face it without wanting it, God can touch broken lives and make them whole again.
- When possible, couples should pursue every option to avoid divorce. At times, however, the unthinkable occurs. God is there to help us pick up the pieces.

*Victims of divorce do not need to be judged or condemned by the church.*

***If any brother has a wife who does not believe, and she is willing to live with him, let him not divorce her. And a woman who has a husband who does not believe, if he is willing to live with her, let her not divorce him. For the unbelieving husband is sanctified by the wife, and the unbelieving wife is sanctified by the husband . . . But if the unbeliever departs, let him depart; a brother or a sister is not under bondage in such cases. But God has called us to peace. For how do you know, O wife, whether you will save your husband? Or how do you know, O husband, whether you will save your wife? —1 Corinthians 7:12–16***

- When one spouse becomes a Christian and the other doesn't, the believing spouse should stay in the marriage.
- Paul explained that the marriage bond is so strong that a believer should not willingly break it. Through that union, the unbeliever may become a Christian. In any event, the believer can have a positive influence on the spouse and children.

## PRAYER STARTER

7

Lord, we know that You hate divorce. You hate what it does to people. You hate the death of a marriage, a family, a dream. And yet, it is a sad reality. We want Your will, Lord. We want what is best for all concerned. I pray today for . . .

## RECOMMENDED RESOURCES

8

*Before a Bad Goodbye,* by Tim Clinton

*Divorce Recovery: For Those Starting Over Again,* American Association of Christian Counselors Courageous Living Video Series, by Tom Whiteman

*Grace and Divorce: God's Healing Gift to Those Whose Marriages Fall Short,* by Les Carter

*Helping Children Survive Divorce: What to Expect; How to Help,* by Archibald D. Hart

# Domestic Violence

> *During the six months following an episode of domestic violence, 32% of battered women are victimized again.*
> —Bureau of Justice Statistics:

## 1 PORTRAITS

- Marge stared in the mirror at the new bruise on her face. She had never imagined that this would happen to her. She knew her husband Paul was sorry. He had told her so again and again last night after he had seen the marks on her face where he had hit her. This morning before he left for work, he promised that it wouldn't happen again. "Just give me another chance," he said.
- Janet didn't know what to do. The wedding was only weeks away. She had always thought that she and Randy had made such a good couple, but lately he was become more controlling of her time and demanded to know where she was going when he wasn't with her. He was also jealous when some of her other friends spent time with her. But last night was the worst. When she had disagreed with him, he grabbed her arms and shook her. She was afraid. But surely he would calm down once they were married, wouldn't he?
- Tom lived in fear that his wife might explode at any time. Marsha had always had a temper and would occasionally slap him when she got angry. Last night, she had been drinking, and when she attacked him, she really tried to hurt him. Tom knew he couldn't fight back, but he didn't know how much more of this he could take.

## 2 DEFINITIONS AND KEY THOUGHTS

- Domestic violence or intimate partner violence (IPV) may follow a three-step circular pattern.
  1. **Tension builds** until the abuser loses control.
  2. **Battering occurs.** The batterer sometimes feels that the victim deserves it, or that he needs to teach her a lesson. Rationalization about the battering and minimization of the consequences of the abuse are common.
  3. **Remorse**. The batterer is sorry and asks for forgiveness. His tension is gone and he asks for reconciliation. For a while, he may make promises that "it will never happen again" and behave in very loving and contrite ways.
- The third stage of the cycle looks like true repentance. However, it is only an absence of tension and the feeling on the part of the abuser that the victim has "learned her lesson." When this situation changes and the tension again increases, the battering usually reoccurs.

- Domestic violence is fueled by the **batterer's need to control**. When the victim tries to break the cycle, he or she may be in danger of more battering.
- **Biblical headship** in a marriage is based on love and servant leadership, not on the man's control over his wife, and certainly not on physical coercion.
- Abusers and victims of domestic abuse **often grew up in abusive homes**. They simply replicate the examples they saw.
- Many of the predictors of domestic violence are **present in the dating relationship**. Some of these predictors are:
  -Use of force or violence to solve problems
  -Need for the abuser to prove himself by acting tough
  -Rigid concepts of what men and women should be
  -The victim's fears of the abuser's anger
- In public, abusers can often be charming and personable, but they **behave entirely differently in private**. In interactions or counseling sessions, abusers can look quite reasonable and can try to influence you, portraying their wives as irrational or rebellious, and wanting you to see their side.

## CONSEQUENCES

- **Physical**

Women with a history of IPV report 60 percent higher rates of all health problems than do women with no history of abuse.

IPV victims report lasting negative health problems, such as chronic pain, gastrointestinal disorders, and irritable bowel syndrome, which can interfere with or limit normal daily functioning.

The more severe the abuse, the greater its impact on a woman's physical and mental health, resulting in a cumulative effect over time.

IPV also affects reproductive health and can lead to gynecological disorders, unwanted pregnancy, and premature labor and birth among pregnant women.

IPV victims have a higher prevalence of sexually transmitted diseases, hysterectomy, and heart or circulatory conditions.

- **Psychological**

Abused girls and women often experience adverse mental health conditions, such as depression, anxiety, and low self-esteem. Women with a history of IPV experience increased levels of substance use, antisocial, and suicidal behavior.

**56%** of Americans surveyed say they know a victim of domestic violence.

How people say they would react if assaulted by their partner:

**31%** would leave immediately

**29%** would stay and try to work it out

**18%** would call the police and file a report

**16%** would seek help and information

**5%** don't know what they would do

—USA Today, January 6, 2005

*In homes where partner abuse occurs, children are 1,500 times more likely to be abused.*
—DEPARTMENT OF JUSTICE STATISTICS

- **Social**

  Researchers report that children who witness IPV are at greater risk of psychiatric disorders, developmental problems, school failure, commiting violence against others, and low self-esteem. Women in violent relationships experience restrictions in their attempts to gain access to health services, take part in public life, and receive emotional support from friends and relatives.

## VULNERABILITY OF VICTIMIZATION

- Recent research identifies several factors related to IPV:

  History of physical abuse; prior injury from the same partner; having a verbally abusive partner; economic stress; partner history of alcohol or drug abuse; childhood abuse; being under the age of 24; marital conflict; male dominance in the family; poor family functioning.

## 3 ASSESSMENT INTERVIEW

If a couple comes into counseling together and you **suspect abuse, speak to each partner separately** to get an accurate understanding of the situation. To avoid putting the victim in danger, simply say that it is **your normal practice** to speak to each member of the couple individually.

### Rule Outs

**Q1** Do your fights ever get physical? *(This is an easier question to answer than one about violence or abuse.)*

**Q2** Is there use of alcohol or drugs?

**Q3** Do you feel safe with your spouse? *(If you have any questions about the presence of abuse, do not try to address marital issues with the couple together until the issue of safety is thoroughly addressed.)*

*90–95% of domestic violence victims are women. As many as 95% of domestic violence perpetrators are male.*
—WWW.ABANET.ORG

### General Questions

**Q4** Has your spouse ever hurt you physically or tried to physically intimidate you?

**Q5** If yes, when was the last time it happened?

**Q6** How often does the abuse happen?

**Q7** Have you ever tried to get help?

**Q8** What have you done to get help?

**Q9** Has it worked?

**Q10** Does your spouse go through the cycle of tension, battering, and then remorse? *(See under Definitions and Key Thoughts above.)*

**Q11** Describe what usually happens.

**Q12** Are you afraid for your children's safety?

**Q13** Do you have a plan for safety if the abuse happens again?

## 4 WISE COUNSEL

**The first issue is safety.** Working out a plan of safety with the victim is essential.

Sometimes what keeps a victim in the abusive situation is the lack of **resources to escape**. Be sure you investigate this need.

## 5 ACTION STEPS

### 1. Provide for Safety

- Reassurance of the person's safety (and that of any children involved) is first priority.
- If necessary, encourage the person to separate from the abuser, and provide resources for aid and shelter.

### 2. Have a Plan

- Help the person develop a plan for the next time abuse occurs.
- Be sure that the victim has numbers to call—police, a family shelter or hotline, and a trusted friend or counselor.
- If she decides to leave, where will she go? Who will she call?
- Advise her to have bags with essentials packed and in an easily accessible location so she and the children can leave quickly if needed.
- Have her photocopy important documents and have them packed as well.
- She should think through how she can access money, car keys, and important documents if she needs to leave suddenly.
- If she needs to leave at some point after an abusive incident, tell her that no argument or discussion should happen at this point, but to calmly

*Domestic violence crosses ethnic, racial, age, national origin, sexual orientation, religious and socioeconomic lines. By the most conservative estimate, each year 1 million women suffer nonfatal violence by an intimate. By other estimates, 4 million American women experience a serious assault by an intimate partner during an average 12-month period.*
*—WWW.ABANET.ORG*

exit and go to a location she has predetermined and meet the people at that location.

### 3. Follow Up

After the first conversation, put a follow up plan in place for the person to get continued help.

### 4. Reassurance

- Reassure the person that abuse is never "deserved," but is always wrong.
- A husband's role of headship in a marriage never includes the right to control or abuse.

### 5. Relationships

- Assess how much support the person has, and encourage her to reach out to others for help.
- A victim of abuse is often isolated, both out of shame about her situation and the abuser's need to control.

Nearly 5.3 million intimate partner victimizations occur each year among U.S. women ages 18 and older. This violence results in nearly 2 million injuries and nearly 1,300 deaths.

Estimates indicate more than 1 million women and 371,000 men are stalked by intimate partners each year.

Intimate partner violence occurs across all populations, irrespective of social, economic, religious, or cultural group. However, young women and those below the poverty line are disproportionately affected.

- Center for Disease Control & Prevention: Statistics on Intimate Partner Violence

6

## BIBLICAL INSIGHTS

***Yet your father has deceived me and changed my wages ten times, but God did not allow him to hurt me. —Genesis 31:7***

- Trust involves being trustworthy and being willing to trust someone who has earned it.
- Jacob had originally fled from home because he had deceived his brother (Genesis 27:43); here he fled because he had been deceived by his father-in-law. Violated trust can destroy relationships.
- We need to build a bond of trust with those closest to us.

***And Moses and Aaron gathered the assembly together before the rock; and he said to them, "Hear now, you rebels! Must we bring water for you out of this rock?" Then Moses lifted his hand and struck the rock twice with his rod; and water came out abundantly, and the congregation and their animals drank. —Numbers 20:10-11***

- Anger can be the most damaging of all emotions, causing people to say or do things they regret. Out-of-control anger can ruin friendships, marriages, and children.
- Some people live with the consequences of choices made in a moment of heated anger. People who struggle with destructive anger need to find help to discover alternative ways to manage it. This begins by turning it over to God.

***Then he went to his father's house at Ophrah and killed his brothers, the seventy sons of Jerubbaal, on one stone. But Jotham the youngest son of Jerubbaal was left, because he hid himself. —Judges 9:5***

- The tragic story of Abimelech pictures extreme violence used for selfish reasons. This illegitimate son of Gideon and a concubine (Judges 8:29-31) brought disaster upon the rest of Gideon's family. Violence and murder became his way of dealing with all threats to his power (Judges 9:22-49). In the end, however, his violent ways resulted in his own destruction (Judges 9:50-56).
- Violence doesn't really resolve anything, and ultimately, it leads to more violence.

***And you, fathers, do not provoke your children to wrath, but bring them up in the training and admonition of the Lord. —Ephesians 6:4***

- In their training and discipline, parents should not provoke their children "to wrath." In other words, sometimes a parent's discipline can be overly harsh, unfair, unloving, or irresponsible, causing children to become angry, discouraged, and resentful.
- Parents who discipline fairly, consistently, and lovingly raise their children to be stable, mature, and respectful.

***Fathers, do not provoke your children, lest they become discouraged. —Colossians 3:21***

- Although children are commanded to obey their parents, parents do not have permission to be cruel or unreasonable in their treatment of their children.
- Parents who nag, belittle, or deride their children destroy their self-esteem and discourage them.
- The purpose of parental discipline is to train children. Consistent discipline, administered with love, will help children to grow into responsible adults.

As many as 324,000 women each year experience intimate partner violence during their pregnancy.

Inimate partner violence accounted for 20 percent of all nonfatal violent crime experienced by women in 2001.

44% of women murdered by their intimate partner had visited an emergency department within two years of the homicide, 93% of whom had at least one injury visit.

-Center for Disease Control & Prevention: Statistics on Intimate Partner Violence

## 7 PRAYER STARTER

Today we're worried and frightened, Lord. Your children are in need of great help. One needs help handling anger so that he no longer is abusive. The other needs help to know how best to deal with this situation and get her husband the help he needs . . .

## 8 RECOMMENDED RESOURCES

*No Place for Abuse: Biblical & Practical Resources to Counteract Domestic Violence*, by Catherine Clark Kroeger and Nancy Nason-Clark

*Refuge: A Pathway Out of Domestic Violence and Abuse*, by Donald Stewart

*Refuge from Abuse: Healing and Hope for Abused Christian Women*, by Nancy Nason-Clark and Catherine Clark Kroeger

# Eating Disorders

> *Approximately 30-35% of college-age women have a diagnosable eating disorder.*

## 1 PORTRAITS

- Lindsay had binged a few times during middle school and early high school. She didn't like vomiting, so she used laxatives afterward and exercised a lot.
- Madeline and Maggie were twelve-year-old twins whose anorexia began because of their intense competition with each other. They obsessed over who ate the least and exercised the most.
- Don was a seminary student who found that he was very good at keeping track of food intake. After he graduated, his food obsession went with him to his job as a youth pastor.
- Jennifer would binge and purge for weeks every time she started dating someone new or broke up with a boyfriend. After getting married in her early 20s, her binging stopped for a while. When it returned, she started getting cavities from the vomiting, and she finally decided she had to tell her husband.
- Richard ate when he felt discouraged, and Richard felt discouraged a lot. Eating made him feel better, at least for a little while. In the last couple of years, he has gained 80 pounds.

> *Experts now estimate that 1 of every 100 women between the ages of 12 and 25 suffer from anorexia, while 1 of every 7 women in the same age group develops bulimia.*
> —INTRANET.MICDS.ORG

## 2 DEFINITIONS AND KEY THOUGHTS

- People with eating disorders are characterized by a primary **obsession with food** (either eating a lot or not eating enough) and compulsive behaviors related to eating. Often these behaviors are attempts to gain control of life and deal with **anxiety and stress.**
- Compulsive overeating and milder forms of obsession with food or weight can also be considered eating disorders if they produce **unhealthy and obsessive behaviors** and/or altered thought processes or body image.
- 90 percent of those with eating disorders are women.

### Anorexia Nervosa

- Anorexics (those with *anorexia nervosa*) **starve themselves** in order to feel and look thin.

- Even when weighing 20-30 pounds below the lowest recommended weight for their age and height, anorexics **still believe they are fat.** Body image is extremely distorted.
- Anorexics consider hunger pangs to be good—evidence of their success at weight loss. They **obsess over what they eat** and how much they exercise..
- Some studies indicate that as many as 20 percent of anorexics may **die of starvation**.
- Most anorexics are **girls between the ages of 14 and 18**. A symptom of the disease is that they stop menstruating or never start.
- Many anorexics come from homes where parents held them to **high or perfectionistic standards**, which they were successful in meeting early in life. They may resort to anorexia when standards become unclear, for example when rigid parental standards are challenged by permissive societal expectations.
- The attempt at perfection is fueled by several fears:
  - Fear of fat
  - Fear of failure
  - Fear of being less than perfect
  - Fear of rejection
  - Fear of losing control

*Only one in ten people receives treatment for their eating disorder. Approximately 80 percent of those who do access treatment for anorexia nervosa don't receive the intensity of treatment they need to in order to being the road to recovery.*

—ANOREXIA.CHRISTIANET.COM

### Bulimia Nervosa

- Bulimics (those with *bulimia nervosa*) **binge on high-calorie, fatty, and/or sweet foods**, secretively eating hundreds or thousands of calories at a sitting. Afterward, to counteract the effect of this eating, they **self-induce vomiting**, overdose on laxatives, or exercise excessively.
- Bulimia tends to occur in girls in **late adolescence**, such as the last years of high school and early college.
- Bulimia can lead to complications related to **electrolyte imbalances and destruction of tooth enamel.**
- Bulimics are often of **normal weight**. While they are worried about fat, they do not suffer from the severe distortion of body image that plagues anorexics.
- Unlike anorexics, bulimics are often not particularly thin, yet they are similarly **obsessed with food and body weight**.
- While anorexics feel they are right in their extreme diets, bulimics know that their binging and purging is **not normal**.

### Common Barriers to Treatment

There are often multiple barriers that keep a person from receiving proper treatment for an eating disorder.

**Access:** Sometimes finding treatment from someone who specializes in eating disorders is difficult.

**Considering It an Act of Will:** There are emotional, spiritual, and interpersonal complexities involved in the healing of eating disorders. People with an eating disorder can't simply "will themselves" out of it.

**Denial:** People with eating disorders can have distorted body images and often deny or minimize the level of harm they inflict on themselves.

**Fear of Treatment:** Treatment involves discomfort, facing pain and hurt, and can be a difficult and frightful process. This prevents some people with eating disorders from seeking treatment.

*Just as lies fuel bulimia and anorexia, lies will be used to avoid getting the proper help. Love, patience, persistence, and discernment are vital to offering help and encouragement to people in these situations.*
—Jesse Dillinger and Gregory L. Jantz

**Financial Barriers:** Unfortunately, many treatments for eating disorders are expensive.

**Idols:** With eating disorders, food is not about sustenance. It is a preoccupation and obsession with body image, control, or comfort.

**Lack of Faith:** People with eating disorders may not believe any person or treatment can help with their affliction.

**Minimizing the Problem:** Many delay treatment because they minimize the severity of the problem, and they believe it might go away on its own.

**Pride:** It's not easy to admit to self, others, and God that life is out of control.

**Shame and Guilt:** Secrecy and shame may shroud eating disorders for long periods of time. It is very hard for people to admit there is a problem, and they are embarrassed to admit to not eating, or binging and vomiting.

## Warning Signs

Secretive behavior coupled with trips to the bathroom after eating

Laxative or diuretic abuse

Heart palpitations

Depression

Social withdrawal

Restrictive dieting

Frequent and obvious weight fluctuations

Preoccupation with body weight and appearance

3

## ASSESSMENT INTERVIEW

In many cases you will be **approached by a family member** who is concerned about a girl's eating. Your questions need to be probing but nonjudgmental. Family members might be inclined to **blame themselves** for the eating problem or to deny the problem.

First, **rule out immediate medical problems**. Then ask the remaining questions. Some are directed at family members, while others are for the person who is having eating problems. We have used female pronouns since some 90 percent of people with eating disorders are girls or women.

### Rule Outs

**Q1** Is there any medical problem that could account for your (the person's) low weight, vomiting or diahrehia, or weight gain?

**Q2** Are you (Is she) on medication that may account for the problem?

**Q3** How long have you (your loved one) been starving yourself (herself), bingeing and purging, or overeating?

**Q4** What do you (does she) weigh? *(If her weight is 10 percent or more below the recommended weight for her age/height, she should be taken to a doctor for a thorough medical exam. Medical conditions are always a significant concern for those with eating disorders.)*

**Q5** If you (your loved one) purge(s) by vomiting, how long has this been going on? *(If she has done this frequently, she should have medical and dental exams to rule out medical conditions caused by vomiting.)*

*Researchers estimate that eight million American's suffer from some form of an eating disorder. Anorexia statistics show almost one million men and seven million women battle the disease.*

—ANOREXIA.CHRISTIANET.COM

### Questions for the Parent or Other Caring Adult

**Q6** What statements does she express related to body image and fat?

**Q7** Does she view herself as fat, even if she is very thin?

**Q8** Has she been asked to gain weight? If so, how did she respond?

**Q9** What was childhood like for her? Are there issues in the home regarding control or perfectionism?

**Q10** Is she facing a transition? *(Such as, from middle school to high school, from high school to college, or moving from one place to another.)*

**Q11** How has she been influenced by social norms related to beauty?

**Q12** Have you noticed her being particularly sensitive to such expectations?

### Questions for the Woman

**Q6** Do you ever feel helpless? If so when?

**Q7** How do you handle painful feelings, such as fear, hurt, and anger?

**Q8** Describe a time when you felt angry, frustrated, or afraid. How did you express those feelings?

**Q9** What were meals like in your family when you were younger?

**Q10** In your home, was there much focus on food?

**Q11** Has anyone ever told you that you're beautiful? Who and when?

**Q12** How did that make you feel?

**Q13** Why do you think that person said that?

**Q14** Describe your relationship with your parents and siblings. What kind of a child were you?

**Q15** Do you sometimes feel like you aren't good enough?

**Q16** What advantage does weight loss (or purging) afford you? How does it make you feel about yourself?

**Q17** What disadvantages have you seen from those actions?

## 4 WISE COUNSEL

**Do not attempt to treat** an individual whose symptoms are affecting her health. A girl whose eating disorder is endangering her life or health should be in the hospital or an inpatient treatment program.

Even if the eating disordered person needs to be hospitalized, you can help the **family that is hurting**. Focus on them and their needs. Help them to avoid blaming themselves or their child. Help find hope for recovery.

Keep reminding everyone involved that **God is always working,** and He gives hope for recovery. Eating disorders are very difficult, but not impossible to overcome.

Watch for **evidence of suicidal thoughts and words** (see section on Suicide), and get help immediately if you see signs.

If the behavior has gone on for some time, **seek the assistance of a professional** who is a specialist in eating disorders. The young woman's **health will continue to be compromised** until she gets help.

## ACTION STEPS 5

### 1. Identify a Target Weight

- It is important to identify an ideal weight and target weight. *Ideal weight* refers to the best weight for the person when the person's height and body type are taken into account. The body mass index (often abbreviated as BMI) is the most accurate measure of ideal weight, but few people can easily work with this index.
- A *target weight* is the lowest safe weight, which is the bare minimum you want someone with an eating disorder to be at. Target weight is calculated as 90 percent of midpoint of the ideal weight. Agree on a target weight with a doctor or dietician because women with eating disorders often try to negotiate this number.

### 2. Focus on Relationships

- Build a positive relationship with the woman. Those with eating disorders tend to have difficulty being open and accepting help. You will need patience, and also you will need to be willing to speak the truth. Encourage the young woman to be willing to hear the truth.
- Encourage family members to show unconditional love to the eating disordered person. Don't criticize or compare or ask questions in a manner that causes her to feel condemned.
- Healing relationships with people and with God are essential to the recovery process.

*Bulimia affects about 10 percent of college age women in the United States. About 10 percent of individuals diagnosed with bulimia are men.*
—INTRANET.MICDS.ORG

### 3. Take the Focus Off of Food

- If the girl is in immediate danger from starvation or electrolyte problems, take her to a hospital or doctor's office at once. If she isn't in immediate danger, examine what weight loss means to her, what eating stands for, and what she most fears about eating.
- Help the family to take the focus off food at home. They need to see that focusing on food is part of the disease, not the solution.

### 4. Watch for Triggers

- Help bulimics see what triggers her bingeing behaviors and try to identify situations that aggravate it. And for compulsive overeaters, identify recurring, stressful situations that create the urge to eat for comfort.
- Help her to see what is behind her actions. Chances are, some kind of anxiety and stress is driving them.

### 5. Change Thinking Patterns

- Gently question the girl's thinking. Help her begin to see the lies behind the behaviors that are trapping her.

### 6. Examine Perfectionism

- Examine her perfectionism. She may hold herself to excessively high standards.
- Help her to examine these standards and how they compare with God's grace and truth revealed in Scripture.

### 7. Keep a Journal

- Encourage her to write a journal about her feelings and the events of each day. She may have difficulty identifying feelings. Help her to view her feelings—even painful ones—as normal and acceptable.

## 6 BIBLICAL INSIGHTS

***Now the mixed multitude who were among them yielded to intense craving; so the children of Israel also wept again and said: "Who will give us meat to eat? We remember the fish which we ate freely in Egypt, the cucumbers, the melons, the leeks, the onions, and the garlic; but now our whole being is dried up; there is nothing at all except this manna before our eyes!" —Numbers 11:4-6***

- Preoccupation with food can indicate an eating disorder. When people become overly focused on food, their dependence on God suffers.
- The Israelites, while not having an eating disorder, experienced a "perspective disorder" because of their focus on food. Their preoccupation with foods caused them to lose sight of God's miraculous and loving provision of manna.
- When people become preoccupied with anything other than God, they can lose their perspective of God's care for them. People with eating disorders need to refocus on their worth in God's eyes and be thankful for God's provision

***Put a knife to your throat if you are a man given to appetite. —Proverbs 23:2***

- Some people attempt to fill the emptiness in their lives with drugs, alcohol, sex, money, or hard work. Others use food, and these people find themselves trapped in emotional eating—leading to problems like obesity and bulimia.
- There is nothing wrong with food. There should be a balance, however, between enjoying what God has provided, and using food to meet emotional needs, allowing it to control our lives.

- The fruit of the Spirit called "self-control" applies to many areas of life, including eating. God desires to fill any emptiness, helping us to lead balanced, healthy lives.

***All things are lawful for me, but all things are not helpful. All things are lawful for me, but I will not be brought under the power of any. Foods for the stomach and the stomach for foods, but God will destroy both it and them. Now the body is not for sexual immorality but for the Lord, and the Lord for the body. —1 Corinthians 6:12-13***

- Some who face an eating disorder—whether it be an addiction to food, or an addiction to going without food—understand the power and damage of their addiction. God provided food for the animals and people He created in order to sustain them. Food is meant for sustenance—"foods for the stomach and the stomach for foods."
- A food addiction takes the focus off God and puts it on our food or on our bodies—both of which will eventually no longer be needed when we meet Christ face to face.
- People who struggle with eating disorders should seek Christian professional guidance to gain a proper perspective and pattern for eating.

## PRAYER STARTER 7

Dear Lord, thank You that my friend is seeking help. Please help her to accept herself and to know that she is loved. Help her family to get beyond their concern or guilt so that they can work on showing love and support. Please comfort this family and be very close to them. Heal their hearts and minds, and protect her from medical problems. Please be with them every step of the way to healing. In Jesus name, Amen.

## RECOMMENDED RESOURCES 8

*Bulimia/Anorexia: The Binge/Purge Cycle and Self-Starvation*, by Marlene Boskind-White and William C. White, Jr.

*Hope, Help, and Healing for Eating Disorders: Anorexia, Bulimia, & Overeating*, by Gregory L. Jantz

*"Mom, I Feel Fat!": Becoming Your Daughter's Alley in Developing a Healthy Body Image*, by Sharon A. Hersh

The Center for Counseling and Health in Edmonds, WA, has a long-term eating disorder program (both inpatient and outpatient) that is relatively reasonably priced. The program is Christian and uses a multi-disciplinary approach. See www.aplaceofhope.com; phone is 888-771-5166. The founder, Gregg Jantz, author noted above.

# Envy/Jealousy

1

## PORTRAITS

- Carolyn spends most of her days looking for new ways to decorate her home. Whenever a friend paints a room or buys a new appliance, Carolyn feels she has to keep up and get something just as good—or better. Her husband Tom complains that they are never able to get ahead because of Carolyn's constant spending.
- Although Jill has an advanced degree and a successful career, she finds herself resenting Lindsey's ability to entertain with such elegance and style. She thinks to herself, "If I had that much time on my hands I'd be able to entertain like Martha Stewar, too!"
- Bill can't seem to control his tongue. He feels it almost impossible to resist the temptation to pass along to his friends the latest "dirt" on someone in the church or at work.
- Sue was thankful that her friendship with Dana was one in which they could talk openly about the hardships and trials they were both experiencing. Now that Dana seems to be receiving one blessing after another, Sue is resentful that Dana's life has taken a turn for the good.
- Jealous of her sister, her friends, and her neighbors, Megan was now jealous of her husband Matt's new coworker. Wallowing in anger and self-pity, Megan was allowing her jealousy to consume her emotions and taint her marriage. Feeling smothered and wrongly accused, Matt was pulling away in frustration. Megan panicked, predicting that Matt would leave her or have an affair. But her attitude increased the odds that her dark predictions would come true.
- Jim always "needs" a bigger boat, the finest fishing gear, and the latest fish-finding technology.

> *The envious man thinks that if his neighbor breaks a leg he will be able to walk better himself.*
> —Helmut Schoeck

2

## DEFINITIONS AND KEY THOUGHTS

- Jealousy and envy are siblings, the perverse children of a **toxic mix** of anger, anxiety-based insecurity and an obsessive habit of comparing ourselves (usually poorly) with others.
- A **root of fear** is usually present in jealousy—the fear of losing love or praise.
- **Envy** wants what someone else has, whether it is status, possessions, lifestyle, relationships, or characteristics.

- **Jealousy** is the fear that something we have will be taken.
- Jealousy also involves **a triangle**—with the jealous person becoming fixated with a (usually misperceived) rival, who is viewed as competing for the attention of the other person.
- Scripture says that love as "strong as death" will produce powerful jealousy that is "as cruel as the grave" (Song 8:6).
- Left unchecked, envy can develop into **malice, contempt, and destruction** of others (see 1 Samuel 18:9—for envy in the life of Saul).
- Envy manifests itself in the **resentment** of others' prosperity.
- Envy surfaces as **anger and bitterness at another person**. The envious person isn't necessarily aware that the anger is prompted by envy.
- Envy is fueled by a **sense of entitlement**—we believe we deserve success and recognition over another person. Envy, therefore, is **closely linked to pride and greed**.
- **Envy is the opposite of love**. Love rejoices over the good of another. Envy seeks the destruction of another for the benefit of our own gain.
- Envy is ultimately a **rebellion** against God's will and God's provision. When people struggle with envy, they reject God's provision and God's purpose for them.
- Scripture tells us that the Lord is "a jealous God" (Exodus 34:14), but the Lord's jealousy is righteous. God is jealous for the church the way a loving husband protects his relationship with his wife from all potential rivals. (2 Corinthians 11:2). Paul warns us not to provoke the Lord to jealousy (1 Corinthians 10:20-22).

> *Envy is a symptom of lack of appreciation of our own uniqueness and self worth. Each of us has something to give that no one else has.*
> —Anonymous

## Causes of Envy and Jealousy

**Dissatisfaction with God's provision.** The person may only see what God *hasn't* provided rather than what God *has* provided.

**Comparison with others.** From early childhood, many people have been conditioned to see themselves only in comparison to others—being smarter than, not as attractive as, more popular than, etc. Comparison—even positive comparison—produces pride, envy, and jealousy.

**Pride.** Envy is driven by the false notion that a person "deserves" to have whatever he perceives will contribute to his own personal gain and satisfaction.

**Low self-esteem/seeking significance.** When a person doesn't feel good about himself, he may try to soothe that pain by seeking significance in his circumstances rather than finding his deepest needs met by Jesus Christ.

**Desire for worldly gain.** The person may seek money, status, appearance, talents, or achievements as evidence of his value and "place" in the world.

## Expressions of Envy and Jealousy

**Resentment toward others.** The person may be highly critical and judgmental of others.

**Competition in relationships.** The desire to be the "top dog" in relationships may be indicative of a struggle with envy. The person may exhibit a drive toward overachievement and exhibit a superior attitude toward others.

**Depression.** The person may become highly self-critical because he has not achieved what is desired and others have passed him in the race for success.

**Lack of contentment.** In our culture, the media bombards us with the false notion that achieving more material gain will lead to greater happiness. A person struggling with envy is rarely content with what God has provided. Complaints are many; thanks are few.

**Gossip about others.** An envious or jealous person constantly criticizes the object of his anger.

**Idolizing or putting others on a pedestal.** Prideful people often see others as "all good" or "all bad."

**Beginning thoughts with the statement "If only . . ."** Discontent is often expressed in wishing that things were different.

*O, beware, my lord, of jealousy; it is the green-eyed monster which doth mock the meat it feeds on.*
—Shakespeare, Othello, Act III, Scene 3

## Stages of Envy and Jealousy

The **initial stage** of envy is desiring what someone else is or has.

When a person doesn't face his own envy, it **produces contempt** for another person simply because he doesn't want to deal with the reminder of his failures.

Envy can also **develop into malice** in which a person tries to destroy the good he sees in another's life. This person believes that if he can't have what another person has, then he will destroy any pleasure that person receives from it.

Jealousy can **dominate and strangle the life out of a relationship**. Some spouses, having faced abuse or abandonment in their childhood, bring this pathology into a marriage. **Deep wounds** create great needs and can be the impetus to a vicious cycle of dysfunctional jealousy.

A chronically jealous partner uses self-pity, lies, threats, and other manipulations to control a relationship. When the other resists, the jealous person reacts by becoming more controlling. With each incident, the **consuming cycle** gains momentum and heads toward disaster.

## ASSESSMENT INTERVIEW

3

Other issues often mask envy. A person may speak of **the unfairness of life,** "bad luck," or the harm caused by another person. The person may have a **need to always be the best** at every task to prove himself.

Be aware that the issue of resentment involves a **lack of forgiveness,** in which the person experienced hurt and desires revenge.

**Listen to the core issue.** Is the person resentful toward someone? Has someone else achieved something that he has not?

**Don't label** the person as being "envious" or "jealous." Listen and acknowledge the person's struggle and experience, and deal with the issues of comparison, anger, bitterness, perceptions, expectations, and demands.

Q1 What is the situation that has prompted painful feelings for you?

Q2 Do you get upset when others advance in their career or social standing?

Q4 Is it difficult for you to celebrate the blessings of some of those around you?

Q5 Do you sometimes feel that God has disappointed you in His provision for you?

Q6 Do you find yourself often thinking "If only (fill in the blank ________, we had more money, more friends, etc.)?

Q7 Where do you find that most of your money goes?

Q8 Do you feel secretly pleased when someone you admire experiences a setback?

Q9 Do you sometimes want to sabotage another's blessings?

Q10 Do you struggle with feeling critical or judgmental of others?

Q11 Do you find that you aren't content unless you are the "best" at something?

Q12 Do you struggle with depression?

Q13 Do you identify more with the "best and brightest" rather than those on the fringe of a group?

Q14 Do you find that you tend to put others on a pedestal?

Q15 Tell me about your marriage.

Q16 How do you feel about your spouse's friendships or activities?

Q17 Has your spouse ever given you reason to doubt his/her faithfulness or love for you?

*Charity rejoices in our neighbor's good, while envy grieves over it.*
—THOMAS AQUINAS

4

## WISE COUNSEL

The core to overcoming envy or jealousy is **threefold**:

- Understanding God's love
- Being content with His provision
- Loving others as God loves you

Envy and jealousy are **futile attempts** to fill our deepest longings for significance and security by seeking what someone else has or by controlling what someone else does.

The person who is struggling should be gently and consistently pointed to the **love and sufficiency of Jesus Christ,** so he can accept God's provisions and give thanks for them, and take steps to show kindness toward those she has resented.

In addition, **offer encouragement** that the person is willing to address this issue and look honestly at his/her own sin.

5

## ACTION STEPS

### 1. Be Honest

- We all deceive ourselves in a multitude of ways. We may not feel we are experiencing envy or jealousy, but may be disguised as criticism, contempt, gossip, self pity, manipulation, etc.
- Ask God to reveal your motivations and feelings. Write down in a journal or notebook what God has shown you in your heart.
- Confess your heart attitudes to Christ and experience his forgiveness.

*Envy is counting the other fellow's blessings instead of your own.*
—Harold Coffin

### 2. Focus on Jesus Christ

- God sees you as His own beloved child.
- In the morning when you wake up, before your feet touch the floor, commit yourself and the day to God, asking for His guidance and presence throughout the day.

### 3. Develop a Lifestyle of Gratitude and Worship

- Count your blessings often, whether you feel thankful or not.
- Read the psalms as personal prayers, praising God for all He is and what He has done.
- At the end of each day, reflect on the blessings you received throughout the day. Thank God for His constant love and care.

## 4. Avoid Activities that Encourage Comparison

- Spend time in malls only when there is a specific item you need to purchase.
- Read books that encourage reflection on the beauty of life and God's creation.
- Minimize exposure to magazines, media, etc. that focus on material gain.
- Limit (or avoid) times with people who enflame feelings and thoughts of envy and jealousy.

## 5. When Feeling Envious

- Pray for God's blessing to be poured out on your life and give thanks for God's provision.
- Remind yourself of Jesus' counsel that "one's life does not consist in the abundance of the things he possesses" (Luke 12:15). Ultimately, "things" are shallow substitutes for the presence of God in your life.
- Remind yourself of who you are as one of God's chosen children. "From the beginning [God] chose you for salvation through sanctification by the Spirit and belief in the truth" (2 Thessalonians 2:13).
- Ask yourself what it is about another person that you envy. Does this person have strong social skills? Is she deeply compassionate? Is he more successful than you? Does she receive more praise? Thank God for the redeeming qualities you see in that person and ask God to form those qualities in your own heart. You will then move from envy to admiration. Give thanks for the qualities that God has established in your own heart.
- Talk to a friend or counselor about your envy. Be honest, listen, and look for clear steps to resolve the problem in your perspective and your heart.

> *A sound heart is life to the body, but envy is rottenness to the bones.*
> —Proverbs 14:30

## 6. When Feeling Jealous

- Be honest with yourself, and back off from controlling or manipulative statements.
- Spend time with God—soak yourself in prayer and God's Word. Ask Him to transform your need for security into dependence on and confidence in Him.
- Transform your mind—instead of allowing your anxious thoughts to lead to dark suspicions, ask God to cleanse your heart and mind. Ask Him to

help you truly love ("love does not envy . . . thinks no evil," 1 Corinthians 13:4-5). Remember all the positives in your relationship. Do something—right then—to show your love. Make a call, send an e-mail.

- Talk to a friend or counselor to get a fresh perspective and hold you accountable to arrest negative thoughts and replace them with truth and thanksgiving.

*For where envy and self-seeking exist, confusion and every evil thing are there.*
—James 3:16

**7. Grow**

- Create a plan to develop the gifts and abilities God has uniquely given you.
- Evaluate your spiritual gifts and talents.
- Practice spiritual disciplines.
- Spend time memorizing Scripture, and make a commitment to pray for particular situations and people in your life.
- Ask God to bring believers into your life who can encourage you in your relationship with Christ.

**8. Consider Follow Up**

For some people, a chronic struggle with envy may be indicative of deeper unresolved pain from their past. In these cases, working with a professional therapist may be the best course of action.

## 6 BIBLICAL INSIGHTS

***This is the law of jealousy . . . —Numbers 5:29***

- The ancient Israelites had a complex ritual for dealing with jealousy. Their process (Numbers 5:11-31) recognized the destructive potential of a jealous husband or wife. The most important part was that they dealt with this issue before the Lord (Numbers 5:30).
- Jealousy can destroy any relationship, and in a marriage, it can drive in a wedge of mistrust.
- Protection from the wedge of jealousy begins with honesty. Each person should honestly evaluate his or her own tendency toward jealousy, answering the question, "What makes me jealous?"

***Then Saul was very angry, and the saying displeased him; and he said, "They have ascribed to David ten thousands, and to me they have ascribed only thousands. Now what more can he have but the kingdom?" –1 Samuel 18:8***

- Saul became jealous of David's victory over Goliath and the national attention he received. The young warrior upstaged the king, and Saul's jealousy produced anger, resentment, fear, and attempted murder.

- Like a seething cauldron ready to tip at any moment, uncontrolled jealousy can lead to destruction. We need to take our jealousy to God, asking Him to help us appreciate others' talents while showing us how best to use our own for His honor.

***For I am jealous for you with godly jealousy. For I have betrothed you to one husband, that I may present you as a chaste virgin to Christ. —2 Corinthians 11:2***

- The word "jealous" can be used positively or negatively. Paul said that he was "jealous for" the Corinthian believers "with godly jealousy." Paul's jealousy was not for his own reputation, but for the Corinthians' relationships with Christ.
- Human jealousy, however, often has a less than noble focus—such as another's looks, wealth, popularity, or power—and it harms everyone involved.
- Believers need to be careful to avoid letting jealousy over petty issues harm them or others.

***Therefore, laying aside all malice, all deceit, hypocrisy, envy, and all evil speaking . . . —1 Peter 2:1***

- Believers can cultivate gratitude to replace envy and jealousy.
- We need to "lay aside all envy" because envy causes hurt, dissension, and division.
- People who compare themselves to others instantly feel superior or inferior. God wants us to stop comparing our looks, possessions, jobs, or abilities with those of others, and to focus on being His child and serving Him.

## PRAYER STARTER 7

We want to thank You, first of all, for Your great blessings in Your child's life. He knows that You have done great things, but today he struggles with the inner conflict of desiring more. Help him today to understand the great gifts he has from Your hand and the great contributions he can make to Your kingdom. Help him to learn contentment . . .

## RECOMMENDED RESOURCES 8

*Dealing With Desires You Can't Control,* by Mark R. McMinn

*The Search for Freedom: Demolishing the Strongholds that Diminish Your Faith,* by Robert S. McGee

*Search For Significance,* by Robert McGee

*When God Doesn't Make Sense,* by James Dobson

# Fear and Anxiety

1

## PORTRAITS

- As the only child of a single mother, Janice felt she was born to be a scapegoat. She never knew what would happen when her mother would return after a day at work, but it was often some combination of yelling, blaming, judging, hitting, or ridicule. As an adult, Janice is always wary about new situations or people. She becomes tense even when there is nothing to be anxious about.

*13.3% (19.1 million) of the adult U.S. population is affected by an anxiety disorder.*[1]

- Nadine was considered a "loner," but this façade was a mask for a deep fear of being in groups. She found that she became overwhelmed with panic when she was in a restaurant eating with her coworkers. Even though it seemed irrational, she was afraid of saying something foolish, spilling food on her shirt, or beginning to stutter. When she was alone with one person, she was fine, but as soon as she found herself in a group, even making eye contact with someone seemed painful.
- Frank seemed to exude confidence. He was in control of every situation, and he was driven to win at every contest—every relationship and every event in his life was a contest to him.

2

## DEFINITIONS AND KEY THOUGHTS

### Fear

- While most people experience fear as a negative emotion, **fear also has a positive component**. If you find that you have turned down a one-way street toward oncoming traffic, fear triggers an autonomic response that sends a signal to your brain to "flee" the dangerous situation.

*For God has not given us a spirit of fear, but of power and of love and of a sound mind.*
*—2 Timothy 1:7*

- Fear becomes a problem when a person is **afraid of things that are not real** or when the feeling of fear is **out of proportion** to the real danger.
- Fear is an emotion that draws a person into a **self-protective mode**.
- Fears are often related to **what a person perceives** as a real or potential threat to his security. He may fear losing his job, having his home burglarized, or having conflict in a relationship.

### Anxiety

- **Anxiety is a constant fearful state**, accompanied by a feeling of unrest, dread, or worry. The person may not be aware of the cause of the fear.

- Anxiety is aroused by a number of factors:

  External situations (hearing bad news, fast-paced lifestyle)

  Physical well being (lack of sleep, blood sugar imbalance)

  Modeling (parents who were highly anxious)

  Trauma (significant hurts that were never resolved or healed)

  Recurring threats (situations that may be similar to experiences of the past that caused great pain)

- Anxiety's symptoms can include: Inability to relax; tense feelings; rapid heartbeat; dry mouth; increased blood pressure; jumpiness or feeling faint; excessive perspiring; feeling clammy; constant anticipation of trouble; constant feeling of uneasiness

*$42 billion a year is spent on treating anxiety disorders.*[2]

## Phobias

- Phobias are a **specific fear** of something in particular or fears that are **out of proportion** to the object, situation, activity feared. For example, one may have a fear of spiders. A person exhibits a phobia when seeing a small spider on the ceiling of a room and refuses to ever enter the room again.

*Be anxious for nothing, but in everything by prayer and supplication, with thanksgiving, let your requests be made known to God; and the peace of God, which surpasses all understanding, will guard your hearts and minds through Christ Jesus.*

—PHILIPPIANS 4:6-7

## Panic Attacks

- Panic attacks are **sudden, overwhelming, fearful reactions** with feelings of impending doom.
- In a panic attack, the person feels **out of control**. Symptoms include: being paralyzed by the flight-or-fight response, shortness of breath, racing heartbeat, sweating, dizziness, nausea, diarrhea, ringing ears, choking, or vertigo.
- The person may have **no clear idea** what prompted the reaction and then becomes obsessed with fear of another episode occurring.
- The sufferer may feel like he is **going crazy** or is having a heart attack.
- *Note: More than three attacks in a month or the onset of a person refusing to go out of the house indicates the need for some professional assistance.*

## Relational Fears

- There are four major relational fears that can significantly alter the quality of life: fear of failure, fear of rejection, fear of abandonment, or the fear of death/dying.

## 3 ASSESSMENT INTERVIEW

**Q1** When do you feel afraid/anxious?

**Q2** How long and to what extent has this fear/anxiety been occurring for you?

**Q3** What situation/object/person causes you the most distress?

**Q4** Do you find there are times when you are more anxious than others? If so, when?

**Q5** Of the things that cause you fear, which seem reasonable and which seem unreasonable?

**Q6** When do the feelings of anxiety go away?

**Q7** How have you tried to cope with the anxiety?

**Q8** Do you have any health problems and/or medications that may contribute to the anxiety?

**Q9** What would your life be like if you were free of this anxiety?

## 4 WISE COUNSEL

Fear and anxiety are often **defused by knowledge**. The more a person can defuse the perceived threat, the less anxiety he experiences.

Generally, the person has established an **irrational belief system** that is creating anxiety. **Try to identify** lies or deceptions that contribute to the anxiety.

Most anxiety reactions are **learned behavior**. Encourage the person to develop hope that she will be able to overcome the anxiety/fears by learning new behaviors rooted in truth.

Anxiety can be **contagious**: Those who experience strong anxiety tend to elicit anxiety reactions in those who are around them. Fearful people need to be aware of their anxiety levels and how they cope with anxiety when it occurs.

**Be patient** with the person as he sorts through the feelings of fear. Changing patterns takes time.

*Unless fear, worry, and anxiety are honestly faced and worked through, people can end up in a pattern of avoidance—organizing their lives around people and situations that they must avoid.*
—Archibald D. Hart

# 5 ACTION STEPS

## 1. Thought Patterns

Encourage the person to replace negative thoughts and lies with the truth of Scripture (Philippians 4:8).

## 2. Focus on God

- Help the person move his focus from the fear to the character of God (1 Peter 5:7).
- God wants the person to trust Him and relinquish all fears to Him.
- Reflecting on God's strength, kindness, and purpose brings a growing sense of peace (Isaiah 26:3).

## 3. Watch for Triggers

Assist the person in trying to minimize activities and input that induce anxiety.

*Both faith and fear sail into the harbor of your mind, but only faith should be allowed to anchor.*
—Anonymous

## 4. Move Forward

- Help the person learn from setbacks and resolve to continue to face the fears.
- Gently encourage the person to take risks.
- Focus on the solution, not the problem (Matthew 14:22-23).

## 5. Relationships

Assist the person in finding supportive, positive relationships.

## 6. Be Patient

- Remind the person that growth takes time.
- God will work in the person's life to overcome the anxiety that is keeping him from living life to the fullest.
- Remind the person to try to reflect on God's truth and His grace to provide and protect.

6

## BIBLICAL INSIGHTS

***If you should say in your heart, "These nations are greater than I; how can I dispossess them?"—you shall not be afraid of them, but you shall remember well what the Lord your God did to Pharaoh and to all Egypt: the great trials which your eyes saw, the signs and the wonders, the mighty hand and the outstretched arm, by which the Lord your God brought you out. . . . You shall not be terrified of them; for the Lord your God, the great and awesome God, is among you. —Deuteronomy 7:17–21***

- The Christian life isn't easy. Believers face difficulties, pain, suffering, and sorrow. In situations that seem impossible they sometimes become afraid. Fear is a normal response to a perceived or real threat.
- God told Israel not to be afraid when the battle seemed too great. Instead, they should remember what He had done for them in the past and take heart.
- We should look at our fearful situations in the light of what God has already done for us, remembering that "the great and awesome God" will be going into battle with us.

***Trust in the Lord . . . Delight yourself also in the Lord . . . Commit your way to the Lord . . . Rest in the Lord, and wait patiently for Him; do not fret because of him who prospers in his way, because of the man who brings wicked schemes to pass. —Psalm 37:3-7***

*Do the thing you fear to do and keep on doing it. . . that is the quickest and surest way ever yet discovered to conquer fear.*
*—Dale Carnegie*

- David encouraged God's people to trust in the Lord, delight themselves in Him, commit their way to Him, and wait patiently for Him to act.
- *Trusting God* focuses our faith and deepens our commitment.
- *Delighting* means to experience pleasure in His presence.
- *Committing our way to God* means entrusting everything in our lives to His guidance and control.
- *Waiting patiently* is sometimes difficult, but it often is the ultimate test of our trust in God.

***Surely He shall deliver you from the snare of the fowler and from the perilous pestilence. He shall cover you with His feathers, and under His wings you shall take refuge; His truth shall be your shield and buckler. You shall not be afraid of the terror by night, nor of the arrow that flies by day, nor of the pestilence that walks in darkness, nor of the destruction that lays waste at noonday. —Psalm 91:3–6***

- When believers are afraid, they can run to a "refuge" and "fortress"—God Himself.
- No place could be more safe than the presence of God! Believers can trust that God will protect them in their times of fear.

- This promise doesn't imply that God's people will never suffer or face difficulty; but it promises that they need not be afraid because they are in God's hands.

***Trust in the Lord with all your heart, and lean not on your own understanding; in all your ways acknowledge Him, and He shall direct your paths. —Proverbs 3:5-6***

- It's one thing for people to trust God with their eternal destiny, but it is quite another for them to trust God to handle the challenges and difficulties of daily life.
- God promises to direct, or straighten, our paths. We need to trust God to help us handle difficult situations we face, even in cases where we can't see how He will work.
- If we really want to know God's will for our lives, or even for our actions in a particular situation, we can begin by trusting that God cares about every aspect of life and that He will provide what we need.

## 7 PRAYER STARTER

Today a child of Yours is frightened, Lord—frightened about the fear that has taken hold of his life. He feels helpless and hopeless. He wants to serve You, but this anxiety is debilitating him to the point that he can barely function. We need the healing touch of Your hand and wisdom to handle this anxiety . . .

## 8 RECOMMENDED RESOURCES

*The Anxiety Cure: You Can Find Emotional Tranquility and Wholeness*, by Archibald D. Hart

*Overcoming Anxiety*, by Archibald D. Hart

*Tame Your Fears: And Transform them into Faith, Confidence, and Action*, by Carol Kent

*Thus anxiety is a Janus-headed creature that can impel man to self-improvement, achievement and competence, or can distort and impoverish his existence and that of his fellows.*
—E.E. Levitt

# Forgiveness

1

## PORTRAITS

- Zach can't bring himself to attend his parents fiftieth wedding anniversary. Their lack of interest in him and his family has hurt him so much that he wants nothing to do with them—let alone to honor them for fifty years of marriage.
- Becky can't sleep at night. She keeps having nightmares about her mother, who abused her as a child. Even though her mother has been dead for ten years, Becky still can't forgive her.
- Joanne's "best friend" lied about her to her boyfriend, causing him to break up with her. Now, Joanne's friend and her former boyfriend are dating. Every time Joanne sees them at school, she feels betrayed all over again and can't stop thinking about it.
- Tom found out his coworker has been criticizing him to the boss and making negative comments about his work. The boss has elevated his coworker and demoted Tom. Tom can't stop thinking of ways to get even with his coworker.

*Unforgiveness:*
*-creates moods of stress*
*-puts relationships under strain*
*-harms spiritual well-being*

2

## DEFINITIONS AND KEY THOUGHTS

### What Forgiveness Is and Is Not

"Unforgiveness" is is a refusal to let go of an offense, and it usually results in resentment, bitterness, hatred, hostility, anger, fear, and stress. Unforgiveness is a cancer that eats away at the very soul of an offended person.[1]

"Forgiveness" occurs when the cold feelings of "unforgiveness" are changed to warm, loving, compassionate, caring, and altruistic emotions because of a heartfelt transformation.[2]

In Luke 7:43-47, Jesus tells us the truth that those who have been forgiven much, love much, so the antidote for resentment is a deeper experience of God's love and forgiveness.

*It takes two to reconcile, but only one to forgive.*

Explain the following definitions and parameters. Forgiveness . . .

- doesn't mean that any wrongs done to you were acceptable.
- doesn't diminish the evil done against you, nor is it a denial of what happened.

- sets us free from the bondage of hurt and the desire for revenge.
- doesn't take away the consequences the other person will face because of his/her sin.
- is letting go of your desire to hurt the other person. Simply put, forgiveness means to "cancel a debt."
- is a difficult and uncomfortable process. When you make a decision to forgive, God provides you the grace and courage to forgive and to maintain a heart of forgiveness.
- is not weakness. It is the most powerful thing you can do. Refusing to forgive allows Satan to continue to hurt, but forgiveness stops the destructive power of Satan in our lives.
- is not reconciliation. It takes two to reconcile, but only one to forgive.
- doesn't depend on the other person's actions, and it is not probationary (e.g., "I will forgive you as long as you aren't drinking").
- doesn't require you to become a "doormat," nor does it require you to allow the offender to hurt you again.
- is a gift you give to the offender. Trust, on the other hand, must be earned. You need to set boundaries in any difficult, strained relationship.
- doesn't wait for the offender to repent.
- is about how much you trust God to take care of you.
- produces empathy for the offender, humility about our own sinfulness, and gratitude for being forgiven by God and others.

*There is a difference between mental forgiveness and gut forgiveness. For example, when a person has had an affair, frequently the wronged spouse will choose to forgive with the head right away, but it will take the gut months to catch up.*
—Charles Stanley

### Reasons to Forgive

It sets you free to move on with your life.

It refuses to let the person who hurt you have any more power over your life.

It opens up your relationship with God (Matthew 5:43-48).

It keeps you from becoming bitter.

It keeps you from becoming like the person who hurt you.

Unforgiveness doesn't hurt the perpetrator at all; it only hurts *you*.

Scripture commands us to forgive (Matthew 18:21-35).

## 3 ASSESSMENT INTERVIEW

A person seeks help to forgive, because his inability to forgive has started to **disrupt his personal, emotional, or spiritual life.**

The inability or unwillingness to forgive creates tremendous stress and may be the source of physical problems, such as lack of energy, sleeplessness, headaches, joint pain, or back pain. It also may be the root cause of **depression or anxiety**.

Sometimes the person **doesn't realize** that the origin of his problem is a lack of forgiveness.

*When did Jesus forgive you for your sin? Two thousand years ago on the cross. Two thousand years before you came and begged his forgiveness, forgiveness was there—ready, rich, full and free.*
—Joseph M. Stowell

Consider the following assessment questions:

**Q1** Tell me about significant hurts and disappointments you have experienced.

**Q2** What led you to come to counseling?

**Q3** What do you hope to accomplish?

**Q4** Tell me about the incident or incidents that you are having trouble forgiving.

**Q5** How did the incident(s) make you feel?

**Q6** Tell me about the person who hurt you.

**Q7** What have you already tried to do to help you forgive?

**Q8** How have you protected yourself from being hurt again by this person?

**Q9** How can you tell that you haven't forgiven that person?

**Q10** What were examples of forgiveness or unforgiveness in your home while you were growing up?

**Q11** When is the first time you can remember someone offending you? How did you handle it?

**Q12** Can you see a pattern in how you respond when people offend you?

**Q13** Do those responses help or hurt you?

**Q14** What do you think forgiveness is?

**Q15** What do you think might happen if you forgive the person who hurt you?

## WISE COUNSEL

4

Share some **information about real forgiveness**. Often a person refuses to forgive because he doesn't understand what forgiveness is.

Forgiveness is unique for each individual, and even some individual situations. There are no absolute formulas. Remember, it is both an act and a process. When a person forgives, his heart will begin to heal. When he heals, he will have more love to give (Ephesians 4:31).

If the person doesn't want to let the offender "off the hook," explain that forgiveness **lets *him* off the hook** and protects him from the destructive power of bitterness, setting him free to move on with life.

### Identify Emotions

Empathize with the person and acknowledge the evil that has occurred.

Encourage the person to grieve the offense and the losses that have resulted from the wrong. Explain that hurt and anger are not sinful; they are normal responses to an offense.

It is important for the person to identify and express feelings about the offense committed—how he felt during the offense, and how he feels now.

### Set Boundaries

Work with the person to decipher what needs to be done to protect him from letting the offender hurt him again. This involves the way in which he maintains an ongoing relationship with the offender. For instance, he can be polite (safe boundaries) without being a best friend (unsafe boundaries). Likewise, he can listen without taking advice.

Minimize time with unsafe people. Unsafe people are those who hurt without regard for the damage it creates in another's life.

Don't look for approval from a person intimidates, controls, or harms others.

Help the person recognize that he doesn't need another's approval in order to live a free and fulfilling life.

*Human power alone is not sufficient to reach full forgiveness. There is an element of forgiveness that is divine. It cannot be reached without God.*
—Frank Minirth

### Recognize God's Hand

Know that God can use the offense to promote personal and spiritual growth and dependence on Him.

Ask the Holy Spirit to heal the emotional wounds.

Ask God to help the person love the offender. Those who transgress are often lost, broken, or hurting, so even the one who was wronged can feel compassion for the offender.

Praying for the offender will help the person's feelings move from seeking revenge to wanting the best for the transgressor. That's when he is truly free.

## 5 ACTION STEPS

Everett Worthington, Jr., has developed a useful acrostic for navigating the process of forgiveness. It is known as R-E-A-C-H:[3]

### R: Recall the Hurt

- This is difficult but necessary.
- Don't minimize or deny your pain.
- Don't make excuses for the offender.
- Don't use recall as a means to "fingerpoint," but as a way to objectively review what has occurred.
- Journaling is a great way to work through anger and hurt. It organizes your thoughts and helps you acknowledge the truth in black and white.
- Sometimes writing a letter to the offender is helpful, but *don't mail the letter.*

*When you don't forgive someone, in some way that person is in jail, and you are the warden. You're incarcerated ,too, because you have to make sure the prisoner stays there.*
—Kerney Franston

### E: Empathize with the Person

- Write a letter as if you were the person who hurt you. Tell your thoughts, feelings, insights, and pressures. Make this a letter of apology. Process the feelings that surface with a friend, counselor, or pastor.
- By placing yourself in the shoes of the person who transgressed, you can begin to understand why the person did what he/she did.
- This doesn't remove blame from the offender but serves to show that people who hurt are often hurting deeply themselves.

### A: Altruistic Gift of Forgiveness

- Promote the "giving" of forgiveness. Think of a time when you did something wrong and were forgiven. Reflect on the wrongdoing and guilt you felt. How did it feel to be forgiven? Would you like to give that gift of forgiveness to the person who hurt you?
- Write a blank check of forgiveness. Write in your journal that this day you have released that person from the debt he/she owes you.

- You may want to write down the offenses the person has done and then write "Canceled" or "Paid in Full" over them.
- Through this step, recall the mercy and grace of God toward you.

### C: Commit Publicly to Forgive

- Write a certificate or letter of forgiveness stating that you will not ruminate on the wrongs done to you anymore, but don't send it.
- By participating in an outward expression of forgiveness, you will be more prone to remember that you have forgiven and are freed from the plague of "unforgiveness."
- Also, by disclosing your forgiveness to others, you will be held accountable to your decision to forgive the transgressor.

### H: Hold on to Forgiveness

- Hold on to forgiveness when doubts and resentment arise.[4]
- There is a difference between remembering a transgression and lacking forgiveness.
- Make "Stones of Remembrance." After God parted the Jordan River so the Israelites could go through on dry land, God told Joshua to have each tribe choose a stone to be piled up as a memorial to what great things God had done that day. The stones served as a remembrance for the people and their children in times to come (Joshua 24). It is good to have something "concrete" to help you remember the day you set your offender free.
- Remember to forget! When Corrie ten Boom (a Nazi concentration camp survivor) was reminded of an offense someone had done to her, she responded, "I distinctly remember forgetting that." Though you may never really forget, you can remember that you forgave.

*Intellectual and spiritual forgiveness are important, but you must work through all the stages to achieve emotional forgiveness. You must feel the pain, feel the anger, weep for the losses; then you can forgive with your mind, spirit and heart.*
—Sharon Sneed

## BIBLICAL INSIGHTS 6

***He shall restore its full value, add one-fifth more to it, and give it to whomever it belongs, on the day of his trespass offering. And he shall bring his trespass offering to the Lord, a ram without blemish from the flock, with your valuation, as a trespass offering, to the priest. —Leviticus 6:5-6***

- The Old Testament offerings were designed so that the offender might receive God's forgiveness, but the wrongdoer also had to take responsibility for his or her behavior by making restitution to the person who had been wronged.

- We, too, must take responsibility for the effects of our sins on others. We need to be reconciled not only to God, but also to those we have wronged. Biblical law holds us responsible for our behavior.

***And when [David] had called for Absalom, he came to the king and bowed himself on his face to the ground before the king. Then the king kissed Absalom. —2 Samuel 14:33***

- Despite all that Absalom had done, David allowed for the possibility of reconciliation by forgiving his son. Absalom, however, had no tears, no repentance, and no change of heart. Indeed, Absalom eventually tried to take his father's throne (2 Samuel 15:10).
- One person can forgive, but it takes two to reconcile. Forgiveness doesn't guarantee reconciliation. Forgiveness, however, puts salve on those who are willing to let go of the hurt and wrongs done by others.

***I, even I, am He who blots out your transgressions for My own sake; and I will not remember your sins. —Isaiah 43:25***

- When the guilt of past sins weighs us down, we must remember that when we seek forgiveness, God "blots out" our transgressions and forgets our sins.
- "Blotting out" sins pictures wiping the slate clean. Whatever sins we have committed, God promises to erase them. He knows what we have done, but He treats us as though we have never sinned.
- Because God has forgiven us, we can forgive ourselves.

***Then Peter came to Him and said, "Lord, how often shall my brother sin against me, and I forgive him? Up to seven times?" Jesus said to him, "I don't say to you, up to seven times, but up to seventy times seven." —Matthew 18:21-22***

- Don't even keep count; just keep on forgiving.
- Jesus told a parable about a man who, after receiving great forgiveness for a large debt he owed to someone, refused to forgive a person who owed him a small debt. Jesus was illustrating that we sinners have been graciously forgiven by God—and are being forgiven daily, over and over again. Others' sins against us are relatively small compared to our sins against God.
- We should be just as gracious in forgiving others. To refuse to forgive shows that we have not understood how much God has forgiven us.

***"But if you don't forgive, neither will your Father in heaven forgive your trespasses. —Mark 11:26***

- Jesus stated that God's forgiveness of us is somehow related to how we forgive others. When we accept God's forgiveness of all the wrongs we have done Him, we should be so grateful that we willingly offer that same kind of forgiveness to those who have wronged us.

- We will forgive others only to the same degree that we have experienced God's forgiveness. If we are unwilling to forgive, we need to dig deeper into our own sinfulness and God's incredible forgiveness.

7

## PRAYER STARTER

Lord, Your servant has been deeply hurt. He wants to let go, to be free of the pain, but he is finding it very difficult. The emotions go all over the place, and he doesn't want this pain affecting one more waking moment. Can You help him let this go? Can You help him to forgive this offender as he has been forgiven by You? Can You give him life once again? . . .

8

## RECOMMENDED RESOURCES

*Five Steps to Forgiveness: The Art and Science of Forgiving.* by Everett Worthington

*Forgiveness: Getting Beyond Your Past and Pain*, American Association of Christian Counselors Courageous Living Video Series, by David Stoop

*Total Forgiveness*, by R. T. Kendall

# Grief and Loss

## 1 PORTRAITS

- Mark didn't know what was the matter—it had been almost two years since his wife Sue had died, and he still felt devastated. He still couldn't believe that she was really gone. After Sue's accident, Mark's friends were supportive, and his church had brought meals and had prayed for him, but nothing had seemed to help. There were days, more of them than he cared to admit, when he thought it would have been better if he had been in the car with Sue and had died, too.
- Tina couldn't seem to stop crying. She was furious with her husband Bill for forcing them to move a thousand miles from family and friends. She missed everyone: her church, the friends she had grown up with, and most of all, her family. She didn't want to be here and certainly didn't want to make new friends. The phone bill was huge, but she didn't care. She just wanted to go back home.

*Jesus wept.*
—John 11:35

- Rob couldn't drive past the hospital without feeling that sick, clenching feeling in his gut. He had spent hours watching his dad struggle with cancer. Now, Rob didn't care about anything. During his father's illness, his days, and sometimes nights, had revolved around doing whatever he could to make sure his dad made it, and now he was gone.

## 2 DEFINITIONS AND KEY THOUGHTS

- Grief is **intense emotional suffering** caused by a loss.
- Grieving is like entering the valley of shadows. Grief is **painful,** and it is **hard work**. It is **a lingering process**, a healing journey that can last from one to three years, and for some, a lifetime. In fact, some never get through the process of grieving.
- A **sudden death** can be more difficult to grieve because there is no warning and no chance to say goodbye to begin to prepare for the loss.
- Grief isn't always just about death. It can also be **faced in a divorce, abuse, abandonment, illness, life transitions, disaster, or any other kind of misfortune**.
- Grief is actually a **complex set of emotions,** all of which are "normal." Someone who is grieving may experience his loss psychologically through feelings, thoughts, and attitudes; socially, as he interacts with others; physically, affecting his health.
- Often, friends don't know how to help someone who is grieving and may try to "cheer him up" or "get his mind off his loss." This can actually add to the burden

because the person who is grieving has to either avoid his friends or "fake it" rather than have the chance to share what he is really feeling.

- Sometimes loss is cumulative and **awakens memories of early losses** that were never fully grieved.
- Someone who is grieving may experience **intense feelings of guilt** for not caring enough for the person who has died, or he may feel as if he is being punished.
- Sometimes the feelings of anger and sadness are **projected onto God,** and the grieving person believes God is distant and uncaring.
- Sadness and loss often **intensify during certain times of the year,** such as the month that the person died, family holidays, and the person's birthday or anniversary.

## Stages of Grief

- Grief can be felt in many different ways. It has several stages that were originally identified by Elisabeth Kubler-Ross, in her book, *On Death and Dying:*

    1. **Denial or shock.** Intellectually, the bereaved may comprehend what has happened, but his emotions may not experience the pain yet; he may feel numb.
    2. **Release of emotions,** often in the form of anger toward others. The bereaved may get angry with God. Grieving people become preoccupied with memories of what has been lost and may explode in anger or withdraw for a time.
    3. **Guilt and anger.** The bereaved beats himself up emotionally as he blames himself for not preventing the loss. He feels disorganized and doesn't know how to move on with life.
    4. **Bargaining.** In an attempt to lessen the pain, people who experience loss try to swap a behavior for the hope of feeling better. For example, a grieving widow may pour herself into serving others because she hopes God will reward her by making the pain go away. When it doesn't seem to work, she determines to serve longer hours and more selflessly to see if that will work but it doesn't.
    5. **Sadness.** When people realize bargaining doesn't work, they face the cold, hard facts of the loss. At this point, they feel all the sadness they have been trying to avoid. Depression may haunt them if they don't find someone to help them process this grief.
    6. **Acceptance** of the loss. Reorganizing his life, filling new roles, and reconnecting with those around him are all healthy and important facets of the healing process. A key part of this process is the ability to learn how to feel and express the pain without denial and avoidance.[1]

*Although loss and grief are common, no amount of technology or experience can make the grieving process any easier. The hard news is that the only road to true healing is through the grief process. The good news is that God travels that road with us.*
—H. Norman Wright

- As helpful as it is to understand these stages, they are not neatly-packaged states that a person experiences sequentially. They are a cycle, and the bereaved may experience more than one emotion at a time.
- The goal of grieving isn**'t to get things back to normal**. After a loss, a person's entire life may change. The goal is to find and accept a new "normal."

## 3 ASSESSMENT INTERVIEW

### Rule Outs

**Q1** To determine if the grieving process has cycled downward into a debilitating depression, ask: "On a scale of 1 to 10, with 1 being great and 10 being extremely depressed, where would you put yourself today?" *(If depression is evident, see also the section on Depression.)*

If the person seems severely depressed, ask this question. If not, move on to the others.

*When you feel that all is lost, sometimes the greatest gain is ready to be yours.*
—Thomas à Kempis

**Q2** Do you have any thoughts of hurting yourself? *(If suicidal tendencies are evident, see the section on Suicide and get other help immediately.)*

### General Questions

In the first days after a death, you probably won't ask these questions. Focus instead on just being there and offering practical assistance with needs, such as organizing the funeral, contacting relatives and friends, getting meals, and watering plants at the house. In a few days or weeks after the funeral, you can help the person begin to process the pain. Tailor the questions to fit the person and your relationship, and pick the ones that seem most pertinent.

*Note:* These are directed toward someone who is grieving over a death, but could be recast for the person who is grieving loss for other reasons.

**Q3** Tell me about the person who died.

**Q4** Share your favorite memories of this person.

**Q5** Was the death especially traumatic? *(For example, was it a sudden accident or death at home?)*

**Q6** Where were you when the death occurred? *(Listen for ways that the person may be blaming himself or feeling guilty for what has happened. For example, was he driving the car that had the accident? Was he the passenger who survived a car accident while the other person did not? Process those feelings with him.)*

**Q7** How did you feel after the death?

**Q8** What emotions have you had since the death?

**Q9** What emotions do you currently feel most often?

**Q10** Does this loss remind you of any other loss that you have experienced?

**Q11** Who else knows what you have been going through? Who is supporting you emotionally and spiritually?

**Q12** In what ways will this loss change your life?

**Q13** At what level are you functioning right now? Tell me about a typical day.

**Q14** When are your best times?

**Q15** When are your worst times?

## WISE COUNSEL 4

Address any issues of **wanting to die** or not wanting to live and give a referral for counseling or medication, if necessary.

Assess how the person is **functioning in daily life** and what help he might need.

Reassure the person that the grieving process will **take time** and that the range and intensity of emotions he is experiencing are normal. (If, however, the person is incapacitated by grief, offer additional help and resources.)

Remind him that each person's grieving experience is unique, while at the same time **normalizing the process** by identifying it as one you have seen with all people suffering some important loss.

## ACTION STEPS 5

### 1. Be Patient

- Encourage the person to give himself whatever time that it takes to heal emotionally.
- Encourage him to keep a routine, get lots of rest, and not try to attempt too much, but to direct his energies toward healing.

### 2. Maintain Friendships

- Encourage the person to let others comfort him and to share in the journey toward healing.
- Encourage him not to become isolated, but rather to seek meaningful connection with others.
- Have the person make a list of friends to call.
- Have the person locate a grief support group, and perhaps, go with him the first time he attends.

### 3. Feel the Pain

- Help the person understand that the intensity of the pain is normal, and that eventually, it will begin to subside. The sense of loss may never disappear completely, but it will become bearable.

*Yea, though I walk through the valley of the shadow of death, I will fear no evil; for You are with me; Your rod and Your staff, they comfort me.*
—Psalm 23:4

- Trying to avoid the "terrible pain" only prolongs grief.
- Trying to avoid a loss by hiding the feelings will only cause problems in other areas—rationally, spiritually, or physically.
- Dealing with loss in a healthy manner can be a major avenue to growth and life-transforming change.
- The person can move forward by experiencing grief while at the same time, rejoining the living through acts of giving and receiving.

### 4. "Normalize" the Feelings of Grief

- Grief encompasses a number of changes. It appears differently at various times, and it comes and goes in people's lives.
- It is a normal, predictable, expected, and healthy reaction to a loss.
- Grief is each individual's personal journey. His manner of dealing with any kind of loss—no matter how minor or severe it may appear to others—needs to be respected. It should be gently challenged only when experienced in a manner that is detrimental to him and his relationships.

### 5. Healing

- Help the grieving person process any guilt and anger he is feeling.
- Help him redirect his energies from excessive "if onlys" and wishing that things could be different, in order to focus on healing.

## 6 BIBLICAL INSIGHTS

***Then David lamented with this lamentation over Saul and over Jonathan his son. —2 Samuel 1:17***

- Expressing sorrow is a healthy response to grief. David poured out his sorrow in words that honored the king and his son.
- Putting grief into words is a healthy way to handle the pain and honor those who have died.

*We are healed of grief only when we express it to the full.*
—Charles R. Swindoll

***He is despised and rejected by men, a Man of sorrows and acquainted with grief. And we hid, as it were, our faces from Him; He was despised, and we did not esteem Him. Surely He has borne our griefs and carried our sorrows; yet we esteemed Him stricken, smitten by God, and afflicted. —Isaiah 53:3-4***

- Isaiah's words communicate the suffering of the One who loved us and died for us.
- In our deepest moments of grief and loss, we need only look to Christ on the cross and realize that He understands our pain. He alone can heal the wounded heart.

***Jesus said to her, "I am the resurrection and the life. He who believes in Me, though he may die, he shall live. And whoever lives and believes in Me shall never die. Do you believe this?" —John 11:25-26***

- Because of sin, death comes to all of us (Romans 5:12-14). Many try to ignore death, not wanting to think or talk about it. But feared or embraced, expected or not, death still occurs.
- Jesus experienced those emotions at the death of His good friend Lazarus. Jesus knows the pain of loss and uncontrollable sorrow. He knows the incredible power and pain of death.
- It is natural to feel sad and mourn the death of a loved one. But in our times of sorrow, we can let Jesus hold us in His compassionate arms, knowing that He understands.

*In every pang that rends the heart, the Man of Sorrows has a part.* —MICHAEL BRUCE

***But I do not want you to be ignorant, brethren, concerning those who have fallen asleep, lest you sorrow as others who have no hope. For if we believe that Jesus died and rose again, even so God will bring with Him those who sleep in Jesus. —1 Thessalonians 4:13-14***

- The Thessalonian believers wondered what was happening to their fellow believers who had died.
- Believers have the ultimate assurance. We believe that Jesus died, rose again, ascended, and is coming again, and we also believe that He will bring with Him those who have died.
- One day, all believers will be reunited in the grandest reunion ever seen!

***And God will wipe away every tear from their eyes; there shall be no more death, nor sorrow, nor crying. There shall be no more pain, for the former things have passed away. —Revelation 21:4***

- Revelation describes a better time and a better place where grief and loss will not exist: heaven.
- No matter what we experience here, God promises a perfect future with Him. Through the hard times of today, we can trust this hope for the future.

## 7 PRAYER STARTER

Lord, we wish we understood Your thoughts and Your plans, but sometimes we admit that we just don't get it. We don't understand why You would take a loved one from us. We don't understand why You would allow this to happen when You knew how much it hurts. Yet, Lord, we want to trust You . . .

## 8 RECOMMENDED RESOURCES

American Association of Christian Counselors Life Enrich Video Series

*A Grief Observed*, by C.S. Lewis

*Living with Grief and Loss*, by Freda Crews

*Loss in Marriage/Hope of Heaven*, by Norman Wright

# Guilt

## 1 PORTRAITS

- For the first ten years of her marriage, Lydia lived in a house on the street behind her parents. She visited them every day, and her mother helped babysit her children. She was always very close to her parents. Then her husband got a job in a new location. The move devastated her parents—especially her mother. Lydia feels tremendous guilt over moving away from her parents who had become quite dependent on her.
- When Glen was nine years old, he was asked to go home right after school to check on his great aunt who lived with them. A friend asked him to go play football in the park, and Glen decided his great aunt would be fine for a bit longer. When he arrived home an hour late, there was an ambulance at the front door. Aunt Muriel had suffered a heart attack and passed away that day. Glen carried that guilt with him into his adult life.
- Marjorie stole some money years ago from a previous employer, and she had gotten away with it undetected. It wasn't a lot of money. However, she became a Christian recently and feels a lot of guilt over what she did.

## 2 DEFINITIONS AND KEY THOUGHTS

- Guilt is a **feeling of deep regret or remorse** caused by feeling responsible for a failure or loss.
- Guilt can **lead to shame** if the feelings of guilt are based on an act or acts that were thought to be sinful or displeasing to an authority figure.
- There is a **difference between *feeling* guilty and actually *being* guilty**.

  If a moral law has been violated, a person is guilty, regardless of whether or not he feels guilty.

  On the other hand, just feeling guilty doesn't mean that a moral law has been violated.

- It is important to clarify whether the guilt is caused by a **sinful act or from inappropriate regret**.

  **True guilt** is caused by sin and is God's way of calling us to repentance and restitution.

> *As far as the east is from the west, so far has He removed our transgressions from us.*
> —Psalm 103:12

**False guilt** is a burden of responsibility and blame we place on ourselves for failure to live up to our own or someone else's expectations.

## Dealing with False Guilt

- Often, obsessive feelings of guilt over a situation in which the person committed no identifiable sin come from a sense of unworthiness rooted in **the person's childhood**. He may have been blamed or punished for things that he didn't do, or been told he was worthless.
- It helps for the individual to **tell his story**, not to ask for forgiveness, but to verbalize his feelings and get them out in the open.
- It may help for the person to **verbalize those feelings to the one** who makes him feel guilty. Often the person listening will reassure him that he had no reason to feel guilty, so this conversation can provide some relief. But if the other person is dominating, intimidating, or controlling, don't encourage the person to share his feelings—not until he is strong enough for a genuine confrontation, and then, only with your help in preparation and follow up.
- If he isn't comfortable sharing with that outside person, then the person needs to deal with the guilt by **asking God for wisdom, strength, and healing**.
- A person with extreme guilt over something that wasn't a sinful act needs to work on squaring his views of himself and his behavior with the truth as revealed in Scripture so that he can be released from guilt to a life of peace and freedom in Christ. This process will help him experience a closeness to God that will enable him to realize the depths of God's love and mercy.

*The most marvelous ingredient in the forgiveness of God is that he also forgets, the one thing a human being can never do. Forgetting with God is a divine attribute; God's forgiveness forgets.*
—Oswald Chambers

## Dealing with True Guilt

- Guilt caused by sin requires an understanding of **confession and forgiveness**.
- This kind of guilt is prompted **by the Holy Spirit working in the conscience.** The individual is motivated to confess sin and experience God's cleansing.
- Confession, request for forgiveness, and/or restitution needs to happen if possible (that is, if the person hurt is still alive, or if restitution is able to be made in any form).

# 3 ASSESSMENT INTERVIEW

## General Questions

First, seek to identify if the guilt is true or false, then proceed with the correct set of questions below.

**Q1** What brought you to counseling today?

**Q2** Are your feelings of guilt causing physical or emotional problems?

**Q3** What do you feel guilty about?

**Q4** When did this event occur?

**Q5** What have you done about the feelings of guilt related to this event?

**Q6** Did you commit a sin in this act?

### Questions If It Seems to Be True Guilt

**Q7** Is this guilt affecting your life today? If so, how?

**Q8** What have you done to deal with that sin?

**Q9** What can you do to rectify the situation? (Confession? Apology? Restitution?)

**Q10** Have you shared this guilt with anyone?

**Q11** If you have confessed your sin, do you feel forgiven by God?

**Q12** In what ways are you actually experiencing God's grace?

*If we confess our sins, He is faithful and just to forgive us our sins and to cleanse us from all unrighteousness.*
—1 John 1:9

### Questions If It Seems to Be False Guilt

**Q7** Since no sin was committed, why do you think that you still carry feelings of guilt?

**Q8** Have you shared this guilt with anyone?

**Q9** Tell me about your childhood. How were you disciplined as a child?

**Q10** Tell me about your self-image. How might it affect the way you experience guilt?

**Q11** How might the way you were raised affect the way you feel guilt?

**Q12** Have others made you feel guilty? If so, how?

**Q13** Do you think it would help to talk to these people? Why or why not?

## 4 WISE COUNSELING

A person who seeks help for false guilt probably has **problems of unworthiness and low self-worth.** These often are rooted in childhood. If he was always made to feel that he could not do anything right, or if she was always being blamed for things that were out of his control, then these may have been carried into his adult life.

He needs to be reminded of **God's unconditional love**. Let him talk about his past to provide an opportunity to begin the healing process.

The person dealing with true guilt needs to be given action steps that will pave the way for **confession, forgiveness, and restitution**.

Guilt can trap a person into a life of **unfulfillment and heartache.** He will never be free to experience God's best until the guilt is resolved.

## ACTION STEPS 5

### 1. Pay Attention to the Feelings

- Guilt, like physical pain, is a signal that something is wrong.
- Go to God in prayer and ask for insight and wisdom.

### 2. Determine the Source

- Are the guilt feelings because of sin or because of some issues that were out of your control?
- Seek God patiently. Just because you feel guilty doesn't mean you have sinned, but you may need to let God peel back some layers to reveal a sin long forgotten that needs to be resolved.
- If the guilt feelings are out of your control, you still need to find a way to resolve them.

### 3. True Guilt

- If you are feeling guilty because you have committed a sin, what steps will you take to receive forgiveness from God?
- What steps will you take to receive forgiveness from the person and make restitution?
- If an apology or restitution can't happen (for example, the person has passed away), then plan a way to deal with the guilt. Suggest writing a letter to that person and providing a "ceremony" of sorts where the guilt can be given to God.
- Realize that "telling all" can be a way of inflicting more pain on others. Permanent relief from moral guilt comes from God's forgiveness, not necessarily public confession. The scope of the confession should not exceed the scope of the sin.

### 4. False Guilt

- If the guilt is related to self-worth, make a list of all the things God has done for you, including paying the price to save you. *(Note: You can help with providing suggestions and Scripture verses.)*
- Continuing to punish yourself for being human is useless. Do what you can and move on. (If the person is reluctant to embrace freedom, you may need to talk about reasons people use passivity to avoid the risks of change.)

> *The purpose of being guilty is to bring us to Jesus. Once we are there, then its purpose is finished. If we continue to make ourselves guilty—to blame ourselves—then that is sin in itself.*
> —Corrie ten Boom

### 5. Move On

- Once you've confessed, apologized, and made restitution, don't beat yourself up anymore. Leave it with God.
- Turn off the mental tape player. Satan, not the Holy Spirit, is the accuser (Revelation 12:10). Satan wants to create feelings of condemnation resulting in unnecessary guilt. Turn him off!
- Keep a "guilt pot." Anytime you feel guilt creeping in, write that guilt feeling on a piece of paper and throw it in the pot. (The pot will remind you that God is the Potter, always at work on you, and you are merely the clay—Isaiah 64:8.)

### 6. Keep Active

- Do things for other people.
- Practice being forgiving in your relationships.
- By providing encouragement to someone else, you will receive encouragement back and that will increase your feelings of self-worth.

6

## BIBLICAL INSIGHTS

***So he said, "I heard Your voice in the garden, and I was afraid because I was naked; and I hid myself." —Genesis 3:10***

- Adam already knew he had sinned. He felt an inner awareness of wrongdoing called *guilt*, given by God as an internal corrective.
- The realization of guilt could have brought Adam to repentance and confession. Instead, Adam tried to cope with guilt and shame by avoidance and denial.
- As long as we blame others and refuse to take responsibility for our wrong actions, we remain mired in sin. Guilt cuts us off from God's redemptive healing.
- God invites us to be honest about our sin and confess it to Him. When we do, God is "faithful and just to forgive us our sins and to cleanse us from all unrighteousness" (1 John 1:9).

*Good works never erase guilt.* —Erwin W. Lutzer

***At the evening sacrifice I arose from my fasting; and having torn my garment and my robe, I fell on my knees and spread out my hands to the Lord my God. And I said: "O my God, I am too ashamed and humiliated to lift up my face to You, my God; for our iniquities have risen higher than our heads, and our guilt has grown up to the heavens." —Ezra 9:5-6***

- Despite our mistakes and failures, God is willing to meet us at our point of need.

- Sometimes we can make amends by specific action. At other times we suffer the consequences of our sin, but through repentance, we can experience God's grace and love.

***Then Jesus said to those Jews who believed Him, "If you abide in My word, you are My disciples indeed. And you shall know the truth, and the truth shall make you free . . . Most assuredly, I say to you, whoever commits sin is a slave of sin. And a slave does not abide in the house forever, but a son abides forever. Therefore if the Son makes you free, you shall be free indeed." —John 8:31-36***

- No truth is more glorious to imprisoned people than to be told that they are no longer condemned but are set free! Christ brings that good news.
- Often, however, believers who have been set free still keep themselves behind bars. They feel guilty about their past, or that they can't be perfect in this life.
- The feeling of guilt is healthy and productive when it helps us to know when we have done something wrong. But oppressive guilt can also keep people from being able to rejoice in their new life in Christ. That kind of guilt is a prison. We needn't stay locked up if Christ has set us free.

***There is therefore now no condemnation to those who are in Christ Jesus, who do not walk according to the flesh, but according to the Spirit. —Romans 8:1***

- Failure to keep the law perfectly leads to condemnation. Since no one can keep God's law perfectly, all people are condemned. The law brings guilt because people realize they are powerless to keep it.
- Christ's death for us, however, sets us free.
- If Christ no longer condemns us, then neither should we condemn ourselves.

## 7 PRAYER STARTER

Guilt can be so powerful. On the one hand, we know You use it, Lord, to show us where we have gone wrong, sins we need to confess, ask for forgiveness, or make restitution. On the other hand, it can also become like a prison that keeps us from living for You . . .

## 8 RECOMMENDED RESOURCES

*Deceived by Shame, Desired by God*, by Cynthia Spell Humbert

*Released from Shame*, by Sandy Wilson

*Shame & Guilt: Masters of Disguise*, by Jane Middelton-Moz

# Homosexuality

## 1 PORTRAITS

- Tim painfully recalls feeling different from his brothers. "I remember feeling so alone," he says. "While my brothers were out competing in sports, I was quite content in my room drawing." He continues, "My dad and I never got along. He was a high pressure 'corporate type' and was always putting me down for my 'sissy' interests. As I got older, I became increasingly aware of a longing for other men. I fought fantasies of being hugged and touched by another man. In college I finally decided that I couldn't battle these feelings anymore, and gave in to having sex with men. Even then, I realized it wasn't the sex I was wanting, but love."

- Leah was the youngest daughter with five older brothers. She recalls seeing pictures of herself in pre-school dressed by her mom in overalls and T-shirts. With the exception of her ponytail, it was difficult to determine if she was a boy or girl. In grade school, Leah was often the brunt of her brothers wrestling competition. She despised being born a girl. In high school, Leah developed a close friendship with a girl named Emily who was two years older and took a special interest in her. Leah experienced tenderness from Emily that she had never experienced from her mom. Emily's care for Leah awakened a deep need to be loved. In time, they developed a sexual relationship. As the relationship progressed, Leah started to see not only how controlling Emily was, but how dependent she had become on Emily. Somehow, Emily's love was not enough to take Leah's deep soul pain away.

- Henry spoke in a quiet and controlled manner as he shared the recent news of his son "coming out." "Sure, Jay and I have had a difficult relationship, but I just saw it as his own willfulness. He always seemed to want to push me away. I see this as just another attempt to rebel against everything my wife and I believe in."

## 2 DEFINITIONS AND KEY THOUGHTS

- Homosexuality refers to an orientation and a behavior. The *homosexual orientation*, is a condition in which a person is **sexually attracted** to members of the same sex. *Homosexual behavior* refers to any sexual activity between members of the same gender. Female homosexuality is generally called "lesbianism."

- Homosexuality and lesbianism are rooted in a **variety of psychological, biological, social, and spiritual factors**.

- Though countless studies attempt to identify the cause of homosexuality, many of these disagree. Research indicates that homosexuality may have its roots in a **breakdown of relationship with a same-sex parent**, creating a deficit in the child's sense of identity and feelings of being loved.

Male homosexuality has some correlation to an **absent or detached father and an over-involved, controlling mother**. As a result, the child over-identifies with his mother, while at the same time, craving the attention and affection of his absent father.

Lesbianism may be related to an **emotionally or physically absent mother**, resulting in an over-identification by the daughter with her father and a craving for affection from women. Lesbianism can have roots in verbal, physical, or sexual abuse from the opposite sex (possibly a father) creating distrust of men and a feeling of safety and nurture in relationships with women.

- **Other factors** that may play a part in the development of same sex preferences are:

  -Sexual abuse

  -Fear of the opposite sex

  -Exposure to pornography

  -Seduction by peers

  -Willful rebellion

  -Moral relativism

- **Experimentation in the adolescent years** can cause confusion for the teenager about his/her sexual identity as he/she seeks to meet legitimate needs for love through sexual involvement with same sex partners.

- Currently, research does not support a "gay" gene, and **no conclusive evidence for biological basis** of homosexuality has been found. Even in the unlikely case of such evidence being discovered, such would only prove what is already known—that people are fallen beings, physically, emotionally, and spiritually imperfect. An inborn tendency toward a particular sin does not justify that sin; it reinforces the need for a Savior.

- Homosexual behavior, like all human behaviors, is a **matter of choice**. People choose what to do with their desires.

- Homosexuality and lesbianism, from a medical and spiritual perspective, **can be redeemed.** People can find healing from past wounds and experience redemption from sinful behavior patterns as they seek to live in obedience to God.

*Like all complex behavioral and mental states, homosexuality is . . . neither exclusively biological nor exclusively psychological, but results from an as-yet-difficult-to-quantitate mixture of genetic factors, intrauterine influences . . . post-natal environment (such as parent, sibling and cultural behavior), and a complex series of repeatedly reinforced choices occurring at critical phases of development.*

—Jeffrey Satinover

- God's intent for sexual expression is within a covenant marriage between a man and a woman (Genesis 2:24; Hebrews 13:4). Adultery and fornication are denounced in Scripture, along with homosexual behavior.
- In the Old Testament, homosexual behavior is condemned as an "abomination" (Leviticus 18:22; 20:13).
- In Romans 1:24-27, the practice of homosexuality is referred to as an unnatural state rooted in fallen human nature. Homosexual behavior is condemned as "vile" and "shameful." In 1 Corinthians 6:9-10 and 1 Timothy 1:9-11, Paul lists homosexual practices alongside drunkenness, fornication, murder, and other vices.
- In 1 Corinthians 6:11, Paul preaches to former homosexuals and celebrates their deliverance with the words, "Such were some of you. But you were washed, but you were sanctified, but you were justified in the name of the Lord Jesus and by the Spirit of our God."

## 3 ASSESSMENT INTERVIEW

### For a person struggling with homosexuality:

**Q1** Are you a follower of Jesus Christ? *(If not, this is the first arena that needs to be addressed.)*

**Q2** Since you are a believer, do you want to change your homosexual behavior? *(For many, what has kept them in the homosexual lifestyle is ambivalence and fear. Ambivalence because the homosexual lifestyle has temporarily numbed deeper emotional pain. They are afraid of revealing themselves and dealing with their deep pain and whatever caused it.)*

**Q3** Are you experiencing distress over your homosexual behavior?

**Q4** Are these just "feelings," or have you actually committed homosexual acts? *(If the person has had homosexual sex, it is important that he begin the process of seeking forgiveness and repentance by confessing past behavior and restoring moral fences.)*

*There is a huge difference between loving a homosexual and supporting homosexuality.*

**Q5** If you have been acting out your sexual desires, how long has this pattern been occurring? *(Evaluate the extent of the involvement in the homosexual arena—has it been in only one relationship? Many relationships? An allegiance to the homosexual lifestyle? )*

**Q6** Tell me about your family life. What was your relationship with your mom like?

**Q7** Tell me about your relationship with your dad.

**Q8** Have you ever experienced:

-Sexual abuse?

-Fear of the opposite sex?

-Exposure to pornography?

-Seduction by peers?

-Willful rebellion?

**Q9** Are you part of a local church or Christian fellowship? *(If so, does the church provide support for those who are seeking healing from the homosexual condition?)*

### For a parent of a child who is homosexual:

**Q1** What has been your reaction to finding out that about your son/daughter's sexual orientation? *(The person may have a variety of reactions: feeling shock, betrayal, sadness, fear.)*

**Q2** Describe what your relationship has been with your son/daughter in the past.

**Q3** Describe your relationship now.

**Q4** What has your son/daughter communicated are his/her expectations of you now that he/she has shared this information?

**Q5** How do you feel about your own role in this situation? *(It is important to evaluate how the person is seeing his own effectiveness as a parent. There may be guilt or regret about how he or she parented this son/daughter.)*

**Q6** How do you feel your son/daughter is handling this?

**Q7** Does your son/daughter feel free to express his/her feelings with you?

## WISE COUNSEL 4

Evaluate **your own perceptions and feelings** about homosexuality. If you feel fear, anxiety, or anger toward homosexuals, then you should not counsel a person with this condition. Unconditional acceptance of the homosexual and a genuine regard for the person are essential.

Homosexuals seeking counseling may have **repressed many fears, anxieties, hostilities, and painful memories**. Therefore, it is crucial that you communicate safety and a deep respect for the person.

The pathway to healing from homosexuality is long and difficult but is extremely rewarding. Ultimately, the course of healing and redemption for the homosexual is found in a **deep and radical obedience to Jesus Christ,** while at the same time, facing honestly the wounds and sins of the past.

The outcome of the healing journey is to be a person who walks with integrity, **willing to sacrifice all fleshly desires** to be identified with Christ.

## 5 ACTION STEPS

### If the person is a homosexual:

### 1. Seek Help from a Trained Counselor or Pastor

Ultimately, the person will need to work with a counselor or pastor who has training in this arena.

### 2. Issues to Address

- Explain that, in counseling with the professional, the person will need to address particular issues in the process of healing:

  Submission of his/her sexuality to God, and seeking forgiveness for behavior and choices.

  Choosing to change behavior—terminate homosexual relationships, and choose not to frequent places where homosexual relationships/activity was encouraged.

  Find healing in Christ and accept himself/herself as a child of God.

  Deal with the guilt of the past.

  Face the pain in relationships with same-sex parent or abuse by the opposite-sex parent.

  Establish healthy same-sex friendships.

  Embrace his/her own gender as a heterosexual.

### If the person is the parent of a homosexual:

### 1. Examine Your Heart

- God does not view one sin as more heinous than others. We have all sinned and fall short of God's glory.
- Examine your heart and be aware of your personal struggles and temptations so that you are prepared to show your child the same love and forgiveness God has shown you.

## 2. Avoid Condemnation

- The core of the homosexual struggle is a deep feeling of rejection. Someone does not "choose" to have homosexual feelings.
- "Coming out" isn't an intentional act to hurt the parent. More often than not, the child has kept secret the feelings he/she has struggled with to avoid hurting the parent.

## 3. Avoid Lecturing

- Avoid lecturing on all the risks and problems with homosexuality.
- Rarely does someone respond positively when being told what he/she shouldn't do.

## 4. Maintain the Relationship

- Let your child know that you want to maintain a strong, loving relationship.
- Acceptance of your son/daughter does not mean agreement with his/her choices.
- Withdrawing your love and affection will only make the relationship more difficult.

## 5. Pursue Dialog

- Talk with your child and listen. It may be tough, but try to get your child to share the reasons behind his/her choices.
- As you dialog, you will become more comfortable sharing your concerns about the gay lifestyle, and your child may be more open to listening if you have listened.

## 6. Pray Constantly

Pray diligently for God's truth and compassion to speak into your son/daughter's heart.

## 7. Support Group

You may want to join an organization that seeks to minister to homosexuals and where parents can learn more about God's redemptive plan for healing.

*The pro-gay theology is much like the broader gay rights philosophy, in that it seeks legitimization (not just tolerance) of homosexuality . . . When God is reputed to sanction what He has already clearly forbidden, then a religious travesty is being played out, and boldly. Confronting it is necessary because it (the pro-gay theology) asks us to confirm professing Christians in their sin, when we are Biblically commanded to do just the opposite.*

—Joe Dallas

### 8. Maintain Boundaries

- You can still have boundaries in your home. Just as you would not allow your child's opposite-sex boyfriend/girlfriend to sleep with your child on visits, don't allow homosexual sex in your home either.
- Even if they consider themselves "married," you should stand by your values, especially if younger siblings are still in the home.

## 6 BIBLICAL INSIGHTS

***Now before they lay down, the men of the city, the men of Sodom, both old and young, all the people from every quarter, surrounded the house. And they called to Lot and said to him, "Where are the men who came to you tonight? Bring them out to us that we may know them carnally." —Genesis 19:4-5***

- In spite of efforts by some of today's gay theologians to revise and reinterpret Sodom's story, the clear message of Genesis 19 has always referred to homosexual violence. It is generally thought that the Sodomites also practiced bestiality, sex with children and adolescents, heterosexual rape, and adultery, along with other unspeakable forms of sexual perversity and violence. The severity of their punishment shows us God's perspective about the horrors of their behavior.
- Though both homosexuality and rape are consistently condemned in the Scriptures, they are not isolated from other sexual sins, or sin in general. Whether heterosexual sin or homosexual sin, God calls us to forsake all sexual sin and to know the transforming power of His redeeming and healing grace.

*To address the issue of homosexuality is to enter deeply into God's experience: loving the person, hating the sin, and remaining steadfast to God's standards. We know that even when our best efforts to persuade the people we love have failed, God's power is still more than*

***You shall not lie with a male as with a woman. It is an abomination. —Leviticus 18:22***

- This charge against homosexual relations appears in a section including rules against marital infidelity and bestiality.
- This is one of a number of passages in both testaments that, taken together and interpreted plainly, reveal that homosexual conduct is a great offense to God. It is called "an abomination," and was punishable by death. Clearly, homosexual practices violate God's law.

***For this reason God gave them up to vile passions. For even their women exchanged the natural use for what is against nature. Likewise also the men, leaving the natural use of the woman, burned in their lust for one another, men with men committing what is shameful, and receiving in themselves the penalty of their error which was due. —Romans 1:26-27***

- Paul says homosexuality is "against nature" and against what God planned for sexual relations. God created marriage and sexual relations to be between a man and a woman (Genesis 2:24).

- Homosexual acts are called "shameful," and those who live that lifestyle will receive "the penalty of their error."
- God will forgive and strengthen those who turn away from homosexuality and seek to honor Him with their lives.

***And even as they did not like to retain God in their knowledge, God gave them over to a debased mind, to do those things which are not fitting; being filled with all unrighteousness, sexual immorality . . . who, knowing the righteous judgment of God, that those who practice such things are deserving of death, not only do the same but also approve of those who practice them. —Romans 1:28-32***

- Some say that homosexuality is a lifestyle choice or a genetic predisposition—and when confronted with this passage in Romans, some say that these words were meant only for the culture of that day. When dealing with the Old Testament passages condemning homosexual activity (Leviticus 18:22; 20:13), the same argument is often made.
- What is clearly a moral issue in both the Old and New Testaments can't be relegated to the past as just a cultural law. The Bible condemns homosexual conduct because it goes against God's plan for a natural sexual relationship between a man and a woman in marriage.
- As with any sin, the actions of homosexuality can be forgiven, and its powerful temptations can be overcome. God will forgive and accept anyone who desires to be set free from homosexuality.

## 7 PRAYER STARTER

Lord, You love Your precious child. You created him and You have a plan for his life. He is struggling today with the sin nature and feels helpless to overcome its desires . . .

## 8 RECOMMENDED RESOURCES

*Homosexuality*, American Association of Christian Counselors Life Enrich Video Series, by Stan Jones

*Homosexuality: The Healing Journey & Redemption*, American Association of Christian Counselors Life Enrich Video Series, by Mark Yarhouse

*A Parent's Guide to Preventing Homosexuality*, by Joseph Nicolosi and Linda Ames Nicolosi

There are numerous effective Christian ministries that offer help and hope to homosexuals and families of homosexuals, including Exodus International, Desert Stream Ministries, and Redeemed Life Ministries

# Loneliness

## 1 PORTRAITS

- John is 50 years old, and he just lost his wife of 25 years. They never had any children and did everything together. John feels awkward when he's with the friends he and his wife Jenny had together. He spends most of his time now watching television.
- Mary can't stand going to all her friends' weddings. They aren't happy occasions for her. It has been five years since she graduated from college, and she longs to be married. She spends most evenings alone in her tiny apartment.
- Rachel enjoyed her friends in high school, and she looked forward to college. When she arrived, though, it seemed that all the girls she met were very cool toward her. She found out that all of them had formed cliques, but she wasn't in one.

## 2 DEFINITIONS AND KEY THOUGHTS

### A Biblical Understanding of Relationships

Since humans were made in the image of a triune God (who exists in relationship), humans too were made for relationship. This is evidenced in Genesis 2:18, where God sees Adam alone in the Garden of Eden and says it is "not good."

*The man who lives by himself and for himself is apt to be corrupted by the company he keeps.*
—Charles Henry Parkhurst

Humans need both intimacy with God (vertical) and intimacy with other people (horizontal). It is important to find our need for vertical (God) intimacy first, for God says, "I will not leave you nor forsake you" (Joshua 1:5), and Paul writes "nor height nor depth, nor any other created thing, shall be able to separate us from the love of God which is in Christ Jesus our Lord" (Romans 8:39). In contrast, our horizontal (finite, human) relationships can be destroyed by sin, physical death, and other circumstances on this side of heaven.

When humans inherited a sin nature, intimacy was tainted: Adam and Eve clothed themselves, blamed each other, blamed God, and refused to accept responsibility for their disobedience. Through Christ, people can discover the path to genuine intimacy again.

Due to our sin nature, intimacy is difficult to achieve and people often experience loneliness.

## The Nature of Loneliness

- Loneliness is a human response to being alone because God created humans with a need for relationships. From the moment of birth, humans seek attachment and connection.
- Loneliness:
  - is an uncomfortable feeling of **isolation**
  - is a painful feeling of being **disconnected** from others
  - causes a person to feel **alienated**
  - happens when a person feels there is **no one** with whom to share joys and disappointments
  - can result in an overwhelming feeling **of sadness**
  - can cause a person to become **despondent** if nothing is done about it

> *Human beings need both vertical intimacy (with God) and horizontal intimacy (with people) in order to be fulfilled. Without those relationships, they are vulnerable to the complex set of emotions described as "loneliness."*
> —Miriam Stark Parent

## Types of Loneliness

**Situational Loneliness:**

- A response to **physical or emotional separation**.
- Death, divorce, life transitions, and personal mobility are the **most common causes** of situational loneliness.
- In situational loneliness, **intimate relationships are severed, changed, or disrupted** in some way.
- This experience may be **brief and contained or long term and overwhelming**.
- The **longing** that accompanies the separation is intense and compelling.
- When the separation is **permanent** (such as through death), loneliness is **more difficult to handle**.

**Emotional Loneliness:**

- **Emotional separation** can also lead to loneliness.
- People can feel lonely when they are surrounded by those with whom they experience **little or no intimate connection**. The loneliest people are often **in crowds**.
- This sense of **disconnectedness** leads to greater despair.
- This kind of loneliness is often felt as a **form of anxiety**, driving some to frantic efforts at **superficial connections**.

- When physical separation is coupled with emotional separation, the loneliness can seem unbearable.

**Chronic Loneliness:**

- Chronic loneliness can result from **persistent feelings of not belonging or being understood**.
- Chronic loneliness is often rooted in **social deficits or an aggressive sense of shame and worthlessness**.
- The person feeling chronically **alone and isolated** has **no hope of "connecting"** again.
- Chronic feelings of loneliness can lead to **deep personal isolation and despair,** often ending in angry, violent alienation, and sometimes, suicide.

## 3 ASSESSMENT INTERVIEW

*The world's greatest tragedy is unwantedness; the world's greatest disease is loneliness.*
—Mother Teresa

**Q1** Do you feel alone even when you are in a room full of people?

**Q2** Does the loneliness ever go away?

**Q3** When it does, what are you doing?

**Q4** Describe a typical day.

**Q5** Have you talked to God about your loneliness?

**Q6** Do you feel that God understands your loneliness?

**Q7** Do you blame yourself for your loneliness? Do you blame someone else?

**Q8** Do you have a friend you can share these feelings with?

**Q9** Tell me about another time in your life when you were lonely.

**Q10** Do you remember what you did or what got you out of the loneliness the previous time?

**Q11** Do you think you could change your loneliness in a similar way at this time?

**Q12** Tell me about any outside involvements.

**Q13** Tell me about your interests and hobbies.

## WISE COUNSEL 4

- The person needs to understand the source of loneliness.

  Perhaps his loneliness is based on a perception, not an unchangeable circumstance.

  Is the person feeling lonely due to a mistaken perception of the situation?

  Can the situation be changed?

- A person's loneliness may be a healthy part of the grief process as he deals with a loss. That is natural and will eventually pass if the person doesn't let the loneliness cause severe isolation from others.
- The experience of loneliness can cause people to draw closer to God and to others. If we are dealing with loneliness, we need to reach out to God and to others.
- God will bring people into our lives at various times. A person might not always have the same trusted friend to confide in.

## ACTION STEPS 5

### 1. Recognize the Feeling

- Have the person express his feelings.
- Ask the person to determine the source of the loneliness by putting his thoughts and feelings in writing—possibly in a journal.
- Encourage the person to make some social and spiritual changes to move out of loneliness (e.g., become more involved in his community, devote time to communion with God every day, etc.).

### 2. Seek God

- Encourage him to draw closer to God. God wants His children to be dependent on Him for everything. Help the person enjoy his relationship with God. He is the closest friend we will ever have. He will never leave and never disappoint (Hebrews 13:5).
- Focus on the positive and help the person cherish the fact that God has a good plan for each day and each stage of life.

### 3. Get Involved

- Encourage him to join a church committee, Bible study, a community organization, support group, sport, or hobby club.

> *We are born helpless. As soon as we are fully conscious we discover loneliness. We need others physically, emotionally, intellectually; we need them if we are to know anything, even ourselves.*
> —C.S. Lewis

- Invite him to volunteer! Volunteering for a community agency is a great way to help others, and at the same time engage in meaningful relationships.
- If possible, explore additional church activities, such as hosting a meeting, prayer group, or Bible study in his home.
- Point him to others who are actively seeking healthy, close, active and meaningful friendships.

### 4. Be Courageous

- Loneliness can be overcome in time if we take courageous steps to find trustworthy people.
- Even if others are distant, God is near.

## 6 BIBLICAL INSIGHTS

***I have become a stranger to my brothers, and an alien to my mother's children. —Psalm 69:8***

- Loneliness is a heavy burden; people can feel alone even when surrounded by people.
- When our courage and strength fails, and when people seem to have abandoned us, we can take comfort in knowing that God is always with us. When we know Him, we are never alone.

*The soul hardly ever realizes it, but whether he is a believer or not, his loneliness is really a homesickness for God.*
—Hubert van Zeller

***Fear not, for I am with you; be not dismayed, for I am your God. I will strengthen you, yes, I will help you, I will uphold you with My righteous right hand. —Isaiah 41:10***

- God reminds His people that in their loneliness and inadequacy they need not fear or be dismayed. Why? Because He is their God and because He is with them, holding them in His "righteous right hand."
- Everyone feels lonely at times. Sometimes, however, loneliness can become so desperate that it produces inordinate fear. That fear, then, can draw our attention away from God.
- Feelings of loneliness can be alleviated by attending church (Hebrews 10:25), finding a friend (Proverbs 18:24), listening to Christian music, and praying for God to work in and through us to take away the lonely feelings.

***Now Pashhur the son of Immer, the priest who was also chief governor in the house of the Lord, heard that Jeremiah prophesied these things. Then Pashhur struck Jeremiah the prophet, and put him in the stocks that were in the high gate of Benjamin, which was by the house of the Lord. —Jeremiah 20:1-2***

- As we read Jeremiah's prayer journal, we see into the life of an intensely lonely man. On these pages, anger, resentment, and self-loathing compete with praise and confidence. But the fact that he continued to communicate with God meant that he knew he wasn't completely alone.
- The intensity of his painful feelings didn't completely cloud the deeper reality of God's presence. As overwhelming as his gripes and challenges were, he still found comfort in having Someone to whom he could complain.
- When we think that we are alone facing the greatest challenges of our lives, the Spirit of God will continue to shape us and enable us to live for God.

***Let your conduct be without covetousness; be content with such things as you have. For He Himself has said, "I will never leave you nor forsake you." Hebrews 13:5***

- When people feel lonely, they feel like they don't belong, like no one cares, unloved and unwanted. When believers feel lonely, they need to remember God's great promise, "I will never leave you nor forsake you."
- No matter how painful or difficult our situation, and no matter how alone we feel, God is there. We can look to Him for deliverance, commit the situation to His care, and take comfort in His presence. God is always with us.

## 7 PRAYER STARTER

Dear Lord, Your child has come today with deep, painful feelings of loneliness and isolation. God, in this time, please help Your child to know emotionally that You are very present and that You are watching overhead. Please continue to comfort Your child through this time of loneliness. Also God, please help my friend find meaningful relationships and friendships that will be pleasing, and bring honor to You...

## 8 RECOMMENDED RESOURCES

*After the Boxes are Unpacked,* by Susan Miller

*Attachments,* by Tim Clinton and Gary Sibcy

*Loneliness,* by Elizabeth Skoglund

*What Wives Wish their Husbands Knew About Women,* by James Dobson

# Love/Belonging

## 1 PORTRAITS

- Kathy has jumped from one group of friends to another—and then another. No matter where she goes, she just doesn't seem to fit in.
- Ben grew up without a dad, a fact that plagues him every day. He often wonders what it would have been like to have grown up with both parents.
- Sue would like to meet new people, but she doesn't seem to have the necessary skills to do so. She ends up staying at home to avoid being embarrassed.

## 2 DEFINITIONS AND KEY THOUGHTS

### Love

- First Corinthians 13:4-8 describes several characteristics of love:

  Love suffers long and is kind

  Love does not envy

  Love does not parade itself

  Love is not puffed up

  Love does not behave rudely

  Love does not seek its own

  Love is not provoked

  Love thinks no evil

  Love does not rejoice in iniquity

  Love does rejoice in the truth

  Love bears all things

  Love believes all things

  Love hopes all things

  Love endures all things

  Love never fails

*Above all things have fervent love for one another, for "love will cover a multitude of sins."*
—1 Peter 4:8

- In Romans 12:9-21, Paul writes "Let love be without hypocrisy . . . Be kindly affectionate to one another with brotherly love." Paul continues, speaking about love's other remarkable qualities:

Love is fervent in spirit and service, strong and intense

Love is joyful, patient, prayerful, generous, and hospitable

Love blesses persecutors, refusing revenge

Love is compassionate and humble

Love is peaceable

Love overcomes and destroys evil

Love hates/abhors what is evil

> *Condescend to all weaknesses and infirmities of your fellow creatures, cover their frailties, love their excellencies, encourage their virtues, relieve their wants, rejoice in their friendship, overlook their unkindness, forgive their malice, and condescend to do the lowest offices to the lowest of mankind.*
> —William Law

## Belonging

- We are chosen by God, that whoever believe in Christ will have everlasting life with Him in heaven (John 6:27, 47).
- Ephesians 1:4-6 states explicitly that we belong to God, "just as He chose us in Him before the foundation of the world, that we should be holy and without blame before Him in love, having predestined us to adoption as sons by Jesus Christ to Himself, according to the good pleasure of His will, to the praise of the glory of His grace, by which He made us accepted in the Beloved."
- Truly happy and contented people attribute their well-being first to God, and then to their **friends and family**. What they're saying is, "I have been blessed by the love I have received from others."
- While everyone has an emotional need for love and belonging, the **level of that need may vary** from person to person. Some are perfectly content with feeling loved by a few close people, while others thrive on being loved and accepted by a wide variety of people.
- We all need to be loved and accepted, but **no one will be loved by everyone**. A person may receive love from a number of individuals, but **dwell obsessively on the one person** who will not accept him.
- People need to **give love** in order to receive love. The second greatest commandment is to love your neighbor as yourself (Mark 12:31).
- When we love others, regardless of whether they deserve it or not, we are **freeing ourselves to receive love** as well.

> *If you judge people, you have no time to love them.*
> —Mother Teresa

## Love Languages

- In his book, *The Five Love Languages,* Gary Chapman described five different "love languages," or ways that people say, "I love you." We need to help the people determine their love language:

  **Words of Affirmation**—Do you need verbal praise and encouragement? Do you thrive on words of affirmation, kindness, and thank yous? Do you love it when people compliment you to your face and to others (directly and indirectly)? Do you love getting notes and e-mails? Do you need verbal affirmation? Do you do this for others you care about?

**Quality Time**—Do you enjoy having people's undivided attention? Do you like it when people come over and just hang out? Do you like to plan activities to do with others? Do you thrive on quality conversations? Do you enjoy the give and take of asking questions and listening? Do you really like to get inside people's heads and find out what they're thinking?

**Gifts**—Do you value visual symbols of love? Gifts can come in any shape or size—maybe someone just brings you a cup of coffee at work or tosses a candy bar your way. The cost doesn't matter—it's truly the thought that counts. Do you find yourself doing this for others?

*To love is to be vulnerable.*
—C.S. Lewis

**Acts of Service**—Do you like to *do* things for others and have them help you out as well? A friend steps in to help you on a project, or someone washes your car, or makes you dinner—and you eagerly do the same types of things for your friends.

**Physical Touch**—Are you a "toucher"? Do you give pats on the back and hugs—all of which express friendship? Do you appreciate that kind of physical touch from others?[1]

- Determining our own love language, and **understanding the love language of those around us**, goes a long way to communicating love.

## 3 ASSESSMENT INTERVIEW

Nobody comes to us for help saying they need to feel loved and that they need to belong. Instead, **not receiving love and belonging will exhibit itself** in these ways: :

Feeling depressed; lacking energy; having no zest for life; having no desire to be social; not feeling fulfilled.

*Faith, like light, should always be simple, and unbending; while love, like warmth, should beam forth on every side, and bend to every necessity of our brethren.*
—Martin Luther

Determine if depression may have caused withdrawal from meaningful relationships. If this is the case, use the questions in that section of this guide. For those whose feelings of being disconnected are less severe, ask the following questions.

**Q1** Tell me about your hobbies.

**Q2** Do you share these hobbies with other people?

**Q3** What organizations do you belong to?

**Q4** Describe a typical Saturday or day off for you.

**Q5** Who do you love in your life?

**Q6** How do you show that love?

**Q7** Of the five love languages, which is yours? *(Explain these briefly.)*

**Q8** What do you think are the love languages of those closest to you?

**Q9** Who loves you? How do these people show it?

**Q10** Do you think that some people may be showing you love in a different "language," and you're just not understanding it?

**Q11** Do you think that you are showing love to some people, but that your "language" is different from theirs, and they aren't understanding it?

**Q12** Do you deserve to be loved by others? Why or why not?

**Q13** Who doesn't love you?

**Q14** Do you think that everyone should love you? Tell me about that.

**Q15** How do people get to know you?

**Q16** Do you think that they are getting to know the real you, not the you that you want others to see, but the deeper you?

*Joy is love exalted; peace is love in repose; long-suffering is love enduring; gentleness is love in society; goodness is love in action; faith is love on the battlefield; meekness is love in school; and temperance is love in training.*
—D.L. Moody

## 4 WISE COUNSEL

Disconnected people need to take initiative to **include others in their lives**. This can seem uncomfortable or awkward, but it is necessary. We can't sit at home and feel sorry for ourselves or feel that others should come to us.

**The church** is a great way to get involved with other people. It offers the opportunity to minister to others as well as be ministered to. Ask the person how he/she might get involved in the local church.

## 5 ACTION STEPS

### 1. Be Realistic

- Everyone needs to feel loved and accepted, but no one will be loved and accepted by everyone.
- It's OK to have someone angry with you, and it's unreasonable to expect that your friends or family will never be upset or disappointed.

### 2. Refuse to Be Offended

- It doesn't matter who your friends are or what family you belong to or where you work, the opportunity to be offended will come. Wherever people are together, sparks fly. Don't magnify relatively small offenses into capital crimes! Instead, choose to reduce offenses by seeing them objectively. A wise friend can help you get the right perspective.
- Too many people leave friends, jobs, organizations, or even marriages because they have been offended. Running away is not the answer. Work through these situations if you expect to grow into the person God wants you to be.

### 3. Get Involved

- Find an activity that will force you to associate with other people. The actual activity or hobby is immaterial. The goal is to be in situations where other people will get to know you better.
- Join a club, organization, or ministry you haven't been a part of before—and be committed for no less than three months of involvement.
- Write in a journal about the social interaction you experience.
- Call someone from the ministry or club at least once a week.

*Love is an action, an activity. It is not a feeling.*
—M. Scott Peck

### 4. Listen to the Love Language

- Being loved is often the result of showing love to others.
- Listen to the love languages—both what you say and what others are saying to you.

6

## BIBLICAL INSIGHTS

***Two are better than one, because they have a good reward for their labor. For if they fall, one will lift up his companion. But woe to him who is alone when he falls, for he has no one to help him up. —Ecclesiastes 4:9-10***

- The Preacher observed the importance of friendships. God created people to be in relationship with Him and in relationships with one another.
- Friends who work on a task can rejoice together in its accomplishment. Friends can help each other—if one should fall, the other is there to "help him up."
- Those who have both a strong relationship with God and strong friendships with other believers have bonds that strengthen life's joys and limit life's sorrows.
- Friendships among believers are precious because they have the bond of Christ for eternity. We should both *find* good friends and *be* good friends.

*The greatest happiness of life is the conviction that we are loved—loved for ourselves, or rather, loved in spite of ourselves.*
—Victor Hugo

***This is My commandment, that you love one another as I have loved you. Greater love has no one than this, than to lay down one's life for his friends. —John 15:12-13***

- Jesus gave two commandments to His followers: "Love Me" and "love each other." Jesus said that His followers should love each other as He loved them.
- So great is God's love that Jesus gave His life for us, and in response, we are to love others as Jesus loved us. We probably won't have to die for anyone, but we show our love for others by listening, helping, encouraging, and giving. Christ's humble, sacrificial love is our example.

***[Love] bears all things, believes all things, hopes all things, endures all things. —1 Corinthians 13:7***

- "Bears all things" means love shelters or covers.
- "Believes all things" means that love never loses faith in others and is willing to think the best of them. (This, however, doesn't man that we become blind to their abusive behavior, control, and irresponsibility. Loving them means speaking the truth to them, protecting ourselves when necessary, and encouraging them to act responsibly.)
- "Hopes all things" means that love looks forward with optimism, knowing that God works all things together for good.
- "Endures all things" means that love holds on. In the end, love never fails and it never ends.

*Real love is not earned, it is simply received.*

***Beloved, let us love one another, for love is of God; and everyone who loves is born of God and knows God. —1 John 4:7***

- God authored the concept of love. When people become believers, they learn how to "love one another" because the Spirit shows them how as they follow His leading.
- Because Christ is our example, Christian relationships can be the most loving in the world. Christians who meet each other for the first time experience a bond of love that transcends understanding.
- The love that binds Christians produces for solid and eternal relationships. The love in our relationships reveals God in us.

## 7 PRAYER STARTER

Thank You for the love You have shown us through Your Son, dear Lord. Thank You for the others You have placed in our lives. Your child has come today with a feeling of not belonging, of not being loved. I pray that You will reveal to him the special person You created him to be, and show him that love from others is often the result of showing love . . .

## 8 RECOMMENDED RESOURCES

*Bait of Satan: Living Free from the Deadly Trap of Offense*, by John Bevere

*Five Love Languages*, by Gary Chapman

*Freedom in Christ/Abba's Arms*, American Association of Christian Counselors Life Enrich Video Series, by Sandra Wilson

*A Man After God's Own Heart*, American Association of Christian Counselors Life Enrich Video Series, by Ed Hinson

*A Woman and Her God*, American Association of Christian Counselors Life Enrich Video Series, by Beth Moore

# Mental Disorder

## 1 PORTRAITS

- Barbara was a vigorous, energetic woman who loved to help at the local shelter. But occasionally, she stopped her volunteer work and didn't leave her house for weeks. At other times, she' stayed at the shelter for days, not leaving to sleep, being very gregarious, and giving away a lot of cash.
- No one at church knew exactly why Michael seemed so odd. He'd been a star basketball player in high school and college, and he graduated with honors from law school and joined a good firm. But now he was unemployed, supported by his wife. People at church thought he'd damaged his brain with drugs, because he acted so spaced out, but his fall from success was not of his own doing.
- Sandy did everything in extremes. She was dramatic, loving, and enthusiastic some of the time, but then she'd become angry, obnoxious, and belligerent. She was divorced, had held a lot of different jobs, and attended a lot of different churches. She was known among the local pastors as a troublemaker.
- Matt was shy and reclusive. He worked with computers and rarely spoke in Sunday school class. When he spoke, he often voiced bizarre opinions about numerological schemes in the Quran and predictions of the exact time of the end of the world. People thought he was weird.

*Bipolar disorder, also called manic-depressive illness, is a serious disorder of the brain. More than 2.3 million American adults, or about 1 percent of the population in a given year, have bipolar disorder.*
— WWW.NIMH.NIH.GOV

## 2 DEFINITIONS AND KEY THOUGHTS

- Mental disorders cause individuals to **experience extreme problems in functioning** in significant areas of their lives—relationships, employment, education, financial well-being, even spirituality.
- Mental disorder is **not short term, but it is also not necessarily permanent.** By definition, mental problems must endure for a minimum period of time before the disorder can be diagnosed.
- Many mental disorders **resolve after treatment** with counseling, medication, or simply the passing of time.
- Other mental disorders are **lifelong and cause ongoing problems** for those afflicted with them and for their families.
- If someone is mentally ill, he is not simply "odd." **Labels of mental disorder**

**ought never to be applied without a professional assessment**. Mental disorders are—by definition—serious disturbances. These are some common types of mental disorders:

**Psychotic disorders** are those that result in **bizarre, paranoid, or delusional thinking**. The most common is schizophrenia. Individuals with psychotic illnesses manifest the symptoms **most often thought of as "crazy"**—seeing or hearing things that aren't there, making bizarre connections between unrelated events, or showing grossly inappropriate responses to ordinary occurrences.

**Mood disorders** are those that primarily affect a person's **emotional stability**. The most common are depression and bipolar disorder (formerly called manic-depression). Individuals afflicted with depression feel discouraged and hopeless almost every day, have lost interest in activities in which they used to take pleasure, and sometimes consider or attempt suicide. Those with bipolar disorder exhibit cycles of wide swings in emotions and behaviors.

**Anxiety disorders** are characterized by **extreme nervousness, panic, or phobias**. People suffering from anxiety disorders can't calm down, feel panicky much of the time, and have physical symptoms of constant nervousness. Those with post-traumatic stress may experience flashbacks of trauma and may react to loud noises or other reminders of the precipitating event.

**Personality disorders** are disturbances in thinking and behavior that are **a part of a person's basic character.** They result in lifelong patterns of counter-productive behavior. Unlike other mental disorders, personality disorders do not often respond to medications or short-term therapy.

There are many other disorders, some associated only with children, but there is not enough space here to deal with them all.

- There are **huge differences between mental disorder, sin, and demonic influence**. Treatment follows a thorough assessment and careful diagnosis.
- In a church, mental disorder most often **becomes apparent in relationships**. Mentally ill people who are active in church may have difficulty tolerating the opinions of others, getting along on committees, or accepting limits. Other mentally ill people may be on the periphery of the church—a churchgoer's spouse or child who is often the subject of prayer requests.
- Tragically, misdiagnosis and improper treatments are common, and far too many people suffer needlessly. The failure to understand the multiple reasons people suffer—including the distinction between sin, mental illness, and demonic influence—has significant consequences.

Some people only confess sin when they should be taking medication, but

*A special feature in the report America's Children: Key National Indicators of Well-Being 2005 shows that nearly 5 percent—or an estimated 2.7 million children—are reported by their parents to suffer from definite or severe emotional or behavioral difficulties, problems that may interfere with their family life, their ability to learn, and their formation of friendships. These difficulties may persist throughout a child's development and lead to lifelong disability, including more serious illness, more difficult to treat illness, and co-occurring mental illnesses.*

others blame an illness when they should be confessing their sin.

Demons are being cast out of schizophrenics who need medical treatment, and people who need the casting out of demons are put into mental hospitals and drugged to complacency.

- Christians need to understand that even throughout the Scriptures, physicians, balms, salves, and other medicines were used. The church and mental health professionals should value the contribution each can make and work together to relieve human suffering.

## 3 ASSESSMENT INTERVIEW

Keep in mind that much that passes for "insanity" in the general population is simply a brief crisis due to extreme circumstances. **Don't jump to conclusions** or put labels on people.

Some people with mental disorder struggle for **just a short time**. Others are able to live fairly normal lives with regular medication and supportive counseling.

Some **suffer from constant emotional and behavioral chaos**, inability to maintain relationships or jobs, difficulties with the law and with substance abuse. Responses to medications vary widely, and some disorders (such as bipolar disorder) cause symptoms that make afflicted individuals unlikely to stay on medication.

With some forms of mental disorder, **there is the risk of violence** due to severe depression, feelings of hopelessness, or aggression. Ask the "Rule Out" questions to assess for the potential for violence. All the questions are directed toward the family member or concerned friend of a mentally ill person, but they could also be asked directly to the troubled person.

*Four of the 10 leading causes of disability in the U.S. and other developed countries are mental disorders—major depression, bipolar disorder, schizophrenia, and obsessive-compulsive disorder. Many people suffer from more than one mental disorder at a given time.*
— WWW.NIMH.NIH.GOV

### Rule Outs

**Q1** Has your family member ever been violent?

**Q2** Does he or she have access to weapons?

**Q3** Has he or she ever expressed feeling threatened? *(If so, turn to Action Steps 1 and 2.)*

**Q4** Does your family member seem despondent or hopeless?

**Q5** Has she or he ever attempted suicide? *(See section on Suicide for more information on how to handle this situation.)*

**Q6** (If a woman) Has she recently had a baby?

**Q7** Who could be endangered if this person becomes violent?

### General Questions

Q8 Has anyone in this person's family ever been under the care of a psychiatrist or admitted to a psychiatric hospital?

Q9 If so, what reason was given?

Q10 Are you aware of a diagnosis?

Q11 What makes you think that this person has a mental disorder?

Q12 Describe the history of this person's most significant relationships. *(Unstable relationships—or a lack of personal relationships—may be an indicator of underlying mental problems.)*

Q13 Has this individual ever been convicted of a crime? If so, what crime and when?

Q14 Does this person ever speak in bizarre ways or about strange things?

Q15 Does this person express fear that people are "after" him or her?

Q16 Does this person describe hearing or seeing things that aren't there? *(Questions 14-16 address symptoms of psychosis.)*

Q17 Does this person show cycles of emotions or behaviors?

Q18 Does he or she ever go for long periods with little sleep?

Q19 Does he or she ever spend a lot of money recklessly or act grandiose and above the law? *(Question 17-19 can identify symptoms of bipolar disorder.)*

## WISE COUNSEL

4

Though only a small percentage of people with mental disorder become violent, you should still **be vigilant about the risk of violence**.

People who are **paranoid**—who believe that others are working against them, perhaps in an elaborate plot—can feel threatened enough to strike out at others.

**Mania**—feeling grandiose and on top of the world—can also breed violence when the manic individual feels threatened.

**Never risk yourself, your family, or your congregation members** by naively thinking that violence will not occur. If a situation is escalating, it's better to **call 9-1-1** unnecessarily than to overlook the potential of violence.

Police and paramedics are **trained to assess the situation** and to bring people to local emergency rooms if they are exhibiting signs of mental problems. At the emergency room, medical professionals will assess the individual and decide on a course of action. You can help by reporting your concerns to the police or paramedics.

5

## ACTION STEPS

### 1. Lessen the Risks

- If there is any risk of violence, get professionals involved immediately.
- Remove any weapons (guns, knives, anything else sharp, and ropes, scarves, sheets, or belts) and drugs from the home. Try to observe the person until help arrives.

### 2. Watch Yourself

- Explain to family members that if they are present with the person who is expressing extreme anger or paranoia, get out of the way.
- They should not block the individual's exit. Instead, they should let him leave and call 9-1-1.

### 3. Get Professional Help

Encourage family members to talk with a professional if their loved one is

Threatening violence

Causing financial hardship

Abusing substances (see also the section on *Addictions*)

Participating in dangerous or destructive behavior

Disappearing without explanation

### 4. Get Medical Help

Proper diagnosis and medication can help with the person's disordered brain chemistry.

### 5. Support Groups

- There are many support groups for those who love people with mental disorders. The best-known is NAMI, the National Alliance for the Mentally Ill, which sponsors both support and advocacy across the country.
- Other groups can be found by contacting your local mental health agencies.

*Researchers supported by the National Institute of Mental Health (NIMH) have found that half of all lifetime cases of mental illness begin by age 14, and that despite effective treatments, there are long delays—sometimes decades—between first onset of symptoms and when people seek and receive treatment.*

## 6. Practical Help

- Local mental health agencies should have information about financial help, health insurance, supportive counseling, and other interventions that can aid people with mental disorders and their families.
- People with **chronic mental disorder** and need ongoing help may benefit from programs such as day treatment or supportive living facilities.

*If ADHD is suspected, the diagnosis should be made by a professional with training in ADHD. This includes child psychiatrists, psychologists, developmental/behavioral pediatricians, behavioral neurologists, and clinical social workers.*
— WWW.NIMH.NIH.GOV

## 7. Spiritual Help

- God loves those with mental disorders and their families. Be sure to be spiritually sensitive and unbiased in your love and heart to them.
- Help the person with mental disorder understand his need for Christ. Is he a Christian? Does he understand what Jesus can do in his life? (See John 1:12; Romans 3:23; 6:23.)
- Pray for wisdom regarding your approach to helping the person with mental disorder. Does he need professional assisance, medication, advice, encouragement, education, correction, a support system, insight, confession, verbal reinforcement, modeling, or confrontation?

## 8. Live in Peace

- Don't blame the person with a mental disorder or get pulled into arguments with him.
- The person is, indeed, ill and blaming this person is like blaming a patient for his heart attack.

## BIBLICAL INSIGHTS 6

***But the Spirit of the Lord departed from Saul, and a distressing spirit from the Lord troubled him. —1 Samuel 16:14***

- King Saul, who reigned in Israel before David, displayed classic characteristics of mental disorder, including wide mood swings and fits of depression and anger. A person can develop such debilitating emotional symptoms for many reasons. In this case, Scripture indicates that "a distressing spirit from the LORD troubled" Saul.
- Saul had turned from God, so He sovereignly permitted affliction by a spirit of distress—possibly a demonic influence—to occur. Not all mental disorders are a result of demonic influence, but like any sickness or disease, the battle for our minds is a result of the Fall and Satan's presence in this world.

***That very hour the word was fulfilled concerning Nebuchadnezzar; he was driven from men and ate grass like oxen; his body was wet with the dew of heaven till his hair had grown like eagles' feathers and his nails like birds' claws. —Daniel 4:33***

- We are spiritual beings, created by God and incomplete without Him. Also, we are physical beings, and a physical disease can lead to psychological or spiritual problems, and vice versa. Also, we are psychological beings, with minds, emotions, and wills. The interrelationships among these three realms in our humanity mean that specific problems may have mulitple symptoms and causes.
- If believers face a mental problem, they should seek counsel from wise, qualified Christians who can treat them with a comprehensive approach. During this time, other believers can surround the hurting brother or sister in prayer. God promises to help His people through even the most difficult times.

*Mental disorders are common in the United States and internationally. An estimated 22.1 percent of Americans ages 18 and older—about 1 in 5 adults—suffer from a diagnosable mental disorder in a given year.*
— WWW.NIMH.NIH.GOV

***Then they sailed to the country of the Gadarenes, which is opposite Galilee. And when He stepped out on the land, there met Him a certain man from the city who had demons for a long time. And he wore no clothes, nor did he live in a house but in the tombs. —Luke 8:26-27***

- In this case, the man's situation was caused by demon possession. Usually, however, mental disorder has other causes, such as genetics or hormonal imbalances.
- People need assurance of their worthiness before God, as well as professional help. Jesus has the power to heal many kinds of afflictions.

7

## PRAYER STARTER

Dear Lord, I am concerned about my friend, and we have good reasons to be concerned. Please lead us to people who will be able to help us, to offer resources, and to aid this friend we love. Give us strength, patience, and rest. In Jesus' name, Amen.

## RECOMMENDED RESOURCES

*Battling Bi-Polar Disorder*, American Association of Christian Counselors Courageous Living Video Series, by Michael Lyles

*Facing ADHD: Assessment and Treatment of the ADHD Child*, American Association of Christian Counselors Courageous Living Video Series, by Grant Martin

*Psychiatric Medication and the Christian*, American Association of Christian Counselors Courageous Living Video Series, by Michael Lyles

# Money Crisis

## 1 PORTRAITS

- Carl and Laura's credit card debts have run out of control. Carl can't get Laura to stop spending, so they are constantly overwhelmed with bills they can't pay.
- Bill just lost his job—downsized by the corporation. He is trying to find work, but the job market is tough. He's struggling with believing God's care for him is sufficient in the midst of this crisis. His unpaid bills are mounting.
- Sherry's husband of twenty years ran off with another woman. After all the negotiating between the lawyers, Sherry is left with virtually nothing. She hasn't worked for years—how will she make ends meet?

## 2 DEFINITIONS AND KEY THOUGHTS

- Money has to be **mastered** or it will master us.
- **Jesus talked more about money** than about any other single topic. Why? Because our perceptions about money reveal our hearts, and our choices about money chart a path for our lives. Jesus said, "Where your treasure is, there your heart will be also" (Matthew 6:21).
- A person who comes to us to talk about money needs advice about handling the difficult financial situation, but he also needs something deeper—an understanding that, amidst the difficulty, **God still cares and will meet his needs**. The primary need may be for the person to become more responsible.
- It may be important to help the person make some **lifestyle changes** that can help with the crisis. If the crisis is the result of personal irresponsibility, he needs to make changes that will keep this crisis from happening again.

## 3 ASSESSMENT INTERVIEW

### Practical Questions

**Q1** What do you consider to be the cause of the financial crisis you're in today? (If spouses meet with you, do both agree that this is the source of the problem?)

**Q2** What do you think needs to happen in order for you to get out of this crisis?

**Q3** What are some of the effects on you and your family?

**Q4** How are you currently coping with the situation?

**Q5** Who usually handles the bills in your home?

**Q6** Describe the process for handling your monthly financial commitments.

**Q7** What is the shortfall between what you have and what you need in order to meet those commitments?

**Q8** In what areas can you pare back and save some money?

**Q9** Do you think you can commit to "tightening your belt" for awhile?

**Q10** What lifestyle changes do you need to make in order to keep this from happening again?

**Q11** Will you commit to those changes? What is your next step?

### Spiritual Questions

**Q12** How are you doing spiritually?

**Q13** Are you tithing? Why or why not?

**Q14** What do you feel about your relationship with God at this point?

**Q15** What do you feel about prayer? Do you feel you can pray about this situation?

**Q16** In what ways have you seen God answer your prayers?

**Q17** In what ways do you still want Him to answer?

**Q18** Are you refusing any of His answers because of pride? *(For example, has help been offered but refused? Has a job been offered but considered "beneath" the person?)*

**Q19** Is there any sin that may have led you into this situation? Do you want to repent of that sin?

**Q20** What do you think God wants to teach you through this situation?

*The average credit-card holder is carrying a $2000 balance at 18 percent interest and is making minimum payments. At that rate of payment, it will take more than twelve years to pay off the balance, even if the card goes unused during that entire time. And total interest that will be paid on that $2000 balance is $2,231.*[1]

## WISE COUNSEL 4

Some issues the person may be facing include:

**Perspective**—The person may be so completely overwhelmed that he can't function in life and loses perspective of what really matters. You need to help him see that there *is* a way out if he takes a breath, begins to think creatively, and takes action..

**Prayer**—The person may feel he can't pray because the situation is his own fault. You need to help him understand that, no matter what the cause of the crisis, God wants him to pray about it.

**Blame**—The person may blame the entire problem on someone else and focus too much on that person. Help him see that spending all of his time thinking about his anger is not helping his financial situation.

**Quick Fix**—The person may focus on some speedy way to get out of the problem (like winning the lottery or filing for bankruptcy). Help him see that financial management is going to be hard work. It will take some belt-tightening and lifestyle changes in order to solve the problem and make sure it doesn't happen again.

## 5 ACTION STEPS

### 1. Get Perspective

- You need a fresh perspective. The truth is: "Money will not solve all your problems." Sure, money is important, but the more important issue is what God wants to do in your life.
- Credit card companies are not staying awake at night worrying about *you*.
- Go do something free and enjoyable. You have today—enjoy it. Keep on living. Walk the dog, hug your kids, listen to a CD, borrow a movie from the library or a friend.
- Set new priorities. Give back to God, and God promises to provide (Malachi 3:10; Acts 20:35).

### 2. Pray

*Therefore humble yourselves under the mighty hand of God, that He may exalt you in due time, casting all your care upon Him, for He cares for you.*
—1 Peter 5:6-7

- Is it okay to pray about money? Yes, of course. In the middle of a financial crisis, as in any crisis or suffering, God wants you to run to Him.
- In addition, pray for guidance and wisdom.
- If you caused the financial problem, ask God to forgive you and to help you learn so it won't happen again.
- God is concerned about *all* of life. His goal is to make you more like Him. Your financial crisis can be part of that growth.

### 3. Deal with the Immediate Problems

Face the problem and decide what sacrifices or changes may be necessary in the short term, such as:

- Is there sin? Look it in the face and deal with it.
- Do you need professional help? (such as for a gambling addiction)
- Communicate with creditors and set up payment plans.
- Put the credit cards on ice (literally), so you can't get to them. Cut up as many as possible.
- What other urgent issues need to be addressed, such as family conflict, health problems, etc.?

### 4. Develop a Plan

- Prepare a budget. Start with your income; figure fixed payments (rent/mortgage, tithe, utilities, car payments, insurances), then regular expenses per month (food, gas, misc), then other monthly payments (creditors—start with minimum payment amounts).
- List all the "other" expenses from lowest total to highest total.
- After working your budget, how much money can you put toward the "other" bills? If only the minimum (such as with credit cards), start there. (If you can't even make minimums, you will consider other options in #5 below.) Write amounts beside each bill.
- Decide how much you can pay toward each of the "other" bills. Pay that amount toward each bill regularly. As soon as the lowest bill is paid off, add the amount you were paying to that bill to the next bill on the list, and so on. Gradually, you will be adding larger amounts of money to the larger bills.
- Prepare a worksheet that lists all bills. Organize them according to due dates and which will be paid with each paycheck during the month. Make this reproducible so you can use it each month, checking off payments as you go.

### 5. Get Help

Brainstorm ways to get additional money to help retire the debt. (Be sure he understands that any additional money must go toward debt, not to raise his standard of living.)

- Sell something of value.
- Consider consolidating your debt. Take out a home equity loan or refinance an existing mortgage.
- Take on a new job (perhaps the spouse goes to work outside the home, or money is earned from inside by babysitting, tutoring, etc.).
- Get a loan from family or friends. (Be very careful with this one.)
- Obtain advice from an accountant or financial advisor who can help keep you on track (see also Recommended Resources, below).
- Get help from the church or the government.

### 6. Set New Priorities and Parameters

- Do *not* run up any new debt. Leave credit cards for true emergencies only.
- Testify needs vs. wants (Philippians 4:11).
- Decide on a thirty-day moratorium on any purchases over a certain amount of money. You may find you don't want it so badly after thirty days.

***The Motley Fool's Credit Center features several amazing statistics:***

- Total consumer credit: $1.7 trillion.
- Credit card debt carried by the average American: $8,562.
- Total finance charges Americans paid in 2001: $50 billion.
- Percent of U.S. households deemed credit worthy by the lending industry: 78%.
- Number of credit card holders who declared bankruptcy last year: 1.3 million.

-www.fool.com

### 7. Be Patient

- Your crisis is not a permanent condition. It's a turning point and it will get better.
- Don't be ashamed. Hold your head high, trust God for guidance, follow that guidance, and remember that somehow God is going to work all these things together for your good (Matthew 6:25-26).
- Ask: Where is God guiding? What is God teaching? Read Matthew 6:19-21.
- Don't let the crisis turn you from God. Draw nearer to Him, study His Word, and pray for wisdom, protection, provision.

6

## BIBLICAL INSIGHTS

***The sleep of a laboring man is sweet, whether he eats little or much; but the abundance of the rich will not permit him to sleep. —Ecclesiastes 5:12***

- Many people want to be rich, thinking that they will have no more worries. That is a paradox, however. Riches give freedom to do many things, but the chains of worry often ruin true enjoyment.
- God wants us to be content whatever our financial status. All wealth ultimately belongs to God. He created everything, and He entrusts a little of it to us for a short while.

*By committing not to go further in debt, people begin to reverse the process that produced the debt. Then, they can develop a balanced budget that will control spending and will allow them to stay within the parameters of their financial means.*
—CROWN FINANCIAL MINISTRIES

***"You have sown much, and bring in little . . . And he who earns wages, earns wages to put into a bag with holes." Thus says the Lord of hosts: "Consider your ways!" —Haggai 1:6-7***

- People spend money on what they consider most important. Haggai pointed out that the people in Jerusalem were valuing the comforts of their own homes over God.
- We need to reevaluate where we spend our resources. Do our activities and spending habits reflect our dedication to God?

***"Bring all the tithes into the storehouse, that there may be food in My house, and try Me now in this," says the Lord of hosts, "If I will not open for you the windows of heaven and pour out for you such blessing that there will not be room enough to receive it." —Malachi 3:10***

- God's ways are not our ways. People think that to be secure, they need to hoard their money. God disagrees.
- Jesus issued the same challenge: "Give, and it will be given to you: good measure, pressed down, shaken together, and running over" (Luke 6:38). To refuse to give is actually to rob God, but to give generously is to know God's abundant blessings.

***Be anxious for nothing, but in everything by prayer and supplication, with thanksgiving, let your requests be made known to God; and the peace of God, which surpasses all understanding, will guard your hearts and minds through Christ Jesus. —Philippians 4:6-7***

- This verse applies to many kinds of worries—and it certainly fits financial pain. If you're in a financial crisis, the first place you need to go is to God, letting "your requests be made known to" Him.

***For the love of money is a root of all kinds of evil, for which some have strayed from the faith in their greediness, and pierced themselves through with many sorrows. —1 Timothy 6:10***

*The borrower is servant to the lender.*
*—Proverbs 22:7*

- The Bible doesn't say that money is the root of all evil. Money can do good things for God's kingdom. The root of all evil is the *love* of money.
- Those who love money never have enough, and they do any number of stupid, illegal, or risky things in order to obtain more. They are never satisfied.
- How do believers stay away from the love of money? "Godliness with contentment" is the answer. When we are content with what we have, we can give the extra back to Him.

## PRAYER STARTER

7

Lord, my friend has come today with a difficult situation. We know, Lord, that nothing is too hard for You. We humbly ask that You will help him be wise as he prepares a budget, seeks new income, and tries to pay off these debts because we know this honors You. Show him what You would have him do, and we ask for provision and protection . . .

## RECOMMENDED RESOURCES

8

Christian Credit Counselors, www.christiancc.org, 1-888-520-4422

Crown Financial Ministries, www.crown.org

*Debt Free Living: How To Get Out of Debt*, by Larry Burkett

*Margin: How to Create the Emotional, Physical, Financial, & Time Reserves You Need*, by Richard A. Swenson

National Foundation for Credit Counseling, www.nfcc.org to find a credit counseling service in your area

*Priceless: Straight-Shooting, No-Frills Financial Wisdom*, by Dave Ramsey

*The Treasure Principle*, by Randy Alcorn

# Pain/Chronic Pain

## 1 PORTRAITS

- Sally had deteriorating rheumatoid arthritis. The pain had become so bad she could no longer help in the nursery with the toddlers, as she had loved to do for the past 20 years. "What use am I if I can't even do the simplest thing to serve the Lord?" she asks dejectedly.
- Ben, a construction worker, was in a car accident that left him with several crushed discs and constant pain. "Why me?" he asks. "What did I do to deserve this? I can't work, and we can barely get by on my disability check. I feel like I'm hitting a closed door when I try to get answers from God. He doesn't seem to care."
- Kristy had been diagnosed with lupus a year ago. "Every day I feel like I have the flu," she sighs wearily. "The fatigue is debilitating. I can't make any plans with the kids because the day we plan to go to the beach or to a movie I always end up too sick to go. I'm so tired of this stupid disease!"
- Josh's leg had been amputated below the knee due to bone cancer. Now, after months of painful chemotherapy, he has learned the cancer is in the thigh bone and he will have to begin another round of chemo with the chance of losing the rest of his leg. "I don't know what's worse, the pain or the fear," he wonders. "How much more can I stand? I'm so afraid."

## 2 DEFINITIONS AND KEY THOUGHTS

- **God is present** and always working, even in our pain. The **physical, emotional, and spiritual are all connected**. When a person is in pain, he may feel God is not there, but nothing could be further from the truth. He needs to put his faith in God's word, not his feelings.
- Pain can blind the eyes. When a person says, "I'm knocking at God's door, but **He doesn't answer**," his feelings contradict Matthew 7:7 where Jesus says, "Knock, and it will be opened unto you." When a person says, "I pray, but **God isn't listening**," his feelings contradict Isaiah 65:24 where God says, "Before they call, I will answer; and while they are still speaking, I will hear." People need encouragement that God's promises trump their feelings.
- **Illness or chronic pain is not due to a lack of faith.** On the contrary, it is often the suffering itself that drives a person to God, motivates him to grow spiritu-

ally, and helps him to understand that he can't cope alone. We certainly can't conclude that the presence of pain (or illness) implies that a person doesn't have a deep and mature faith, hasn't been praying enough, has sinned in some terrible way, or has neglected his spiritual growth. But a deep faith equips people to endure and cope with their pain.

- **God allows pain for a reason.** If pain is to have meaning, we need to turn to God. Quite often, God uses pain to get our attention. C. S. Lewis said that "pain is God's megaphone." Many who have suffered chronic pain state that if they had to choose between never becoming ill or learning the things they learned through pain, they would choose the pain because of the wisdom they learned and the closeness to God they enjoyed.
- **God's grace is sufficient.** Paul's thorn in the flesh helped him learn that God's grace is sufficient (2 Corinthians 12:7-10).
- What the world considers blessings—health, family, and riches—can sometimes draw a person away from Christ. **When a person has everything, he may forget he needs God.** What the world considers curses—tragedy, pain, and heartache—reveal our need for Him. People run to Him because they have nothing left but Him.
- The Center for Spirituality, Theology and Health, at Duke University has conducted over 25 research studies exploring the associations between religion, mental health, and the need for health services. Hundreds of additional studies around the globe have recently been completed on these issues. This is what they found:

  Many people turn to religious beliefs and practices to **help them cope when they become sick**. When people are anxious, suffering, and at the end of their rope, they often turn to God.

  Religious beliefs and practices are associated with **better mental and physical well being.** Physical wellness includes lower blood pressure, better immune system functioning, a longer life span, etc.

  People actively involved in a religious community, who pray regularly, and who keep religion as an instrumental part of their lives often experience **less depression and anxiety, and greater hope, meaning and purpose**. They also recover more speedily from painful emotions.

  Religious people are **less likely to engage in addictive behavior** such as alcohol or drug abuse. They are less likely to participate in **risky sexual practices** outside of marriage.

  During the most difficult and trying circumstances, the practice of **religion separates those who can cope** from those who can't.

Today, many medical schools teach courses that introduce asiring doctors to the benefits of religious faith and spirituality. Medical students are now being trained on how to partner with religious belief in clinical practice. The June 16, 2004 issue of the Journal of the American Medical Association was entirely devoted to spirituality in medicine.

3

## ASSESSMENT QUESTIONS

### Rule Outs

Q1 On a scale of 1 to 10 with 10 being no depression and 1 being extremely depressed where are you today?

Q2 Do you abuse alcohol or drugs to escape the pain? *(If you suspect that severe depression or substance abuse is present, you should deal with that along with pain management.)*

Q3 Do you ever have thoughts of suicide? *(If you think the person is suicidal, make out a safety contract where he promises not to hurt himself without first calling you. If he calls you, take him to the hospital where he can be placed in a safe environment and get medical help.)*

*In answer to Corrie ten Boom's question, "Why is our Lord allowing this to happen?" during their time in the Nazi death camps, her sister Betsy said, "If we know Him, we don't have to know why."[1]*

### General Questions

Q4 Tell me what brought you to me today.

Q5 When did the pain first start?

Q6 How long has it been going on?

Q7 What are its symptoms?

Q8 How has this changed your life?

Q9 How are your family and friends responding to your pain?

Q10 How would you like them to respond?

Q11 What things have you tried to help manage the pain?

Q12 How have those been working?

Q13 Besides the physical pain, have you had any feelings of anger, doubt, or fear?

Q14 Tell me about these feelings.

Q15 Where do you think God is in all this?

Q16 Why do you think God let this happen to you?

Q17 What are your feelings toward God right now? Be honest.

Q18 What do you want God to do?

Q19 If He chooses not to heal you, how do you feel about that?

Q20 Has anything good come out of your pain? Do you think it can?

## WISE COUNSEL 4

**Empathize with the person about his pain.** He needs to know that you understand the difficulty of the situation and that you care.

Explain that he has experienced a loss that may feel similar to losing a loved one. Make clear to the person that **a loss of health needs to be grieved.**

**Validate the struggle and the strength the person has already shown.** People in chronic pain get down on themselves because they can't do what they used to do and what they see others doings. They may see themselves as weak, pathetic, or useless. Help them identify their strengths and see how strong they are to just cope with the pain each day.

**Explain that God understands and cares what he is going through.** Even if the person can't feel God's presence, He is still there. Share verses that show this truth and talk about how the suffering person needs to trust God's Word.

**Share Paul's story of the thorn in his flesh.** Though Paul prayed to God to remove the thorn, God refused, stating that His grace was sufficient. Ask the suffering person what he thinks grace looks like and how it could be sufficient for him. Ask questions that require the person to think through what grace means in these verses.

## ACTION STEPS 5

### 1. Live within Your Limits

- Part of acknowledging the Lordship of Christ is living within the limits *He* gives. If you need pain medication, take it. If you need a nap, take one.
- There is nothing heroic about going beyond your God-given limits to the point where you are grouchy to everyone around you. Pace your day so you don't get too tired, and ask for help when you need it.
- Good nutrition, exercise your doctor approves of, and sufficient sleep are essential. Make it a priority to get these three.

### 2. Do Things that Improve Your Attitude

- The pain won't defeats you—it will be your attitude toward it that can lead to despair.
- Identify what helps lift your spirits and do it. Some suggestions are:

  -Pray

-Read the Bible

-Sing and praise

-Listen to music that feeds your soul or tickles your fancy

-Watch TV and comedy movies (laughter releases endorphins that im prove mood)

-Try to see the humor in situations

-Have cheerful people around

-Write in a journal or write letters to friends

-Start a hobby or pick up a pasttime you enjoy

-Help someone else

-Learn something new

-Cultivate a grateful attitude

### 3. Get Support

- The only thing worse than pain is bearing pain alone.
- Read books about people who lived with pain and see what helped them.
- Join a support group. Don't isolate yourself. God made us to be in a community with others who can comfort us with the same comfort God gave them (2 Corinthians 1:4).

*God whispers to us in our pleasures, speaks to us in our conscience, but shouts to us in our pain. Pain is God's megaphone to rouse a deaf world.*
—C. S. Lewis

### 4. Keep Truth Before You

- When self-pity and negative thoughts come into your mind, replace them with affirming, positive, powerful truth.
- Write the negative thought and the truth in a notebook. Divide the page in half and on one side write LIES and on the other side write TRUTH. Under LIES, write the self-defeating thought. Under the TRUTH, write the truth that contradicts the negative thought. For example, when you think "God isn't here for me," replace it with "The everlasting God . . . neither faints nor is weary" (Isaiah 40:28).

### 4. Comfort Others

Redeem the pain by comforting others with the same comfort God gives you (2 Corinthians 1:3-4).

6

## BIBLICAL INSIGHTS

***For we do not have a High Priest who cannot sympathize with our weaknesses, but was in all points tempted as we are, yet without sin. Let us therefore come boldly to the throne of grace, that we may obtain mercy and find grace to help in time of need. —Hebrews 4:15-16***

- We have a Savior who can "sympathize with our weaknesses." He understands temptation because He faced it. He understands weakness because He experienced it. He understands pain because He felt it.
- People who live with chronic or acute physical or emotional pain have a Savior who truly understands. Far from sitting in the heavens simply feeling sorry for sick and sinful humanity, He clothed Himself with our humanness, became man, and felt our pain.
- When we come to Christ with our hurts, He reaches out, truly understanding how we feel. He is able to help us. Christ does not always take away the pain, but He invites us to bring it to Him. Whatever our pain or difficulty, we are encouraged to come to Him.

***When Jesus saw him lying there, and knew that he already had been in that condition a long time, He said to him, "Do you want to be made well?" —John 5:6***

- Jesus has the power to heal any pain, but His first priority is to heal people spiritually. He may take away a person's pain, as He did this man's, but He may not take away the pain. He didn't remove Paul's physical difficulty (2 Corinthians 12:7-10).
- Whatever the Lord does, however, He understands the big picture and knows what He wants to accomplish either through healing a person's pain or through giving that person grace and peace in spite of the pain.
- We can pray for healing, but most of all, we need to pray for spiritual growth and maturity, and that God will be honored by our trust in His goodness and sovereignty.

***And lest I should be exalted above measure by the abundance of the revelations, a thorn in the flesh was given to me, a messenger of Satan to buffet me, lest I be exalted above measure. Concerning this thing I pleaded with the Lord three times that it might depart from me. And He said to me, "My grace is sufficient for you, for My strength is made perfect in weakness." Therefore most gladly I will rather boast in my infirmities, that the power of Christ may rest upon me. Therefore I***

***take pleasure in infirmities, in reproaches, in needs, in persecutions, in distresses, for Christ's sake. For when I am weak, then I am strong. —2 Corinthians 12:7–10***

- Those in pain may think that if God would heal them they would be much more valuable and effective in ministry. That assumption, though, isn't necessarily true.
- God's power is often best revealed when He works through human weaknesses. His "strength is made perfect in weakness."

7

## PRAYER STARTER

The pain my friend is facing today is acute, dear Lord. He is suffering and doesn't understand why. He wants to feel better, wants to function better, wants to serve You better, but the pain constantly gets in the way. What are You seeking to teach him through this pain, Lord? What wisdom and comfort can You give him today?

*Pain motivates the Holy Spirit to reveal His comforting, nurturing, consoling, and protecting character—something that often comes to us by no other means but pain. Pain will truly teach that nothing will come between us and God. Pain is the seed to growing a deep faith, to maturing in spiritual strength and wisdom, to becoming more and more like Christ.*

—Siang-Yang Tan and George Ohlschlager

## RECOMMENDED RESOURCES

*Chronic Pain: Biomedical and Spiritual Approaches*, by Harold G. Koenig

*Chronic Pain Management*, American Association of Christian Counselors Counsel Tapes Series, by Siang-Yang Tan

*Pain: The Gift Nobody Wants*, by Paul Brand and Philip Yancey

# Parenting

## 1 PORTRAITS

- "If the principal calls me one more time, I think I'll scream! Why can't that boy just listen?" Martha yells in exasperation.
- Randy and Casey, just one year apart, are constantly fighting with each other. Randy just hit Casey in the face with a soccer ball, which sent Casey running to his mother in tears. It happens all day, every day.
- Little Ruthie was an answer to her parents' prayers for a child. She is so precious, but she just won't behave. She just turned three and seems to test her parents at every turn.

## 2 DEFINITIONS AND KEY THOUGHTS

- God placed certain people in leadership roles over children and called them "parents." **God has ordained parents to be the leaders** in the home.
- Children need both a mother and father. Unfortunately, fathers are often physically or emotionally absent. It is estimated that 40 percent of American children are being raised in homes where no father is present.[1] These children have more physical, emotional, and behavioral problems, and are more prone to incarceration.[2]

*It is said that we live in "fast times, precarious times, even cynical times", and parenting has never been more challenging or more necessary.*[3]

- Raising children is a **high calling** that God has given to parents. We must not take this position lightly.
- Parents **have been given authority** over our children. In other words, we have been handpicked by God Himself to assume the leadership role in the raising of our children.
- Dr. James Dobson says that our role as a parent is to **work yourself out of a job**. While we never really stop being a parent, our role changes as our children grow and mature. Ultimately our role becomes less and less active, and we serve more as an advisor or friend to our adult children.

### Ingredients for Good Parenting

Just as bread needs yeast in order to rise, children also need certain ingredients in order to reach their potential. Let me give you three of these ingredients to ponder. Keep in mind that while the ingredients will be required at all stages of parenting, the amount required at various stages in the parenting process depends on the age and maturity level of the child.

### 1. Love

- Children need hugs, physical contact, words of encouragement and affirmation, quality time—all of these **communicate love**. Love also helps to break down barriers that we can't see with our eyes.
- Adolescent children are very **aware of appearances** and may not want to be hugged in front of peers.
- Sometimes, especially as toddlers and in adolescence, our children can seem like our enemies, but in reality they are simply learning how to think and act on their own. As they learn to be independent, **a certain amount of rebellion is normal.**
- As a parent, you are to love your children even when it is undeserved. That doesn't mean you accept everything they do. Love of the person and acceptance of behavior are not synonymous. Remind them that you **love them even when you disagree** with them or are heartbroken by their actions.

### 2. Discipline

- The Bible cautions fathers **not to discourage** their children (Colossians 3:21), but it also says that those who love their children are careful to discipline them (Proverbs 13:24). **Discipline, unlike punishment, always envisions a better future** for the child.
- **Balance is the key.** As a parent, discipline and train your children, but your discipline doesn't mean you are running a boot camp.
- Follow through with consequences. If you say the child must go to his room if he "does that one more time," and he does it again, **you need to follow through** with exactly what you said. Don't argue—do it calmly and firmly.
- **Consistency is king.** The actual consequence is less important than the consistency of implementing consequences when children misbehave.
- There are **three rules** that may help to serve as a guide in disciplining your children.

  **The KFC Rule**. KFC stands for Kind, Firm, and Consistent.

  **Granny's Rule.** This simply means, "First you do what I want, and then you get to do what you want." For instance, "If you want to go swimming, then first you need to do these chores."

  **The Millennial Rule.** This simply means that if you allow your child to get away with something, it may take a thousand times of correction to retrain him.

*Every 24 hours:*
*-3000 children experience the divorce of their parents*
*-1629 children are put in adult jails*
*-3288 children run away from home*
*-1512 drop out of school*
*-7742 teenagers become sexually active* [4]

—Archibald D. Hart

> Do not withhold correction from a child.
> —PROVERBS 23:13

### 3. Guidance

- As a parent, your job is to **teach your children about life**, and guide them in all areas, especially in God's Word (Deuteronomy 6:4-9).
- Guiding your children may also mean **allowing them to make mistakes**. When a mistake is made and the principal or police officer calls to inform you of the situation, you are about to walk through a crisis with your child. Be prepared to be disappointed with some of your child's choices and behaviors. Don't make the mistake of immediately helping your child get out of difficulties because of his choices and behaviors. More growth takes place through a crisis than anywhere else.

## 3 ASSESSMENT INTERVIEW

Parents often **feel like they have failed** if their child needs help. Being a parent isn't easy.

Reassure parents that **seeking help is proof that they are, in fact, good parents.** Having a family problem does'tt mean that the child is a "problem child." Avoid labeling a child with a titles like this.

If the family is seeking help because the child is unruly or uncontrollable, consider having them **see their family physician** in order to rule out a physical problem. Problems like attention deficit disorder seem to be more and more prevalent, and a professional evaluation may be warranted.

> Children and adolescents deal with issues that were not present a generation ago. "Health education" is now "sex education" and children are often exposed to drug trafficking before leaving elementary school.[5]

### General Questions

**Q1** Tell me about your child's early development.

**Q2** Define the behavior as clearly as you can.

**Q3** When did the problem first begin to surface?

**Q4** How often do you struggle with this issue?

**Q5** How have you addressed the problem in the past?

**Q6** Describe a typical scenario in which everything seemed to fall apart.

**Q7** Are both parents consistent in discipline?

**Q8** Can your children play one of you against the other, or do they know you are united?

**Q9** Do you follow through on promised consequences, or do you often break these promises?

**Q10** What is each member of the family doing when the problem arises?

**Q11** What does each member of the family do after the problem occurs?

**Q12** Has there been a significant change in your family that may have created additional family stress?

**Q13** Tell me about the other children in the family.

**Q14** What would the perfect family look like?

**Q15** How do you want your family to be?

## 4 WISE COUNSEL

Again, convey to the parents that **God has placed them together.** God will help them and show them how to grow as a family.

Changes may need to be made, and while the **changes may be difficult** at first, the family will be able to accomplish those changes with the Lord's help.

Encourage the parents of **tough or strong-willed children** to not panic when considering their child's future. Some of the most successful adults were the most difficult children. Encourage parents to envision a positive future for the child and share that vision lovingly with the child.

Talk about the importance of **spending time together.** In this day, it can be quite difficult to get the whole family together unless there is a crisis.

## 5 ACTION STEPS

Your goal is to help this family develop a plan. This may be a plan regarding:

-The rules to be followed

-How discipline will be handled for infractions of the rules

-What is negotiable and what is not (for example, curfews might be negotiable)

-Setting aside family times (a particular night of the week, or breakfast or dinner together)

-Chores (who does what, what is required, when must the chores be completed)

-Other items as needed

*Almost 75% of children living in fatherless homes will experience poverty and are 10 times as likely to experience extreme poverty.*[6]

### 1. Develop the Plan

- Determine the behaviors, expectations, rewards, and consequences that need to be in the plan? (This varies depending on the ages of the children and the issues involved.)

- Have the whole family talk together and share ideas to be incorporated into the plan.
- Try to incorporate everyone's ideas into the plan. Even the youngest members can have input, but the parents are responsible to be the final say.

*Train up a child in the way he should go, and when he is old he will not depart from it.*
—Proverbs 22:6

### 2. Adjust the Plan as Needed

- If you sense that the parents are immature and won't even be able to develop a good plan (or that their kids will run over them), follow up after they have had their family meeting to look over the plan they developed. You may need to help them be stronger in the parental role or be more realistic.
- If the parents are capable of making the changes and following through, tell them to work through the plan for a couple weeks and make tweaks as needed—always with a family meeting. (For example, if chores are still not getting done, you may need to add stronger consequences.)
- The plan should reward desired behavior and specify consequences for undesired behavior.

### 3. Be Consistent

- Post the plan where everyone can see it.
- Mom and dad must be 100 percent together on this. The kids must not think that they can get one to overrule the other, or that they can pit their parents against each other.

### 4. Pray Together

Ask for God's leading as the parents raise their children to be responsible adults.

*Behold, children are a heritage from the Lord, the fruit of the womb is a reward.*
—Psalm 127:3

### 5. Spend Time Together

- Try to get at least one meal a day together as a family. Eating breakfast together may be more feasible than eating dinner together.
- Most importantly, keep the relationship between you and your child strong.

  Talk with your child

  Listen to your child

  Show your child you love him or her

Spend time playing games with your child

Remember that kids spell love T-I-M-E.

Encourage your child.

Pray with your child.

## 6 BIBLICAL INSIGHTS

***"For this child I prayed, and the Lord has granted me my petition which I asked of Him. Therefore I also have lent him to the Lord; as long as he lives he shall be lent to the Lord." So they worshiped the Lord there. —1 Samuel 1:27-28***

- Parenting is both demanding and rewarding. Many people prepare and study for years to enter a chosen profession, but parenting is usually on-the-job training.
- The goal of parenting is to eventually let the children go as responsible, mature, independent adults.

***For I have told him that I will judge his house forever for the iniquity which he knows, because his sons made themselves vile, and he did not restrain them. —1 Samuel 3:13***

- Eli didn't discipline his sons, even though they were priests under his supervision. These men were treating the sacrifices of the people with contempt (2:12–17) and were committing sexual sin with women of the tabernacle.
- Eli, as parent and as high priest, certainly had the authority to deal with his sons, but he chose not to do anything. Eventually, God stepped in.
- God gives parents authority over their children. Parents should use that authority wisely to guide their children away from sin.

*Children miss nothing in sizing up their parents. If you are only half convinced of your beliefs, they will quickly discern that fact.*
—James Dobson

***Then Adonijah the son of Haggith exalted himself, saying, "I will be king"; and he prepared for himself chariots and horsemen, and fifty men to run before him. (And his father had not rebuked him at any time by saying, "Why have you done so?" He was also very good-looking. His mother had borne him after Absalom.) —1 Kings 1:5-6***

- One of David's apparent weaknesses was the inability to discipline his children.
- David's failures as a father led to a number of failures and sins in his children. Parents always influence their children—for good and bad. There is no substitute for invested, caring, loving parents who discipline when necessary.

***But the mercy of the Lord is from everlasting to everlasting on those who fear Him, and His righteousness to children's children, to such as keep His covenant, and to those who remember His commandments to do them. —Psalm 103:17-18***

- One of the great promises of the Bible is that the mercy of the Lord continues from one generation to the next, even to our children's children.
- The children of believers, however, don't automatically believe in God, but God's mercy and goodness are available to each generation that follows the good example set by the previous generation.
- Parents need to set the right example for their children. They are living not merely for themselves, but they are setting a precedent that will affect generations to come.

*A wise son heeds his father's instruction, but a scoffer does not listen to rebuke.*
*—Proverbs 13:1*

***But you must continue in the things which you have learned and been assured of, knowing from whom you have learned them, and that from childhood you have known the Holy Scriptures, which are able to make you wise for salvation through faith which is in Christ Jesus. —2 Timothy 3:14-15***

- Timothy had been learning the Holy Scriptures from childhood. Christian parents have the God-given responsibility to raise their children to love God and His Word.
- Even young children can learn the great truths and stories found in the Bible that show God's love and power.
- Teaching given to young children will be embedded in their minds, giving them a strong foundation on which to build. That training is able to make them "wise for salvation through faith which is in Christ Jesus."

7

## PRAYER STARTER

Thank You for these parents who have come today, Lord. They want to raise their children well, and they want to be good parents. Right now, they feel like things are going awry at home, and they don't quite know which way to turn. . . .

*A wise son makes a glad father, but a foolish son is the grief of his mother . . . He who gathers in summer is a wise son; he who sleeps in harvest is a son who causes shame.*
*—Proverbs 10:1, 5*

8

## RECOMMENDED RESOURCES

*Bringing Up Boys*, by James Dobson

*The Complete Book of Christian Parenting & Child Care: A Medical and Moral Guide to Raising Happy, Healthy Children*, by William Sears and Martha Sears

*Dare to Discipline*, by James Dobson

*Stress and Your Child: Know the Signs and Prevent the Harm*, by Archibald D. Hart.

*Grace Based Parenting: Set Your Family Free*, by Tim Kimmel

*The New Strong-Willed Child: Birth Through Adolescence*, by James Dobson

*Parenting with Love and Logic: Teaching Children Responsibility*, by Foster Cline and Jim Fay

*Understanding Your Teenager*, by David R. Veerman

*And you, fathers, do not provoke your children to wrath, but bring them up in the training and admonition of the Lord.*
—Ephesians 6:4

# Perfectionism

1

## PORTRAITS

- Genevieve, a young wife, constantly complains to her new husband about the way he hangs his clothes in the closet, parks the car in the driveway, and even how he sets his shoes by the bed. Everything has to be perfect for her, and Randall can't seem to do anything right. He is always on pins and needles.
- Matt always feels his school work and efforts in the hockey rink are never good enough. Matt studies for hours and practices his hockey in the driveway until dark. When he gets anything less than a 95 on a test, he is crushed and often has debilitating headaches.
- Danny and his new boss William constantly but heads. Danny has worked in the same accounting firm for ten years and is fairly set in his ways around the office. William has come in with some very demanding requests, and Danny is about to explode!

2

## DEFINITIONS AND KEY THOUGHTS

- Perfectionism is a disposition to feel that **anything less than perfecttion is unacceptable**. It is rooted in the need for control and affirmation.
- Theologically, perfectionism is the **destructive belief** that people can achieve God's acceptance by being good enough or doing well enough. Some perfectionistic people think they should be like God: all-knowing (omniscient), all-powerful (omnipotent), everywhere at once (omnipresent), and generally without human frailty.
- Perfectionistic people **think**:

  they should **know everything,** so they beat themselves up for mistakes.

  they should be **totally powerful,** so they become upset when things are out of their control.

  they should **accomplish the work of ten people** in a given day, so they become depressed and discouraged over what "little" they can accomplish.

*Perfectionists need to find their worth not in what they do or how well they do it, but in being God's creation.*
—Chris Thurman

- Perfectionistic people **are:**

  **idealistic** in that they frequently think about how things "should" be, not how they really are.

  always **setting impossibly high goals,** which lead to discouragement, failure, and ultimately quitting.

  **afraid of failure**, equating failure to achieve their goals with a lack of personal worth.

  **tied up in the "shoulds"** of life. With such an overemphasis on "shoulds," perfectionists rarely take into account their own wants and desires.

  **product-minded,** believing that contentment, happiness, and a sense of accomplishment are not permissible until their current project or activity has been completed. The "process" is overlooked because the end result hasn't been reached, and there is no "joy in the journey."

- Perfectionistic people **feel:**

  that they **have to be the best** at what they do. To simply do their best isn't good enough.

  that their **worth is determined by their performance**. Since day-to-day performance in various areas of life fluctuates, a perfectionist's sense of worth fluctuates as well.

*If you are a perfectionist, it is likely that you learned early in life that other people valued you because of how much you accomplished or achieved. As a result you may have learned to value yourself only on the basis of other people's approval. Thus your self-esteem may have come to be based primarily on external standards. This can leave you vulnerable and excessively sensitive to the opinions and criticism of others. In attempting to protect yourself from such criticism, you may decide that being perfect is your only defense.*

—WWW.COUNS.UIUC.EDU

## Personality Types

- Type A people:

  are usually very **strict, demanding, and rigid**.

  have a certain way for things to be done, and **flexibility is not an option**.

  need to be **on time,** and have problems with people who are more relaxed with time.

  are often described as **workaholics** and driven.

  were probably given **conditional love** at some time in their lives. That is, reward and acceptance were given only if a standard was met.

  are more likely to **suffer heart attacks** at an earlier age.

- Type B people:

  are usually more **laid back** and carefree with their time.

  are not so rigid and are considered **more flexible** in their relationships.

  tend to **cope with daily stress** in a more positive way.

- Many references in the Bible use the word "perfect": "Therefore you shall be perfect, just as your Father in heaven is perfect" (Matthew 5:48). We need to help people understand that **perfection is not something God expects** from them. God knows we can't do it or He wouldn't have had to send His Son.
- As Christians, we need to be **more concerned with our relationship with God**—allowing Him to help us grow—than with being perfectionists. A mature, loving heart will do more to insure a life of healthy relationships and a good self-worth than any perfectionist's rigid schedule or ways will.

## 3 ASSESSMENT INTERVIEW

*Are you so foolish? Having begun in the Spirit, are you now being made perfect by the flesh?*
—Galatians 3:3

**Q1** Describe perfectionism for me.

**Q2** Do you feel that you have to be the best at everything?

**Q3** Do you feel that you need to be in control?

**Q4** What kinds of goals do you set for yourself?

**Q5** Do you have those goals pretty much across the board in every area of life? That is, are your expectations as high at home as they are at work or in school?

**Q6** Do you see life as "all or nothing," "black or white"?

**Q7** Do you find it difficult to be flexible?

**Q8** Tell me about your growing up years. When did you feel most loved by your friends and family?

**Q9** Did you ever feel that you were only loved based on your performance?

**Q10** Have you always been this way?

**Q11** How do you feel when you don't get things done to perfection?

**Q12** How do you feel about someone who enjoys relaxing more than you do?

**Q13** Would you define yourself as a Type A or Type B personality? *(Explain the difference.)*

**Q14** Do you think one personality type is better than the other?

**Q15** Does God say you have to be perfect?

## 4 WISE COUNSEL

Your job is **not to totally overhaul an individual's personality or makeup**. Wouldn't you prefer to have a perfectionist performing heart surgery on you than someone who just is willing to be "good enough"? We need to celebrate what they bring to their work but help them manage it in a manner that minimizes damage to themselves and others.

Perfectionism is a problem if it **adversely affects the person's health or self-esteem**, or if it **affects others** at work or at home and causes stress.

Remind the person that **God is all-powerful**. He can help the perfectionist relax and become more flexible in what he demands of other people.

If the person is **struggling with someone** who is a perfectionist, then there is a good chance that the person is a Type B dealing with a Type A. He needs to understand how the Type A individual thinks: Type A people are more demanding on themselves than on others.

## 5 ACTION STEPS

### 1. Determine Your Personality

Take a personality inventory, such as the Myers-Briggs or other similar tests that are available online. This is a great way of discovering what makes you tick. Seeing yourself on paper and realizing that you have personality tendencies that are similar to others can be part of your life journey in discovering the *you* God made.

### 2. Change Is Not the Issue

You don't need a radical personality change, but you need to understand your God-given nature, how to use it when appropriate and reign it in when not appropriate.

### 3. Learn Flexibility and Acceptance

- Realize that the statement, "I am more rigid with my time and you are more flexible," is okay and doesn't mean that I am better than you.
- Ask, "What's the worst that can happen?" The answer (for example, that the report goes through with one typographical error) probably isn't worth losing sleep over.
- God's love is unconditional. You don't have to earn His love by being a perfectionist or by setting unrealistic standards for yourself or others.
- God sets no conditions that we have to meet in order to be His children. We, in turn, need to be unconditional in how we accept others.

*Being confident of this very thing, that He who has begun a good work in you will complete it until the day of Jesus Christ.*
—Philippians 1:6

> *Living your life as a perfectionist will also set you up for continuous rejection and self-putdowns—and deny you peace of mind—because demanding perfection usually results in failure. And even if you achieve an exceptional result, chances are that you'll still be unhappy, as you'll find additional reasons for not being good enough. That's the destructive nature of perfectionism and that's why it destroys self-esteem. Nothing is ever good enough.*
> —HTTP://UB-COUNSELING.BUFFALO.EDU

### 4. Laugh a Little

Don't be so judgmental of yourself and others. Find humor in who you are! (God made all of us, so He must have had a sense of humor, right?)

### 5. Be Realistic

- You're not going to be God, so stop trying.
- Look at life as it *is*, not as you think it *should be.*
- Meet people halfway.
- Don't expect the impossible—of yourself or others. Set attainable goals and reasonable time limits.
- In your life, determine where high standards are appropriate and where they aren't. Learn to accept "good enough" on certain tasks.
- Realize that many positive things can be learned from making mistakes.

### 6. Grow in Your Love for God

- We are all "in process." Paul told the Philippians that even he hadn't arrived and hadn't attained perfection, so we shouldn't expect it either. We won't be perfect until we see Jesus face to face. Our goal now is to know, love, and follow Christ, not attain perfection.
- Spiritual growth is a climb up a mountain with wonderful views and some grueling stretches. We keep going by taking some good friends along and staying nourished on prayer, Bible study, serving, and giving.

## 6 BIBLICAL INSIGHTS

***Therefore you shall be perfect, just as your Father in heaven is perfect. —Matthew 5:48***

- Jesus was not commanding His people to be perfectionists. The standard of perfection reveals our sinfulness and our need for a Savior.
- One day Christ will make us perfect, but during our time on earth, we should be striving for Christlikeness, always realizing that we have much room to grow.

***I am indeed a Jew, born in Tarsus of Cilicia, but brought up in this city at the feet of Gamaliel, taught according to the strictness of our fathers' law, and was zealous toward God as you all are today . . . —Acts 22:3-4***

- Paul could have been considered a "perfect" Jew. He had the right pedigree, the right training, the right desires, the right enthusiasm. But being "perfect" in our own eyes doesn't take away sin. Only Christ can accomplish that..

- No one's pedigree, training, background, wealth, abilities, gifts, appearance, or anything else can be perfect enough to earn salvation. We should not be enslaved to the "perfectionism" of this world that is ultimately worthless.
- Only when we trust God and allow *Him* to use our backgrounds, training, and gifts for His glory will we find complete fulfillment.

***For by grace you have been saved through faith, and that not of yourselves; it is the gift of God, not of works, lest anyone should boast. —Ephesians 2:8-9***

- God is perfect, but all of us are sinful. Fortunately, God doesn't require people to reach a certain level of perfection before He will accept them. Otherwise, no one could ever be saved!
- God provided a perfect way of salvation—His grace.

***For by one offering He has perfected forever those who are being sanctified. —Hebrews 10:14***

- Believers have been made perfect in God's eyes because of the death and resurrection of Jesus Christ. At the same time, however, we "are being sanctified," growing through our walk with Him.
- Instead of measuring perfection by worldly standards, we should seek to obey God, looking forward to the day when He will finally make us perfect with Him in our perfect eternal home.

*And He said to me, "My grace is sufficient for you, for My strength is made perfect in weakness." Therefore most gladly I will rather boast in my infirmities, that the power of Christ may rest upon me.*
—2 Corinthians 12:9

## 7 PRAYER STARTER

Lord, we know that You want me to follow you, but Your child needs to understand better what that means. He wants to do well at everything he does, and that's a good quality. Unfortunately, his drive for perfection is ruining his life and his relationships . . .

## 8 RECOMMENDED RESOURCES

*Control Freak: Coping with Those Around You, Taming the One Within*, by Les Parrot

*When Perfect Isn't Good Enough: Strategies for Coping with Perfectionism*, by Martin Antony and Richard Swinson

# Pornography

## 1 PORTRAITS

- Sharon couldn't shake the nagging feeling. She finally asked Paul if he has ever been involved in pornography, and he replied defensively, "I have but I have, it under control now. You have nothing to worry about." Sharon wept as she described her horror in finding obscene pictures on their computer that he had downloaded from the Internet. "I trusted him," she said.
- Fifteen-year-old Andrew remembers the first time he viewed sexually arousing material. He was at his friend's house and was checking his e-mail. He got a message from someone he didn't recognize with a file attachment. He opened the file and saw a photo of man and woman engaged in sexual activity. Andrew felt flush with excitement and guilt. Soon he was going online when no one was home to view similar sites because he liked the feeling it gave him.

## 2 DEFINITIONS AND KEY THOUGHTS

- Pornography is the viewing of **sexually explicit material** that dehumanizes, objectifies, and degrades men and women for the purpose of sexual arousal. Often it is photos, but or videos; sometimes it takes the form of stories or comic-book drawings.
- Pornography **promises "sex without consequences"** and self-gratification.
- Generally, a **man will come** for help because he has **been found out** by someone at work or a loved one. Or sometimes, a man will seek counseling because he has intense feelings of guilt and shame.
- A **woman may come** for counseling because she either **suspects or has found evidence** that her husband has been involved in pornography, and she doesn't know what to do.
- A **teenager may come** in for counseling at the insistence of **his or her parents**.
- Many who engage in pornography **rationalize their behavior as "harmless"** because they think they aren't actually committing adultery.
- Eventually, use of pornography **loses its power to stimulate,** and the user is enticed to involve others (usually strangers) in sexual activities.
- Pornography is often used as a **stress reliever** that gives **escape** from life's perceived hardships.

- Pornography use may be a **symptom of a deeper issue** (low self-esteem, loneliness, past sexual abuse).
- Many use pornography **to avoid emotional or sexual intimacy with their spouse**.
- Consistent use of pornography promotes the perception that **women are only objects** and that **sex is unrelated to love**, commitment, and marriage.
- Viewing pornography **increases the likelihood of sexual addiction**.
- Use of pornography can create **unrealistic sexual expectations** from a spouse.
- The user of pornography often **struggles** with anger, guilt, shame, increasing anxiety, and oppressive memories.
- It is not uncommon for many people to have their **first exposure** to pornographic material during the **junior high** school years.
- Many adolescents begin viewing pornography because of **curiosity** and as a release for hormonal tension.

- Pornographic Web sites: 4.2 million (12% of total Web sites)
- Daily pornographic search engine requests: 68 million (25% of total search engine requests)
- U.S. adults who regularly visit Internet pornography websites: 40 million
- Promise Keeper men who viewed pornography in last week: 53%
- Christians who said pornography is a major problem in the home: 47%
- Average age of first Internet exposure to pornography: 11 years old
- 8-16 year olds having viewed porn online: 90% (most while doing homework)

—WWW.FAMILYSAFEMEDIA.COM

3

## ASSESSMENT INTERVIEW

### For the person who is viewing pornography

Recognize that the person who is struggling with this issue probably feels a **great deal of shame** and may be reluctant to speak about it.

It is important to **communicate acceptance** and your willingness to understand the struggle in the person's life instead of immediately condemning him.

Approach the person with grace rather than judgment. Cite Romans 3:23, "For all have sinned and fall short of the glory of God."

**Be patient** in encouraging the person to explain how the struggle began, how it progressed, and what is currently happening.

In the assessment process, **evaluate the length of time** the person has been involved in this activity and **the extent of the involvement.** (Is it daily or sporadic? Is it reaching the level of an addiction? Is it affecting his or her work or home life?)

In addition, it is important to evaluate the degree to which the person feels **sorrow and regret**, and to test his **willingness to change**.

**Q1** How long has this pattern been going on?

**Q2** What prompted you to start?

**Q3** When do you find you most often engage in viewing pornography? (at night? when stressed? when you are on the computer and no one is around?)

**Q4** What is it like to admit to this?

**Q5** How do you think this is affecting your relationship with your spouse/friends/family?

**Q6** When do you find yourself most tempted?

**Q7** Have you made any attempts to stop? If so, how?

**Q8** What are you willing to do about this?

**Q9** How do you see God in your life right now?

### For the spouse seeking counsel

*But each one is tempted when he is drawn away by his own desires and enticed. Then, when desire has conceived, it gives birth to sin; and sin, when it is full-grown, brings forth death.*
—James 1:14 - 15

If the person coming for help is a wife of someone suspected of using pornography, she will probably **express a variety of emotions,** from anger to shame to guilt (feeling as if she is somehow at fault).

In the initial interview, **listen carefully and provide hope** that God will show a way through this difficult experience.

**Evaluate her options and plan**. She may be dealing with fear of confronting her husband. She may be struggling with thinking clearly about this situation and needs to talk it through with you.

**Q1** When and how did you find out about this?

**Q2** Have you made any attempts to talk with your husband about this?

**Q3** If not, why not? Are you afraid of his reaction?

**Q4** If so, how did you approach it and what did you say?

**Q5** How did he respond?

**Q6** Have you seen any unusual changes in his behavior lately?

**Q7** How are you feeling in regards to finding this out?

**Q8** How specifically can I help you?

**Q9** Would you like me to talk to your husband? Do you think he will be willing to talk to me?

**Q10** What are some things that will help rebuild trust between you?

**Q11** What are some next steps for you to take?

## 4 WISE COUNSEL

### For the person who is viewing pornography

Evaluate how **honest** the person is being with himself and you.

**Repentance is a crucial spiritual component** in the healing of sexual sin. Explain and discuss David's confession of sin in Psalm 51.

Determine how **willing the person is to take steps to change**. Words are cheap, but courageous steps forward can begin to rebuild damaged relationships.

**Identify the triggers** that are involved in tempting the person. Some narrow down most of the moods associated with triggers with a simple acronym: HALT, which stands for:

Hungry

Angry

Lonely

Tired

Provide hope that he will be able to experience victory over this problem.

Let him know that there will be times of temptation, and possibly some setbacks, but God is faithful to forgive and restore.

Assure him of your continued support through this process.

Instruct him to structure a system of accountability with a trusted friend.

## 5 ACTION STEPS

### For the person who is viewing pornography

#### 1. Flee Temptation

- Help the person identify all the locations, web sites, and activities that tempt him.
- Avoid bookstores that sell pornographic magazines.
- Only use the computer when someone else is in the room.
- Purchase software that blocks access to undesirable Internet sites.

## 2. Identify Emotional Triggers

- Are there work associates, times of the day, or particular stressful situations that trigger the temptation?
- Identify which part of HALT (Hungry, Angry, Lonely, Tired) is the person's strongest trigger.
- Encourage the person to take specific steps to minimize the triggers.

## 3. See It as Sin

- It is important that the person see the behavior as sin and no longer minimize or justify it.
- Discuss how God views his sin, the nature of forgiveness, and God's unconditional love. Help him grasp the freedom, joy, and power of Christ's forgiveness.

## 4. Refocus on Christ

- Help the person develop a plan to strengthen and deepen his relationship with Jesus Christ.
- Help him set up daily Scripture reading and prayer.
- Encourage memorization of Scripture so that he can bring "every thought into captivity to the obedience of Christ" (2 Corinthians 10:5).

## 5. Get Support and Accountability

Promote involvement in a local Christian ministry that supports men who are experiencing this struggle.

## 6. Check in on the Marriage

Evaluate his relationship with his spouse (if married) and invite them to meet with you to explore the effects of this behavior on their relationship and find healing for their wounds.

## 7. Refer

- Pornography use can contribute long-term problems of sexual addiction and depression.
- If this has been a **long-standing pattern** with a high degree of involvement, **enlist the support of professional** trained in the arena of sexual addiction and a local Twelve Step Group.

### For the spouse seeking counsel

If the husband will not come in and talk with you, or if the wife doesn't want him to know about her conversation with you, then you will need to encourage the wife to be strong and courageous as she confronts her husband at the right time.

### 1. Watch for Triggers

- The wife can identify the locations and activities that provide temptation.
- She can help her husband avoid bookstores that sell pornographic magazines (for example, don't send him late at night to the local 7-Eleven on an errand).
- Move the computer out of isolation. If her husband is willing to be helped, he will go along with this. If not, she can explain that she doesn't want the kids to find pornography.
- Purchase software that blocks the access to undesirable Internet sites.

*Let us walk properly, as in the day, not in revelry and drunkenness, not in lewdness and lust, not in strife and envy.*
—Romans 13:13

### 2. Identify Emotional Triggers

- Does she sense that there are work associates, times of the day, or particular stressful situations that trigger the temptation? What can she do to help?
- Which part of HALT (Hungry, Angry, Lonely, Tired) is the strongest trigger? What can she do to offset those?
- If her husband is willing to be helped, she can talk to him about these triggers and how she can be his ally in minimizing them.

### 3. Continue to Love Him

- Nagging, anger, or humiliation don't work. Continue to love your husband, even if you feel "cheated on." Ask God to help you choose to love him through this.
- Let him know that you want him to come back from the darkness, and you want your marriage unhindered by these "other women."
- Tell him how you feel when he views pornography.
- Ask him if he wants his children similarly enslaved when they are older.
- Explain to him that eventually pornography won't satisfy, and he will need more, other types, or will be led into an affair.

### 4. Pray for Him

- Pray that your husband will realize the damage he is inflicting on himself and his family, and ask God to motivate him.
- Let God work in your husband's life.

### 5. Be Supportive

- Encourage him to join a support group or men's Bible study that will provide accountability.
- Do whatever it takes to free him up to attend such a group.

## 6 BIBLICAL INSIGHTS

***Now Israel remained in Acacia Grove, and the people began to commit harlotry with the women of Moab. —Numbers 25:1***

- Sexual sin always progresses, drawing people farther and farther from God. What may start as an "innocent" flirtation with sin can lead to deadly consequences.
- Dabbling around the edges of sexual sin can take hold and consume a person, leading to intense pain and brokenness.

***For this is the will of God, your sanctification: that you should abstain from sexual immorality; that each of you should know how to possess his own vessel in sanctification and honor, not in passion of lust. —1 Thessalonians 4:3–5***

- The Bible is very clear about sexual sin. God created sex as a beautiful expression of love in marriage, but Satan took that beauty and distorted it.
- Sexual sin encompasses a wide range of activities forbidden by God. No matter what society allows, believers need to look to God for instruction in this serious matter.
- Christians need to avoid activities or thoughts that warp what God intended for building oneness in marriage.
- Believers should have no part in sexual sin. God knows its power to destroy people, and His commands are for our good.

*Beloved, I beg you as sojourners and pilgrims, abstain from fleshly lusts which war against the soul.*
—1 Peter 2:11

***I am He who searches the minds and hearts. And I will give to each one of you according to your works. —Revelation 2:23***

- Sometimes people think they can hide parts of their lives from everyone.
- Christ searches minds and hearts—nothing is hidden from Him. No sexual sin can escape His notice. People may think they are getting away with it, but God knows.
- Everywhere we go and everything we say, think, or do is seen by God. That understanding should help us to steer clear of sexual sin.

## 7 PRAYER STARTER

Oh Lord, this family is being devastated by sin. Help this family to deal with the pain that pornography is causing. We ask that You strengthen Your child to stand firm in his commitment to be free from the addictive power of pornography . . .

## 8 RECOMMENDED RESOURCES

*An Affair of the Mind: One Woman's Courageous Battle to Salvage her Family from the Devastation of Pornography*, by Laurie Hall

*Every Man's Battle: Pornography*, American Association of Christian Counselors Life Enrich Video Series, by Steve Arterburn

*Female Sex Addiction*, American Association of Christian Counselors Life Enrich Video Series, by Marnie Feree

*Healing the Wounds of Sexual Addiction*, by Mark Laaser

*Male Sex Addiction*, American Association of Christian Counselors Life Enrich Video Series, by Mark Laaser

*The Silent War: Ministering to Those Trapped in the Deception of Pornography*, by Henry J. Rogers

*I Surrender ALL. Rebuilding a Marriage Broken by Pornography*, by Clay and Renee Crosse

# Prejudice

## 1 PORTRAITS

- Joey is president of his church youth group, but he struggles with accepting Ellie, a new member. Ellie and her family have just moved to Joey's town from across the country. Even though she claims to be a Christian, Joey is suspicious of her and feels she is faking just to get accepted. He likes his youth group just the way it is and resents this foreigner (even though Ellie is a citizen) who eats different foods and talks with an accent.
- Janna is a young adult who is serious about her career in Human Resources. She has risen to a position to where she is hiring personnel. Janna interviewed a sharp young woman who is very qualified for the position. After the interview, her boyfriend picked her up outside Janna's office. She's white, and he's black—and Janna found reasons to give the job to someone else.
- Matt grew up in a small town where there were "two sides of the tracks" and he was always taught that he was on the "right" side. The summer after his high school graduation, he became a Christian. Matt won an athletic scholarship to a prestigious college. Upon arriving at college in a large cosmopolitan city, he encountered teammates who were from "the wrong side of the tracks." He struggles with his resentment againt "people who don't belong" and his new faith in Christ.

## 2 DEFINITIONS AND KEY THOUGHTS

- Prejudice is **an emotional response** based on fear, mistrust, and ignorance, is usually directed at a racial, religious, national, or other cultural groups, although it can also focus on other differences, such as financial.
- Prejudice is also a mindset of superiority that often is **passed on from one generation to the next**. Children who watch their parents model prejudice toward others' religion or ethnicity (for example) often become adults with those same prejudices.
- Expressions of prejudice vary from mild to severe, from showing preference for "people like us" to verbal assault and physical violence.
- Prejudice causes the whole body of Christ to suffer: "For as the body is one and has many members, but all the members of that one body, being many, are one body, so also is Christ" (1 Corinthians 12:12).

> *He who oppresses the poor reproaches his Maker, but he who honors Him has mercy on the needy.*
> —Proverbs 14:31

- Some argue that prejudice is a matter of personal opinion, and say, "I can't help the way I feel." However, Christians are instructed to **exercise personal choices** based on what they see in the character of God.
- Second Chronicles 19:7 states: "Now therefore, let the fear of the Lord be upon you . . . for there is no iniquity with the Lord our God, no partiality . . ." Romans 2:11 says that God does not show favoritism: "There is no partiality with God."
- God's unbiased love for everyone is the basis for John 3:16: "For God so loved the world that He gave His only begotten Son, that whoever believes in Him should not perish but have everlasting life."
- The prejudiced person:

  needs to address **deep issues** of anger and superiority, which often masks feelings of inferiority.

  fails to reach out to people who are different.

  has a **false view of himself**—seeing himself as uniquely separate and better than others.

  has an **incorrect understanding of God** and His creation of and love for all people.
- A prejudiced person eventually **alienates himself** in our global, multicultural world.
- Prejudice can lead to **discrimination**—acting on resentful attitudes, thoughts, and opinions into action.
- If the person had a negative experience with someone from another culture that led to prejudice, he needs to **be realistic** about his assessment. For example, if he had a bad experience with a doctor, would he never go to see another doctor?

> *Although a world without prejudice may be impossible, we as Christians are to demonstrate impartiality in our individual lives . . . We must increase our exposure toward those who are different in order to engender feelings of similarity instead of feelings of separation.*
>
> —Sabrina D. Black and Paris M. Finner-Williams

## 3 ASSESSMENT INTERVIEW

**Q1** Have you ever thought about why you have prejudices?

**Q2** Did you learn this attitude toward this group of people from your parents? Explain what your parents taught you about this.

**Q3** Did you ever have a negative experience with a person from this culture?

**Q4** Does one negative experience make all of those people bad?

**Q5** How have you expressed your prejudice? Have you been discriminatory?

**Q6** Why do you feel this person deserves this kind of treatment?

**Q7** Have you ever been misunderstood?

**Q8** Has someone ever showed a prejudice toward you for being a Christian? How did that make you feel?

**Q9** Has someone ever made fun of you personally or where you are from? How did that make you feel?

**Q10** When you feel prejudice toward someone, how does that make you feel?

**Q11** What does it mean to you when you hear, "Walk a mile in someone's shoes"?

**Q12** How did Jesus treat those who were different from Him?

## 4 WISE COUNSEL

Don't assume that the person has any **knowledge of life outside** his own cultural boundaries. As a society, we are becoming more globally-minded, but many of us are still very narrow-minded in their understanding of differences in cultures.

Share some **examples of how other cultures live or think**. Differences between American culture and other cultures don't mean that we're right or that they're right—we're just different.

Help the person understand that he should learn to **celebrate differences** instead of judging the differences.

As the love of God flows through Christians, we are drawn together as one body; our relationships with one another are rooted in biblical teachings like:

"Be kindly affectionate to one another" (Romans 12:10).

"Be of the same mind toward one another" (Romans 12:16).

"Love one another" (Romans 13:8).

"Pursue the things which make for peace and the things by which one may edify another" (Romans 14:19).

"The members should have the same care for one another" (1 Corinthians 12:25).

"Through love serve one another" (Galatians 5:13).

"Be kind to one another, tenderhearted, forgiving one another" (Ephesians 4:32).

"Bearing with one another, and forgiving one another" (Colossians 3:13).

*If a stranger dwells with you in your land, you shall not mistreat him.*
—Leviticus 19:33

## 5 ACTION STEPS

### 1. Cross-cultural Appreciation

- Examine your own cultural roots and become more personally aware of who you are and where your ancestors came from (we are a nation of immigrants—everyone came from somewhere else, unless you're a Native American).
- Look up information about the culture in question (the one enflaming the prejudice). Give one specific item to look up—for example, meals or special celebrations. This item of information should be brought to the next conversation.

### 2. Get Personal

- Think of a time when you were made fun of. Remember how it made you feel.
- How is that any different than the prejudice you are showing toward someone? (Encourage the individual to answer this—this may really stretch his thinking and bring him to a point of realization.)

### 3. Avoid Stereotypes

- Would you want to be generalized as a "dumb blonde" or a "tough German" or a "loud Italian"? Then don't do that to others.
- We sometimes make generalizations about people without regard to their uniquenesses.
- Usually, generalizations are used to avoid relating to the person as an individual.

### 4. Practice Empathy

- "Walk a mile in someone else's shoes" before you make a judgment about that person. Get into his head, think about what feeling prejudice would really be like for him. This is called *empathy*.
- Consider how you would feel landing in another country where you don't know the customs or the language.

### 5. Do What Jesus Would Do

- Remember your common bond in Christ with fellow believers. This common bond tears down any walls of prejudice (Colossians 3:11).

*Always remember that children model adult behavior. What parents say and how they act concerning others will influence impressionable minds. Racist jokes, generalized statements or hateful expressions plant unwanted seeds—in the victim and in the offender. Instead, plant healthy seeds in the tender soil of your child's heart, building respect toward others.*

—WWW.FOCUSONYOURCHILD.COM

- Changing your deeply-rooted attitudes and beliefs will not come overnight. As you continue to examine your own beliefs and talk to others about them, change will occur.
- People who want to overcome prejudice can renew their minds (Ephesians 4:23). By studying God's Word, Christ will then melt your heart and remove the prejudice that can do harm to your ability to relate to others.

## 6 BIBLICAL INSIGHTS

***Gilead's wife bore sons; and when his wife's sons grew up, they drove Jephthah out, and said to him, "You shall have no inheritance in our father's house, for you are the son of another woman." —Judges 11:2***

- Jephthah was rejected by the rest of his family because his mother was a harlot (prostitute). His half brothers' prejudice against him was so intense that they drove him out of their home.
- Prejudice can cause people to turn away from a good friendship or working relationship.
- The Bible teaches that we should not be prejudiced against anyone, because all people are created by God and all believers are one in Christ (Galatians 3:26–28).

*There is neither Greek nor Jew, circumcised nor uncircumcised, barbarian, Scythian, slave nor free, but Christ is all and in all.* —Colossians 3:11

***But he disdained to lay hands on Mordecai alone, for they had told him of the people of Mordecai. Instead, Haman sought to destroy all the Jews who were throughout the whole kingdom of Ahasuerus—the people of Mordecai. —Esther 3:6***

- Haman's prejudice was focused against one Jewish man and then was extended to the Jewish race and religion.
- Prejudice is a powerful tool of Satan of putting one person in a superior position to another. That should never be the attitude of the followers of Christ.
- Believers ought to see all people as created in the image of God and should accept all other believers as part of God's family. In love, they should also readily share Christ with lost people of all races and nations.

*It shall be that I will gather all nations and tongues; and they shall come and see My glory.* —Isaiah 66:18

***Then he said to them, "You know how unlawful it is for a Jewish man to keep company with or go to one of another nation. But God has shown me that I should not call any man common or unclean." —Acts 10:28***

- In the early church, it was hard for Jewish believers to comprehend that Gentiles might also become Christians. At this critical time in the growth of the early church, however, God made it clear that the Good News would be for everyone.

- Today, we should not allow any prejudice to keep us from sharing the message of salvation with the world.

***There is neither Jew nor Greek, there is neither slave nor free, there is neither male nor female; for you are all one in Christ Jesus. —Galatians 3:28***

- This verse describes how Christ breaks down all barriers.
- All believers have personal identities which provide rich variety in the church, but all have also been made "one in Christ Jesus." As part of a huge, diverse family, we should not allow prejudice to separate us from other believers.

*But in every nation whoever fears Him and works righteousness is accepted by Him.*
—Acts 10:35

***If you really fulfill the royal law according to the Scripture, "You shall love your neighbor as yourself," you do well; but if you show partiality, you commit sin, and are convicted by the law as transgressors. —James 2:8-9***

- James warned the believers against showing prejudice. They were not to fawn over a rich person while ignoring a poor one.
- People often want to be associated with those who are successful, popular, and powerful. God demands impartiality, however, because all people are equally valuable in His eyes.
- Favoritism goes against God's command to love our neighbor as ourselves. God wants us to respect all people and treat them equally, regardless of their background or economic status. Each person is God's creation.

## 7 PRAYER STARTER

Thank You, Lord, that Your child has come today to deal with this issue of prejudice. The reasons run deep, but not so deep that You can't heal. Help him to see that You created all people in Your image and because of that all people have dignity and value . . .

## 8 RECOMMENDED RESOURCES

*Living in Color: Embracing God's Passion for Ethnic Diversity,* by Randy Woodley

*No Partiality,* by Douglas R. Sharp

*Through Gates of Splendor,* by Elisabeth Elliot

# Premarital Sex

## 1 PORTRAITS

- Laurie was in high school and was devastated when she broke up with her boyfriend. Only her best friend knew that her emotional pain was heightened by the knowledge that she'd surrendered her virginity to this boy.
- Jake is a good Christian kid who attends youth group. His parents were shocked to discover that he has contracted a sexually transmitted disease.
- Kim is twenty years old and in college, but has just discovered that she's pregnant. The young man who got her pregnant has shown himself to be immature and possibly addicted to drugs.
- Dave has been having sex with his girlfriends since middle school. He really doesn't understand what all the fuss is about.

## 2 DEFINITIONS AND KEY THOUGHTS

- Sex is a **God-given appetite** that needs to be controlled
- According to the Bible, **sex outside of marriage is wrong**—no matter how old you are or how much you love your partner.
- Sex can be defined a few different ways. Typically, it refers to intercourse between a man and a woman, but a more accurate definition might be **any activity that causes at least one partner to experience orgasm**. This much broader definition dispenses with the distinctions that allow people to have sex without calling it sin.
- Many teens think "it's not really sex" if it's **oral sex**. The Bible teaches that any sexual engagement with another outside of the covenant of marriage is sin. Additionally, most teens do not understand that **STDs (sexually transmitted diseases) can be transferred** during oral sex.
- Our society has been sexualized by media who **use sex to sell and to entertain**. The situation for teenagers is very different from what their parents experienced. Now they regularly laugh at homosexual and extra-marital sex on TV, and they seldom are reminded of the negative after-effects of sex or of the fact that God labels these behaviors sin.
- **Divorce may contribute** to early sexual activity as teens seek attention because parental guidance is lacking.

*I say then: Walk in the Spirit, and you shall not fulfill the lust of the flesh.*
—Galatians 5:16

- Divorced or widowed parents present **mixed messages** to their children if they tell their teens to wait to have sex but are sexually active themselves.
- Kids who are **not allowed on dates** by themselves may be less likely to indulge in risky sexual behavior.
- Teens whose parents **speak to them openly** about sexual ethics will be more informed and more thoughtful about their behavior. Ignorance can lead to recklessness.
- More than anything else, **drugs and alcohol** contribute to risky sexual behavior and impulsive decision-making.
- **Teen girls who develop early** often struggle to accept their sexuality. They are frequently treated as sex objects by boys whose sexuality is just awakening, and they are rejected by other girls who are envious of the attention they get.
- Girls who **strive for acceptance** and rarely assert themselves may be susceptible to boys who tell them they must have sex or they won't date them any longer.
- Whether true or not, the statement **"everybody is doing it"** is frequently cited by teens to justify sexual acting out.

## 3 ASSESSMENT INTERVIEW

Most people who seek counseling for a sexual indiscretion will be hyper-attuned to criticism. This may be particularly true if the encounter involved a person of the same sex. You will have to make every effort to **appear nonjudgmental**. If you feel repulsed or angered by the individual's behavior, then you may need to refer the person to someone else.

Teens may **seek counseling for an unrelated problem** and then slowly—if trust develops—admit to premarital sex, pregnancy, or abortion. The following questions will help you to assess the situation once it becomes clear that sexual misbehavior has occurred.

### Rule Outs

**Q1** Were you forced to have sex? If so, when did this take place? *(If the person is a minor, the rape should be reported.)*

**Q2** Is there any possibility that you are pregnant? If so, what are your thoughts? *(If she is considering abortion, see the section on Abortion.)*

**Q3** Sexually transmitted diseases can be caught through oral sex as well as intercourse. Have you engaged in unprotected oral sex or intercourse? *(If so, the person needs a medical exam immediately. If infected, tthe person should contact every person he or she has been with, at least within a particular window of time, so they can be tested.)*

*Keep your heart with all diligence, for out of it spring the issues of life.*
—Proverbs 4:23

**Q4** Has your sexual experience caused you to feel depressed? Have you considered harming yourself? *(If yes, see the section on Suicide.)*

**Q5** Have all of your sexual encounters been heterosexual? If not, how long have you been having sex with someone of the same gender?

**Q6** If you have engaged in homosexual activity, has this been continual or just experimental? *(If homosexuality is an issue, see the section on Homosexuality.)*

### General Questions

**Q7** When was the first time you had sex?

**Q8** How often do you have sex?

**Q9** Do you always enjoy it? If not, why do you do it?

**Q10** With how many partners have you had sex?

**Q11** Do you always use protection?

**Q12** Do you plan your sexual activity ahead of time, or does it just happen?

**Q12** Are alcohol or drugs involved in your sexual activities?

**Q13** Do you believe that your behavior is right and healthy, or do you want to change it?

**Q14** If you want to change, what strategies have you tried? How well have they worked?

**Q15** Have you ever been pressured into having sex? What would you do if it happened again?

**Q16** Is there any relationship between love and sex? If so, what is the relationship?

**Q17** Are you feeling guilty? What do you plan to do with your feelings?

**Q18** Do you think that God can forgive you?

**Q19** What do you think you should do now?

*Put off, concerning your former conduct, the old man which grows corrupt according to the deceitful lusts, and be renewed in the spirit of your mind.*

—Ephesians 4:22-23

## 4 WISE COUNSEL

If you allow the person to **talk without judging** him, he will be more open.

Through processing the behavior, the person will probably come to the conclusion that the act was wrong and that the **behavior needs to change**. If that does not happen, you at least will have built a strong relationship and can begin gently teaching the person biblical values.

To repeat, **if you are repulsed or angered** by the person's behavior, you need to **refer him or her** to another counselor.

## ACTION STEPS

5

### 1. Talk It Out

- If the person is young, help him or her feel comfortable. Simply listen and encourage the person to talk.
- The person may not have come in with issues about premarital sex, but you may discover that it underlies presenting issues such as self-esteem, guilt, anger, depression, etc.

### 2. Refer If Needed

- If you discover that the woman is pregnant (or a man has gotten a woman pregnant, encourage disclosure to family members.
- Refer to a crisis pregnancy center to discuss the options for raising the child or giving it up for adoption.

### 3. Confess Sin

The person needs to be willing to admit and confess the sin. Confession, forgiveness, and repentance are crucial elements in the healing process.

### 4. Accept God's Forgiveness

- The person may be suffering from intense feelings of guilt. Help him or her process these feelings, confess the sins, and experience forgiveness.
- Sometimes using a guided visual meditation to teach a biblical truth helps the person to feel forgiven. He or she can imagine placing all the sins into a trash bag and turning it over to Jesus. He deals with it by destroying it, and then covers the person with a clean, perfect coat. It is important to help some people feel God's presence and experience His leading as part of their healing journey.
- Focus on God's love and forgiveness. Passages like Psalm 51 remind us that God forgives even the worst of sinners and heals their pain.
- Explain that even though the person has lost his/her virginity, he/she can start over with God. Encourage a commitment from now until marriage to remain pure.

### 5. Discover the Reasons

Help the person understand why he or she engages in sex. Is it:

- A search for intimacy?

- A desire to prove manhood or womanhood?

*Our culture promotes individual dating as opposed to group dating, placing young couples who feel strongly attracted to each other in settings that increase the likelihood of their violating their own and God's standards. Group settings help take some of the pressure off of couples seeking to control their urges, while helping them develop healthy social skills. Yet ultimately, the battle gets fought in the mind.*

—WWW.FAMILY.ORG

Over 2 million teens are infected with STDs (sexually transmitted diseases) every year.

With divorce rates around 40%, premarital sex is no longer an issue of importance only for adolescents.

According to Archibald Hart, sexual experimentation is beginning earlier. Forty years ago, the average age for first sexual contact was 17 or 18. Today it is 14 or 15, and dropping.

- A need to be accepted or popular with others who are having sex?
- A need to hold on to a particular boyfriend or girlfriend?
- A pleasant physical sensation?

**6. Remain Pure**

- Having sex is like many other life-dominating, impulsive behaviors. Brainstorm ways to avoid having sex outside of marriage in the future. This might include:
- Not being alone with the girlfriend or boyfriend, at least until new norms are established
- Ending the dating relationship if the other person does not share the conviction that sex should stop
- Seeking out new friends who believe in preserving sex until covenantal marriage
- Searching for activities that will help to refocus sexual drives
- Being physically active on a daily basis
- Asking every day for God to take over and sanctify your sexual drive

6

## BIBLICAL INSIGHTS

***But it happened about this time, when Joseph went into the house to do his work, and none of the men of the house was inside, that she caught him by his garment, saying, "Lie with me." But he left his garment in her hand, and fled and ran outside. —Genesis 39:11-12***

- Lust has no logic. Sometimes you can't talk someone out of doing wrong—you just have to get out of the way.
- Joseph knew only one answer to this moral challenge: View it from God's perspective. He concluded that violating his sexual integrity would be a "great wickedness" and "sin against God."
- Sexual sin hurts our relationship with God and can destroy relationships with others. Joseph realized that he had no choice but to run!

***I am my beloved's, and his desire is toward me. —Song of Solomon 7:10***

- Throughout the Song of Solomon, the husband and wife exult in each other's physical attractiveness. These explicit descriptions of their love underscore the importance of the soul relationship and their commitment to one another.

- When a man and a woman become one in marriage, the bond of physical intimacy strengthens their relationship. Within the bonds of marriage, God approves of and encourages sexual pleasure

***Do you not know that your bodies are members of Christ? Shall I then take the members of Christ and make them members of a harlot? Certainly not! —1 Corinthians 6:15***

- Sex is more than a physical act. In sex two people "become one flesh" (Genesis 2:24). Sex is meant by God to be a holy union in which a man and a woman share a deep bond.
- Sex itself is not evil—God created it but people pervert it. Believers need to practice sexual integrity.
- God's people need to abstain from sex outside of marriage. Within the bonds of marriage, a husband and wife should be faithful, always seeking to lovingly meet each other's needs.

*According the Center for Disease Control and Prevention (www.cdc.gov), approximately 50% of youths in grades 9-12 have had sexual intercourse, 35% are sexually active and 15% have had four or more sexual partners. -www.cdc.gov*

## 7 PRAYER STARTER

Dear Lord, thank You that my friend is seeking help. Please aid him/her to see Your plan for sexuality. Help him/her to learn new strategies to handle temptation. We know that once we ask for Your forgiveness, we have it. We praise You for this reality and thank You for Your forgiveness. Please be with us every step of the way as we seek to preserve purity in the days to come. In Jesus' name, Amen.

## 8 RECOMMENDED RESOURCES

*Don't Date Naked,* by Michael and Amy Smalley

*Female Sex Addiction:* American Association of Christian Counselors Life Enrich Video Series, by Marnie Feree

*Male Sex Addiction:* American Association of Christian Counselors Life Enrich Video Series, by Mark Laaser

*The Naked Truth: Sexual Purity for Guys in the Read World,* by William Perkins

*Purity Under Pressure,* by Neil Anderson and Dave Park

*Each year in the United States, between 800,000 to 900,000 adolescents younger than 19 years old become pregnant. -www.cdc.gov*

# Self-Esteem

## 1 PORTRAITS

- Jennifer is plagued by thoughts that she's not good enough for her husband, her children, and her friends—and especially, for God. She feels that apart from her husband and children, she has no purpose in life. Her husband keeps reminding her that without him, she's nothing.
- Henry has lived his entire life trying to please his parents. At 40 he still sees every decision he makes as an opportunity to win the favor of his father. He is sad and discouraged, and he can't seem to hold a job or a long-term relationship.
- From the time she was a young child, Sandy has been told that she is ugly and stupid. When she was 18, she didn't go to college because she was afraid she might fail—and she knew she couldn't handle that.
- Jill has had multiple boyfriends. She feels frustrated and pressured to give in to their sexual advances to please them.

## 2 DEFINITIONS AND KEY THOUGHTS

- Self-esteem refers to an **inner sense of worthiness** that gives a person resilience and resistance to discouragement or criticism.
- Generally speaking, each person has a **concept about his self-worth** (which may or may not be accurate), and self-esteem is how he **feels about (or evaluates) that concept**.
- Having good self-esteem **does not mean being proud** or having an over-blown view of our own importance. Paul encourages us to "think soberly" when it comes to evaluating ourselves (Romans 12:3). This means to assess ourselves with honesty and fairness.
- **Low self-esteem** can manifest itself in many ways:

  feelings of self-hate, believing that we are unworthy or incompetent

  refusal to get close to people, believing we don't deserve strong or supportive relationships

  refusal to trust others

  inability to accept ourselves as special and unique

  rejection of what God intended the person to be in Him

> *And because you are sons, God has sent forth the Spirit of His Son into your hearts, crying out, "Abba, Father!" Therefore you are no longer a slave but a son, and if a son, then an heir of God through Christ.*
> —GALATIANS 4:6-7

depression

suicidal thoughts

a need for large amounts of attention

a competitive or argumentative spirit

poor decisions made that are based on fears and not reality

- An individual's self-esteem is in trouble when he **allows others to determine his value or significance** instead of the One who created him.

- Poor self-esteem is often the result of **prolonged periods of negative feedback** in a person's life, resulting in deep wounds and pain. As a counselor, you need to apply active listening skills in order to determine **how far back the negative influence has gone.**

- Society is **constantly assessing our value**. At work, we have performance evaluations, we are graded in schools, and we are evaluated for loans. Assessment of our value begins early in life and continues even after we die.

- Often, another person's value judgment of us is **a means to an end**. An example of this is the young lady who finds herself in the back seat of a car with a boy who says, in effect, "If you want me to value you, you will have sex with me."

- God has determined our value based on **His love and purpose for creating us** in the first place and on the **price He has paid** to redeem us for all eternity.

- Many Christians believe it is prideful to even address the topic of self-esteem. This of course is true when a person has an over-inflated sense of worth resembling conceit. However, people often come to us with a **damaged or painful sense of their worth**. Searching for God's perspective on our worth or significance is worthy of our time and energy.

- Most who struggle with low self-esteem **believe lies about their significance to God**.

- The **goals** of interacting should be to:

  Correct false or erroneous beliefs about the individual's worth and significance

  Make an accurate, genuine assessment of that person's strengths, gifts, significance, and potential

  Bring a healing from deep relationship wounds

  Help the person get over the distortions and be able to honestly admit his strengths as well as his weaknesses

  Help the person on the journey to adopt God's perspective of his worth

*Each person's life touches a lot of others. The effects of what you do ripple outward, influencing people in larger and larger circles—people you've never even met. A small courtesy may have a far-reaching effect. So look at your life from this wider perspective.*
—JOAN LLOYD GUEST

3

## ASSESSMENT INTERVIEW

Most people feel bad about themselves **without having ever identified the problem**. They may feel like failures or have strong feelings of inadequacy that can result in periods of depression and anxiety.

Some people with poor self-image have been **sexually abused and still feel dirty and worthless**. If your discussion uncovers sexual abuse, address that issue or refer the person to someone else more skilled.

Many individuals with poor self-esteem have come from families where a **divorce** made them insecure or where they were blamed for the divorce.

Some may simply have **overly sensitive personalities** that make them vulnerable to slights or criticism.

Use "normalization" to help build rapport and **make it clear that the person's feelings are normal.**

*God has each person's life in His hand; He created each person for a purpose. Every believer should stand tall with high self-esteem by understanding who he or she is in Christ.*
—Archibald D. Hart

**Q1** Have you ever been told that you have low self-esteem? If so, by whom and when? Do you agree?

**Q2** Do you ever feel that you can't feel good about yourself unless you meet some standard in your life that someone else has set for you?

**Q3** Do you consider failures or mistakes as a direct reflection of your worth?

**Q4** Has your need for approval from others ever caused you to make decisions that you knew were not beneficial?

**Q5** Do you ever avoid taking risks because you are afraid you will fail?

**Q6** Do you ever tell yourself that you are stupid and can't do anything right?

**Q7** Do you ever have unrealistic expectations for your family/loved ones to affirm you? Or, do your loved ones complain that you expect too much from them?

**Q8** Is it difficult for you to forgive?

**Q9** Have you been told that you are unforgiving?

**Q10** Do you obsess about your weight and appearance for unhealthy reasons?

**Q11** Do you consider yourself competitive?

**Q12** Do you often find yourself wishing you were another person—or that you had the talent or looks of another person?

**Q13** What kind of supportive friendships do you have?

**Q14** In what situations do you feel most self-conscious? Least self-conscious?

**Q15** What does it mean to you to be a child of God?

**Q16** Do you believe that God loves you? Can you "feel" God's love or is it more of an intellectual understanding that God loves you?

**Q17** How many siblings do you have? Where are you in the birth order?

**Q18** Tell me about life in your family.

**Q19** How were you treated as a child when you did something wrong or failed at something?

**Q20** Did your parents have high expectations or low expectations of you? Or neither?

**Q21** Did anyone in your family play favorites? Who was the favorite and how did that feel?

**Q22** Have you ever been sexually abused or raped? Did you report it? How was it handled and what happened?

**Q23** Describe the people in your life who made you feel good about yourself. Where are they now? Are any still in your life?

**Q24** What makes you feel good about yourself?

*I have been crucified with Christ; it is no longer I who live, but Christ lives in me; and the life which I now live in the flesh I live by faith in the Son of God, who loved me and gave Himself for me.*
—Galatians 2:20

## WISE COUNSEL 4

Helping a person with low self-esteem **does not mean telling him untruths**. Instead, help the person develop a **realistic assessment of his unique set of skills, abilities, and character traits.** And, help this individual develop a **strong sense of God's love and forgiveness**.

Give the person **hope.** Encourage him to see that he is on a journey. **Encourage patience and prayer** along the way.

Remind the person of the story in John chapter 5 where Jesus healed the crippled man who had lived for 38 years with brokenness and pain. Jesus asked him if he *wanted* to be healed. Why would Jesus ask? It seems that a person can live for so long with brokenness that he may not want to do the work that it takes to receive healing. Is the person willing to **do the work to receive healing?**

5

## ACTION STEPS

### 1. Recognize Your Value

- There is a difference between having an inflated ego and simply understanding your significance based on your God-given gifts and value to Him.
- Make a list of ten talents, character traits, physical traits, abilities, accomplishments, etc., that set you apart. (You can give this as homework—the person will come back with the list in hand and be ready to share it with you.)
- Make another list of five traits that you perceive are negative. Write down some ideas for how you can turn these negatives into positives.
- You mentioned a few people who make you feel good about yourself (Assessment Question #23). Are these people still in your life? If not, is there a way you can get them back into your life?
- Identify other positive people and spend more time with them.

*See, I have inscribed you on the palms of My hands; Your walls are continually before Me.*
—Isaiah 49:16

### 2. Stop Harmful Thought Patterns

- Consider some of the thought patterns and other factors that are leading you to believe lies about your worth.
- Rent and watch the movie, *It's a Wonderful Life*. George Bailey felt like a failure until the angel showed him how much different—and worse off—the world would have been without him. Everyone influences others, and you have had a positive influence on some people.
- Think back on things you've done—taught a Sunday school class, helped with Boy Scouts, gave a perfect gift to a relative, taught a child to shoot a basketball, took a bag of groceries to a food pantry, invited a new coworker to lunch. List all of those big and little things done for others. Then consider the impact they had on those people.

### 3. Begin New Thought Patterns

- Each negative thought can be countered with God's assessment of your value. For example: If you feel your self-worth fizzle when a coworker with less experience is promoted over you, stop the negative thoughts before they take hold of you. Ask yourself if there might be any good reason this person received the promotion over you. If not, remind yourself that life isn't always fair.
- Remember that God has your life in His hands. Not receiving that promotion may end up being a blessing in disguise.

### 4. Be Patient

- It has taken years of bad habits to get to shape your self-esteem. Healing will not happen overnight and will require replacing the bad habits with good ones.
- It may take awhile until your reflex action is quick to respond in a proactive way to negative thinking.

### 5. Read God's Word

- Study what the Bible says about your worth to God. Explore what God says about His love for you and His purpose for your life. (Give him the verses from Biblical Insights.)
- Keep a journal to record significant breakthroughs.

## BIBLICAL INSIGHTS

6

***But Moses said to God, "Who am I that I should go to Pharaoh, and that I should bring the children of Israel out of Egypt?" —Exodus 3:11***

- Moses was certain God was making a mistake by choosing him to lead the Israelites. His five excuses indicated a lack of confidence in his ability to get the job done. He had a crisis of identity ("who am I?" 3:11), a crisis of authority ("what is His name?" 3:13), a crisis of faith ("they will not believe me," 4:1), a crisis of ability ("I am not eloquent," 4:10), and a crisis of obedience ("send . . . whomever else," 4:13).
- But God was with him, and Moses led the nation to freedom. With God's help and guidance, great things are possible.

***What is man that You are mindful of him, and the son of man that You visit him? For You have made him a little lower than the angels, and You have crowned him with glory and honor. —Psalm 8:4-5***

- Insignificant, sinful human beings don't seem worthy of God's care. But God does care. He created people "a little lower than the angels" and crowned them "with glory and honor."
- He loves us so much that He sent His Son to die for us. We are important to God.

*For You formed my inward parts; You covered me in my mother's womb. I will praise You, for I am fearfully and wonderfully made; marvelous are Your works.*
*—Psalm 139: 13-14*

*Your eyes saw my substance, being yet unformed. And in Your book they all were written, the days fashioned for me, when as yet there were none of them. How precious also are Your thoughts to me, O God! How great is the sum of them! If I should count them, they would be more in number than the sand.*
—Psalm 139: 16-18

***But now, thus says the Lord, who created you, O Jacob, and He who formed you, O Israel: "Fear not, for I have redeemed you; I have called you by your name; you are Mine." —Isaiah 43:1***

- Society determines people's importance based on what they do or what they know. God chose Israel to be His covenant people and to display His glory to the nations. As a nation, Israel failed to recognize their Messiah, and God established His new covenant with all who would trust Jesus Christ as Savior.
- God's people know that Christ is their God, Savior, and King. Our self-esteem is not based on what we do, but on who we are in Christ.

***Are not two sparrows sold for a copper coin? And not one of them falls to the ground apart from your Father's will. But the very hairs of your head are all numbered. —Matthew 10:29-30***

- Jesus described God's loving concern for every person, explaining that "the very hairs of your head are all numbered." God cares even for small birds—"not one of them falls to the ground apart from your Father's will"—so imagine how much more He cares for His people.
- What a boost of encouragement! We are important to God—created in His image and loved. He loves us so much, in fact, that He "gave His only begotten Son, that whoever believes in Him should not perish but have everlasting life" (John 3:16).

***Behold what manner of love the Father has bestowed on us, that we should be called children of God! —1 John 3:1***

- No one can love more than God. The thought of God's astounding love lavished on sinful humanity is beyond understanding. It's incomprehensible that while we were still sinners in rebellion against God, Christ died for us (Romans 5:8).
- Through that sacrifice, God brought His own to Himself, bestowing the title and relationship of "children." He allows us to call Him Father. We aren't alone, worthless, or unimportant. Everyone who has faith in Christ is a beloved child of God!

7

## PRAYER STARTER

Thank You that my friend is here today, Lord, to talk about how he feels of so little value. Lord, help him to see that he is of great value to You. Help him to see the gifts You gave him and the special "package" that he is—his background, interests, abilities, and ideas make him Your special creation. . . .

## RECOMMENDED RESOURCES

*Finding Truth: Dispelling the Lies that can Destroy Your Life,* American Association of Christian Counselors Courageous Living Video Series, by Chris Thurman

*The New Building Your Mate's Self-Esteem,* by Dennis and Barbara Rainey

*The New Hide or Seek: Building Self-Esteem in Your Child,* by James Dobson

# Sexual Abuse

## 1 PORTRAITS

- Jean had never told anybody what had happened when she was growing up. She had hoped if she never talked about it, it would go away. The first time her uncle touched her, she felt a powerful but confusing mix of guilt and pleasure. He kept offering to stay with her when her parents left on trips, and the touching escalated to intercourse. She had never told her parents because she didn't think they would believe her. She had avoided her uncle as often as she could. She really didn't think it made sense to talk about it now.

- Betty had tried to tell him "no," but he had kept touching her. She had been so excited to have been asked out by an older guy that she tried to act more sophisticated than she felt. Now she kept having flashback about what had happened and didn't know what she should do.

- When Phil was in junior high school, one of the boys on his football team cornered him after practice in the locker room after everybody else had left. The boy demanded that Phil give him "a blow job." Phil knew what that meant, so he tried to run away. The boy grabbed him and hit him, throwing him to the ground. If Phil refused, the boy threatened to beat him up every day, so reluctantly, he performed the act. Phil has felt like scum since that day, and today, he's 27 years old.

## 2 DEFINITIONS AND KEY THOUGHTS

- Abuse is taking **unfair advantage of a difference of power** in order to take control of someone else, including rape, incest, fondling, and indecent exposure.
- Sexual abuse occurs when a **person exploits another** to satisfy the abuser's desires. It consists of any sexual activity—verbal, visual, or physical.
- Sexual abuse is most often perpetrated by an adult who has access to another by virtue of **real or imagined authority** or kinship.
- In child sexual assault, **the child often knows and even loves the abuser**, the emotional confusion and damage can be intense. Statistics say that by age 18, 1 in 3 girls and 1 in 6 boys will be sexually abused by someone they love or should be able to trust.[2]
- Sexual abuse **violates personal boundaries**. The abuser crosses the victim's boundaries to take what he/she wants. A key to helping the abused person is to set up boundaries that can't be crossed.
- Though studies vary, a large retrospective study on the prevalence of childhood sexual abuse found 27% of women and 16% of men reported abuse.

*According to recent surveys, about 1 in 4 women during their college years, and 1 in 33 men, have experienced an attempted (or completed) rape. Moreover, according to a national survey of high school students, approximately 9% reported having been forced to have sexual intercourse against their will.[1]*

## Consequences

- Physical:

  Long-lasting physical symptoms and illnesses have been associated with sexual victimization, including chronic pelvic pain, premenstrual syndrome, gastrointestinal disorders, and a variety of chronic pain disorders, including headache, back pain, and facial pain.

  A significant number of rape victims contract sexually transmitted diseases, including HIV.

  A longitudinal study in the United States estimated that over 32,000 pregnancies result each year from rape.

- Psychological:

  Immediate reactions to rape include shock, disbelief, denial, fear, confusion, anxiety, and withdrawal.

  Victims may experience emotional detachment, sleep disturbances, and flashbacks. Approximately one-third of rape victims have symptoms that become chronic.

  Rape victims often experience anxiety, guilt, nervousness, phobias, substance abuse, sleep disturbances, depression, alienation, suicidal behavior, and sexual dysfunction. They often distrust others, replay the assault in their minds, and are at increased risk of revictimization.

- Social:

  Rape can strain the victim's relationships because it negatively affects the victim's ability to treat and communicate with family, friends, and intimate partners.

  Victims of sexual violence are more likely than non-victims to engage in risky sexual behavior including having unprotected sex, having sex at an early age, having multiple sex partners, teen pregnancy, and trading sex for food, money, or other items.

  Rape and incest victims are more likely than non-victims to smoke cigarettes, overeat, drink alcohol, and are less likely to use seat belts.

- As you counsel a person who has been sexually abused, be aware of the limits of confidentiality:

  Sexual abuse is **illegal. If the person is a minor, it must be reported to the appropriate agencies,** such as local law enforcement, the Department of Social and Health Services, or Child Protective Services.

  You must report it **within a period of time,** usually between twenty-four hours and seven days.

  Usually you can **report by phone, in writing, or in person**.

  Even if the victim doesn't admit the abuse occurred, if you suspect it, you should **report your suspicions**.

*To be abused is to be touched by evil. Chronic childhood abuse does damage to the body, the mind, the emotions, and the ability to relate to another person.*
—Diane Langberg

If the person is over 18 and discloses childhood sexual abuse occurred, reporting abuse may not be mandatory. However, **if the abuser still has access to children**, you may have an ethical obligation to report the abuse to protect those other children.

3

## ASSESSMENT INTERVIEW

Consider any **risk of suicide, depression, or medical concerns** (especially if the abuse was recent).

*I waited patiently for the Lord; and He inclined to me, and heard my cry. He also brought me up out of a horrible pit, out of the miry clay, and set my feet upon a rock, and established my steps. He has put a new song in my mouth.*
—Psalm 40:1-3

Assess for the **type of abuse** perpetrated—its degree and its history. Sometimes the person is **seeking help for other problems** that actually stem back to sexual abuse. Ask the victim to get him/her to talk about that core issue.

### Assume three things in the process of treatment:

1. The problem is treatable and the victim will be a survivor.
2. The victim is not responsible for the abuse; she is only responsible for her recovery.
3. The victim needs to express, accept, and be prepared to deal with her feelings in order to heal.

**Q1** What has happened that has brought you here today?

**Q2** Is this the first time you've sought help?

**Q3** Tell me about your family. How are things going at home?

**Q4** Tell me about your past. Have you had any painful or unusual things happen—even a long time ago?

**Q5** How long did that go on? How many times did it happen?

**Q6** Can you tell me who was doing that to you? *(If the person seems reticent, explain that you need to know in order to help her, others who might be abused, and the abuser himself. In addition, if she is a minor and still in contact with the abuser, immediate action must be taken.)*

*It is very healing for survivors of abuse to see that Jesus also lived in a body that was abused. He was hit, spit upon, humiliated, and left naked in front of others. The Healer, who is scarred for all eternity, knows the pain of abuse.*
—Diane Langberg

**Q7** Do you know if others were or still are being abused?

**Q8** What problems are you currently having as a result of what has happened? *(Listen to how the abuse affected her. No two people are alike in the story or the consequences of abuse. Be aware that victims tend to minimize the impact of the abuse.)*

**Q9** Tell me how you feel about what has happened to you. *(She needs to have permission to feel her true emotions.)*

**Q10** Do you feel responsible for the abuse? *(Reassure her that she isn't alone, and that she isn't responsible for the abuse.)*

**Q11** What do you believe about yourself? *(Dig down for unhealthy beliefs that have developed as a result of abuse. For example, what does she think about herself that she would allow this abuse to continue?)*

Q12 What do you believe about the person who is abusing you? *(Listen for rationalizations. "He couldn't help it; he was drunk." These defenses have helped her cope but have also made her less capable of seeing herself as a true victim of abuse.)*

Q13 Have you ever tried to stop the abuse? What happened?

Q14 What would you like to have happen as a result of our meeting today?

Q15 What kinds of boundaries do you think need to be set up to protect you?

Q16 Who else have you told about this?

Q17 How did that person respond?

Q18 Who can help you maintain the boundaries that you set? Who will be your ally?

Q19 Where do you think God has been in all of this?

Q20 What do you need in order to heal from this wound?

## 4 WISE COUNSEL

People who have been abused have had their boundaries violated in a horrible way. Healing from abuse involves **restoration of healthy boundaries and of trust.** The healing process should be gentle and not contribute to an unintentional re-wounding or shaming of the person.

Follow the victim's lead in the telling of his story. Reassure her that the abuse was **not her fault**.

One of the questions often asked by someone who has been sexually abused is "Why me?" Almost always, feelings of **shame and worthlessness** result from sexual abuse.

As a friend, you need to **keep your own anger in check** to provide a safe environment for her to be open and honest.

## 5 ACTION STEPS

### 1. Be Patient

- Healing from sexual abuse is a process and people vary in the amount of time required for their healing.
- It takes courage to seek help for healing, to talk about your experience, and to bring what was once in darkness into the light.

### 2. Grieve Your Loss

- Much has been taken from you, so you are allowed to feel the pain and grieve the loss.
- Allowing yourself to feel the pain will help you regain some of the power you need.

### 3. Regain Control

- Being able to say what happened and having someone believe you is the first step.

- You have permission to stand strong, to say "no," to be empowered over the one who has exerted power over you.

**4. Find Support**

Attending a group for survivors of sexual abuse can be an excellent next step.

*In 8 out of 10 rape cases, the victim knew the perpetrator.*

*- www.cdc.gov*

**5. Establish Boundaries**

- You now need to learn how to take care of yourself and re-establish healthy boundaries. What are some healthy boundaries you need to establish?
- Be sure a few trusted people are aware of your boundaries so they can help you. You may need their help in dealing with the abuser.
- This will take the form of (1) speaking the truth to the abuser, (2) having the support of others in the Christian community, and (3) informed withdrawal from the abuser.
- If the abuser will not honor the boundaries, then other strategies may need to be put in place, such as a restraining order issued by the courts.

**6. Know that You Will Heal**

- You have a bright future. You're not a victim, but a survivor.
- You may have lost a lot, but you are not "ruined" for the future. God can heal you and restore you.

*Based on a review of state records, 86,830 children in the United States experienced sexual abuse in 2001.*

*- www.cdc.gov*

**7. Trust God**

- God didn't abandon you, and He wasn't working against you as this abuse occurred.
- Plan on several more talks to discuss the concept of God's love even in the midst of painful circumstances.

**8. Get Professional Guidance**

- As much as you can help with the spiritual aspect, the person may need some professional guidance in order to truly deal with the depth of pain that sexual abuse causes.
- Refer to a Christian counselor with expertise in this area.

6

## BIBLICAL INSIGHTS

***When Shechem the son of Hamor the Hivite, prince of the country, saw her, he took her and lay with her, and violated her. —Genesis 34:2***

- Shechem first "lay with" Dinah and "violated her," then claimed to love her and to want to marry her.
- A young man may think he is in love, but to force a woman to have sex with him violates and abuses her. That's not love.
- The consequences of abuse, no matter how a person tries to justify it, are far-reaching and destructive.

***But as for you, you meant evil against me; but God meant it for good, in order to bring it about as it is this day, to save many people alive. —Genesis 50:20***

- If anyone had good reason for revenge, it was Joseph. His brothers' jealousy provoked them to horrible abuse—selling him as a common slave to be taken away forever (Genesis 37:11–28). Before being raised to power in Egypt, Joseph had lost thirteen years of personal freedom.
- Joseph wisely understood that God had sovereignly overruled his brothers' abuse, making their evil turn out for good.
- Such a response can only come from those who trust God to rule in their lives.

*The National Women's Study found that 84% of women did not report their rapes to police. - www.cdc.gov*

***Beloved, do not avenge yourselves, but rather give place to wrath; for it is written, "Vengeance is Mine, I will repay," says the Lord . . . Do not be overcome by evil, but overcome evil with good. —Romans 12:19, 21***

- God knows all that has occurred in our lives. He was present in the darkness, and continues to walk with us. The offenses done to us were done to a child He loves.
- He promises to repay. Our task is to heal.
- Don't let the evil overcome you, and don't give the abuser any more power in your life. Overcome the evil by doing good to others and to yourself.

***All the churches shall know that I am He who searches the minds and hearts. And I will give to each one of you according to your works. —Revelation 2:23***

- Sometimes people think they can hide portions of their lives from everyone. They try to hide angry tempers, deep jealousies, or sexual sin.
- In His message to the church in Thyatira, Christ clearly stated that nothing is hidden from Him (Revelation 2:23).
- Your abuse has not escaped His notice. The abuser may have thought he got away with it, but God knows, and God promises to judge appropriately.

## 7 PRAYER STARTER

We are facing an extremely difficult situation here today, Lord, a situation that You know about, but is now just coming into the light for people whom we know and love. Give us wisdom to handle this situation correctly. Bring healing to this child of Yours who has been used so wrongly . . .

## 8 RECOMMENDED RESOURCES

*Caring for Sexually Abused Children: A Handbook for Families & Churches*, by Timothy Kearney

*Counseling Survivors of Sexual Abuse*, by Diane Mandt Langberg

*Helping the Struggling Adolescent*, by Les Parrott III

*Set Free*, by Jan Coates

# Singleness

## 1 PORTRAITS

- Janelle uses online dating services and speed dating experiences, yet rarely finds anyone who interests her and is interested in her.
- Bart was divorced within a year of a disastrous marriage. Now he can't seem to succeed in any relationship.
- Single again after 15 years of marriage, Ana struggles to figure out who she is by herself.
- Ricardo lives with his mother and rarely dates. He is painfully shy and feels that he probably will never marry.

## 2 DEFINITIONS AND KEY THOUGHTS

- Singleness means **being without a spouse**. People can be single because they **never married** or because they have **lost a spouse** through death or divorce.
- Some people remain **single by choice**, while others **have not met anyone** who attracts them and who is attracted to them.
- Since **women have not been encouraged to be the initiators** in romantic relationships, singleness may feel like a problem that is out of their control.
- Those with **mental, emotional, or physical disabilities face particular challenges** in finding a spouse.
- **Widowers often remarry** soon after the wife's death, while **widows often remain single**.
- **Being single and being lonely are two different things**. Many single people would not characterize themselves as lonely at all.
- It is very helpful when churches **make single people feel welcome**. Not every activity should be for families. Smart churches seek to use the gifts of the single people in their congregation.

## 3 ASSESSMENT INTERVIEW

Some churches provide a welcoming atmosphere for singles, while other churches are so family-oriented that singles feel out of place. Either way, singles may come to your for help. If they are seeking aid, then they may be uncomfortable with their singleness.

**Q1** Do you consider being single a problem? What is the reason that you are single, in your opinion?

**Q2** Is your singleness your choice or not?

**Q3** What is your parents' attitude toward those who aren't married?

**Q4** Are family members pressuring you to get married?

**Q5** Have you ever been in a close relationship—something that might have led to marriage? What happened?

**Q6** Describe your support system—friends and family members who are "there for you." Does your support come primarily from other singles or from married people as well?

**Q7** Do you have many opportunities to meet other singles?

**Q8** What does it mean to be a "well-adjusted single"?

**Q9** Do you think you fit that category?

**Q10** Do you have any leisure pursuits, such as sports, hobbies, or volunteer work?

**Q11** What is your first thought when people tell you they want to "set you up" with a friend or acquaintance of theirs?

**Q12** What, if anything, makes marriage preferable to singleness?

**Q13** What advantages do you think married people have?

**Q14** What, if anything, makes singleness preferable to marriage?

**Q15** What advantages do you think single people have?

**Q16** From the following list, choose four words that best describe what singleness means to you, then explain your choices:

- Loneliness
- Independence
- Self-focus
- Freedom
- Poverty
- Spontaneity
- Burden
- Outward focus
- Isolation
- Deprivation
- Wealth
- Inward focus

> *Single people must not let family or friends put undue pressure on them to get married. If they feel like they have to be in a relationship in order to be accepted by others, then they are susceptible to being used and hurt by others, or they will use and hurt others in order to be in a relationship of convenience.*
> —Alan Corry

**Q17** Does our culture view singleness (especially celibate singleness) as a positive or a negative state?

**Q18** Why do you think so many Christian singles made to feel "incomplete"?

**Q19** What does the Bible teach about people who are single?

4

## WISE COUNSEL

Encourage the person to closely **examine his assumption—even prejudices—about singleness.** Investigate the messages that the person received from his family of origin. (Some parents communicated to their children that girls without dates are flawed and boys without girlfriends must be gay. These destructive messages can leave an adult without feelings of self-worth and independence.)

Our culture pictures those who marry as "victors" who have won "conquests" and "prizes." What does that mean for the single person? Help the person (and your congregation) to understand the **unbiblical values exhibited by those who put down singles.**

*In the United States, in 2000, statistics show that the average age of marriage for women was 26, and for men was 29.*
—WWW.UNSTATS.UN.ORG

Paul made it clear that **singleness is a high calling** that allows the single person to **focus more intensely on God.**

The single person needs to **come to terms with being single**—knowing that he is **complete and whole** as an individual in his relationship with Christ.

The longing to be married may be extremely intense. **Single parents** may be particularly needy, as parenting keeps them from pursuing many social engagements. They may also worry—rightly—about the effect of dating relationships on their children.

5

## ACTION STEPS

### 1. Accept Your Singleness

- Live life to its fullest as you seek God's purpose and direction. Accept your singleness as a high calling with the ability, like Paul, to do things for Christ that you might not have the opportunity to do if you were married.
- Seek God in all you do. Never rush to get married.
- Realize that you are a complete and whole person in your relationship with Christ.

### 2. Remain Celibate

- You may be frustrated by your singleness because you are not sexually fulfilled.
- Discuss reasons for remaining celibate (if needed, see the section on Premarital Sex). To be celibate is the spiritual ability to have complete control over your sexual desires. This doesn't necessarily mean you have the *gift* of celibacy—just that you have a biblical mandate to live a chaste life.
- Discuss sexual temptations and drives. Help the person to discover methods for coping with these in positive ways. Remaining chaste involves more than refraining from sexual activity—it also means bringing all sexual desires under submission to God.
- We can allow God to be at the center of our lives to help us handle our fears, desires, hopes, and dreams.

*Chastity is a requisite of Christian singleness. Furthermore, chastity is possible. There will always be somebody to suggest that such thinking is legalistic, unreasonable, and unlikely to succeed. My reply can only be: "When it's bigger than I am, so is God."*

—Rosalie de Rosset

### 3. Get Involved

- Pursue hobbies, sports, or volunteer work so you can meet new people.
- Find a church that has a strong singles program. Lacking that, find a church that provides opportunities for all church members to mix and have fun together. The same activities will encourage fellowship and help singles to get to know new people, including other singles.
- You need a community of friends whom you can trust and with whom you can share activities and interests.
- You need a balance of male and female friends.

### 4. Learn to Love the Quiet

- Instead of resenting times when you are alone, learn to value them. Fill them with meaningful pursuits, such as hobbies, journaling, listening to music, writing, studying for an advanced degree, or calling friends.
- Learn to listen to God in the undistracted quiet.

## 6 BIBLICAL INSIGHTS

***And the Lord God said, "It is not good that man should be alone; I will make him a helper comparable to him." —Genesis 2:18***

- God's provision of a "helper" for Adam was not a condemnation of singleness but an approval of marriage. God was concerned for Adam's loneliness. He created people to have relationships—with Him and with others.
- In one way or another, all of us have potential problems of aloneness, such as isolation, insecurity, and feelings of rejection. Being "unattached" can foster destructive responses, or it can encourage the development of a deeper relationship with God. There's nothing wrong with being single—just don't go it alone!

***Then Miriam the prophetess, the sister of Aaron, took the timbrel in her hand; and all the women went out after her with timbrels and with dances. —Exodus 15:20***

- Miriam, most likely a single woman, played a significant role in the spiritual life of Israel, and she is the first woman to be called a "prophetess."
- Singleness never denotes inferiority—God has special work for all of His people, whether they are single or married.

***Now there was one, Anna, a prophetess, the daughter of Phanuel, of the tribe of Asher. She was of a great age, and had lived with a husband seven years from her virginity; and this woman was a widow of about eighty-four years, who did not depart from the temple, but served God with fastings and prayers night and day. —Luke 2:36-37***

*There is never a place in the Bible where it says that marriage makes you happy. It says over and over again that God makes you happy.*
—Dick Purnell

- Anna was very young when her husband died, and she had been a widow for 84 years. Anna remained single, choosing to give her life to serving God through fasting and prayer.
- People may be single for a number of reasons, and they respond to singleness in different ways. Some single people, like Anna, seek to serve God without concern about marriage, but others long for a spouse.
- It is important to remember that the key to a fulfilled single life is contentment in God. He has places of service for all people—married or single.

***But I say to the unmarried and to the widows: It is good for them if they remain even as I am. —1 Corinthians 7:8***

- Some have understood this passage to mean that all single people should remain that way, but Paul's words must be understood in the cultural context and his mission.

- As a single man, Paul understood the need for people to do whatever it took to share the gospel with unbelievers. He knew that persecution could come at any time, and his words reveal his total commitment to his call.
- He encouraged single people not to apologize for their singleness. God has an important calling for single people, since they can "serve the Lord without distraction" (1 Corinthians 7:35).
- A married person has many responsibilities, while a single person can be freer to work for the gospel. Neither state is better than the other. Different circumstances create different opportunities.
- Singleness can be used for God's glory. Whether a person has never been married or has become single by way of divorce or bereavement, single people are not set aside by God. He has great things for single people to accomplish for His kingdom.

> *In the United States, in 2005, there are 103 women for every 100 men.*
> —WWW.UNSTATS.UN.ORG

## PRAYER STARTER 7

Dear Lord, my friend is feeling uncomfortable with being single. Please reveal to him Your special purpose for his life as a single person. Encourage him, and bring friends and family around him who can help him appreciate his singleness. Give him the wisdom to see his opportunities for service and enable him to serve You with joy . . .

## RECOMMENDED RESOURCES 8

*1st Class Single*, by Cheryl Martin

*I Kissed Dating Goodbye*, by Joshua Harris

*Sassy, Single, and Satisfied: Secrets to Loving the Life You're Living*, by Michelle McKinney Hammond

*The Sexual Man*, by Archibald D. Hart

*Your Single Treasure: The Good News About Single Sexuality*, by Rick Stedman

# Spiritual Warfare

## 1 PORTRAITS

- Nothing's ever easy for Jenny. No matter what she does, it ends in heartache and failure. She's beginning to think that she shouldn't try anything. Her mind is plagued with thoughts that she's always been a failure, and she always will be.
- Jim's spiritual life began with many marks of God's favor. He soon became a leader in the church, but in the past year, old temptations to look at pornography have come back—and they're stronger than ever! "I thought I was past all that," he complained.
- Pastor Scott's first year in the ministry was harder than he ever imagined. He had to combat one obstacle after another. Now he's added depression to his list of barriers.

## 2 DEFINITIONS AND KEY THOUGHTS

- Spiritual warfare can conjure up all sorts of images of demonic possession and exorcisms. Other images might include people speaking in an unknown voice, having convulsions, or not having control of their own actions. For the purposes of this guide, **the definition is broader and simpler** than those images may imply. It often involves temptation, accusation, and confusion, and in limited cases, oppression and demonization.
- **Spiritual warfare, is a struggle between light and darkness.** God has secured the victory, but Satan still attempts to wage war against God and His people. *Light* is sourced in God and infuses all that is good, but *darkness* is sourced in Satan and permeates all that is evil.

  Some passages about light and darkenss are:

  **Psalm 18:28**—"For You will light my lamp; the Lord my God will enlighten my darkness."

  **Isaiah 9:2**—"The people who walked in darkness have seen a great light."

  **John 1:5**—"The light shines in the darkness, and the darkness did not comprehend it."

  **John 3:19**—"This is the condemnation, that the light has come into the world, and men loved darkness rather than light, because their deeds were evil."

> *You are but a poor soldier of Christ if you think you can overcome without fighting and suppose you can have the crown without the conflict.*
>
> —St. John Chrysostom

**John 8:12**—"I am the light of the world. He who follows Me shall not walk in darkness, but have the light of life."

**John 12:46**—"I have come as a light into the world, that whoever believes in Me should not abide in darkness."

**Acts 26:18**— ". . . to open their eyes, in order to turn them from darkness to light, and from the power of Satan to God, that they may receive forgiveness of sins and an inheritance among those who are sanctified by faith in Me."

**2 Corinthians 4:6**—"For it is the God who commanded light to shine out of darkness, who has shone in our hearts to *give* the light of the knowledge of the glory of God in the face of Jesus Christ."

**2 Corinthians 6:14**—"Do not be unequally yoked together with unbelievers. For what fellowship has righteousness with lawlessness? And what communion has light with darkness?"

**Ephesians 5:11**—"Have no fellowship with the unfruitful works of darkness, but rather expose them."

**Colossians 1:13**—"He has delivered us from the power of darkness and conveyed us into the kingdom of the Son of His love."

- All believers face spiritual warfare. If you belong to Jesus than you will engage in a war against the darkness. Sometimes it is very **clear and evident**, but at other times it is more **subtle and elusive.** Regardless of our awareness, we all engage in the battle.
- The victory is in direct proportion to our willingness to surrender to Jesus Christ. We don't win by our own strength or by our own intelligence or strategies. **We win by submitting to Jesus and resting in His authority over Satan.**
- Romans 6:16 says, "Do you not know that to whom you present yourselves slaves to obey, you are that one's slaves whom you obey, whether of sin leading to death, or of obedience leading to righteousness?" We all submit to something. Submitting to darkness leads to death, but submitting to the Lord leads to righteousness.
- Putting on the full armor of God is key in battling against evil.

**Ephesians 6:11-16**—"Put on the whole armor of God, that you may be able to stand against the wiles of the devil. For we do not wrestle against flesh and blood, but against principalities, against powers, against the rulers of the darkness of this age, against spiritual hosts of wickedness in the heavenly places. Therefore take up the whole armor of God, that you may be able to withstand in the evil day, and having done all, to stand. Stand therefore, having girded your waist with truth, having put on the breastplate of

*In heaven we shall appear, not in armor, but in robes of glory. But here these are to be worn night and day; we must walk, work, and sleep in them, or else we are not true soldiers of Christ.*

—William Gurnall

righteousness, and having shod your feet with the preparation of the gospel of peace; above all, taking the shield of faith with which you will be able to quench all the fiery darts of the wicked one. And take the helmet of salvation, and the sword of the Spirit, which is the word of God."

- We don't have **a magical formula** that defeats the enemy when recited like a mantra. Paul's description of armor is a biblical truth conveyed in a word picture. For example, putting on the belt of truth simply means that we are to know and to adhere to the truth as spelled out for us in God's Word.
- Don't **overemphasize** demonic influences, but at the same time, don't **underemphasize** the fact that we do have an enemy who leads an army of demons. Their job description is to steal, kill, and destroy (John 10:10).
- The enemy wants to harm us, but God promises to protect us. When we step **outside of God's will,** we open up the door for the enemy to sow seeds of destruction. This doesn't mean that all struggles involve demons, but consistently opening ourselves to evil can make us vulnerable to temptations. Discernment becomes important when determining demonic involvement in a person's life.
- Sometimes spiritual warfare occurs because a person is right **in the middle of God's will.** Bible giants such as Daniel, David, Paul, and even Jesus himself, fought against the schemes of the devil.

## 3 ASSESSMENT INTERVIEW

People don't often come in for counseling complaining about the struggles of spiritual warfare. We need **discernment** to be able to ascertain when and why people are engaging in spiritual warfare.

*The Christian life is not a playground; it is a battleground.* —Warren W. Wiersbe

We should look for:

**doors that were opened** or places in the person's life that were repeatedly exposed to sin. (For example, pornography opens the door for sexual problems and dissatisfaction, which, if left untreated, can lead to sexual addiction.) The person has stepped outside of God's will and needs to repent.

**projects, people, or victories** in the person's life that could shed light on why Satan is after him. The person may be in God's will and needs to put on all the armor, stay strong, and continue to resist the devil.

**Q1** Tell me what brings you here today.

**Q2** When did you first begin to experience these problems?

**Q3** Can you tell me about your life when these problems first began?

**Q4** What was your relationship with the Lord like during that time period?

**Q5** Was anything happening in your life that brought conviction from the Lord?

**Q6** Is there anything in your life that has an addictive element in it? If so, explain.

**Q7** Do you ever feel like you do things that you shouldn't?

**Q8** Are there thoughts that seem to plague you?

**Q9** What temptations have you faced recently?

**Q10** Is there anything that you don't feel like you have control over?

**Q11** What solutions have you tried?

## 4 WISE COUNSEL

"Therefore submit to God. **Resist the devil** and he will flee from you" (James 4:7). **This is the promise** that we can lean on.

Temptation can wear people down over time. Too often, people don't resist long enough. Meditate on this promise and resist until you experience God's strength. Replace the tempting thoughts with healthy, God-honoring ones.

## 5 ACTION STEPS

Dean Sherman writes in his book, *Spiritual Warfare*, that there are three battlefields that need to be fortified against an attack. Theses battlefields are the mind, the heart, and the mouth.

If the person fortifies his life in these three areas, he will be waging war from a point of strength, and he will be closing any of those "open doors" that began the battle in the first place. The enemy will not have a way into his life, and therefore, will not be able to influence him. God will have free access.

### 1. Confess Any Known Sin

- The only way to get free from Satan's grip is to know where he's holding on.
- Honestly determine the source, then confess and willingly give up your sin.

### 2. Fortify Your Mind

- Take every thought captive to Christ (2 Corinthians 10:5).
- Think about pure, noble, and godly things (Philippians 4:8).
- A person can't think of two things simultaneously, so he can combat impure thoughts by purposely thinking pure thoughts.

## 2. Purify Your Heart

- When the Bible uses the word "heart," it refers to our thoughts, emotions and attitudes.
- Be on guard against any bitterness (Hebrews 12:15). Too often, people open up the door to bitterness because they have been treated unfairly and think they have a right to retaliate. Let God take vengeance for you (Romans 12:19).
- If you hold onto it, the bitter root will blossom into pain for you. Remember that your emotions should be filtered through God's Word. If you aren't careful, unchecked emotions may lead to sin (James 1:14-27).

*Spiritual warfare is part of every Christian's daily life. We triumph as we walk by faith in Christ, who turns us from darkness to light, from the power of Satan to God, forgiving sin, and giving us a place among those who are sanctified by faith.*
—David Powlison

## 3. Guard Your Mouth

- Proverbs 18:21 says that death and life are in the power of the tongue. The tongue is small, but can do great damage (James 3:2-12).
- Be careful to speak true and God-honoring things.

If resisting the devil is needed because of victories in the faith—big projects that Satan wants to hinder, ministries Satan doesn't want to happen, etc.—encourage the person to daily dress himself in the whole armor of God:

## 1. Pray for Insight

- Be sensitive to God's leading if indeed there is sin in your life. Never assume there isn't!
- Be sensitive to what might be happening in the spiritual realm regarding the situation. Ask God for discernment.

## 2. Get Dressed!

- Gird your waist with truth—the belt was the foundation for the Roman soldier's armor. The truth of the gospel is the foundation of the Christian life, the standard by which we measure everything else. When Satan speaks lies, counterhis lies with the truth from God's Word.
- Put on the breastplate of righteousness—the breastplate protected a soldier's vital organs, covering his body from neck to thighs. The righteousness you put on is not your own, but Christ's, bought for you by His precious blood. You are God's child, so when Satan attacks with doubts and strikes at the vital parts of your faith and life, counter with the righteousness you have because of Jesus. You are protected because you are His child.

- Put on shoes of the preparation of the gospel of peace—you have peace with God because of what Christ has done, and peace to carry you through life because of Christ's promise: "Peace I leave with you, My peace I give to you; not as the world gives do I give to you. Let not your heart be troubled, neither let it be afraid" (John 14:27). When Satan wants to make you worry or keep you up at night, remember your shoes of peace.
- Take the shield of faith—a soldier's shield protected him in hand-to-hand combat and against "fiery darts" being shot from a city's walls. Your faith is your total dependence on God. When you hold your shield of faith, you can block his attacks.
- Take the helmet of salvation—every soldier protects his head. You were saved when you trusted Christ as Savior. The helmet of salvation can protect your mind from the doubts that creep in. When you know beyond a doubt that you are saved, Satan's accusations can be cast aside.
- Take the sword of the Spirit, which is the Word of God—your offensive weapon is your knowledge of God's Word. With it, you will be prepared to answer all of Satan's attacks.

*The devil does not sleep, nor is the flesh yet dead; therefore, you must never cease your preparation for battle, because on the right and on the left are enemies who never rest.*
—Thomas a Kempis

## BIBLICAL INSIGHTS

6

***How you are fallen from heaven, O Lucifer, son of the morning! . . . For you have said in your heart: "I will ascend into heaven, I will exalt my throne above the stars of God" . . . Yet you shall be brought down to Sheol, to the lowest depths of the Pit. —Isaiah 14:12–15***

- Although Isaiah's message was directed against the king of Babylon, many believe this imagery parallels the fall of Satan. The Evil One may have power on earth for a brief time, but God's judgment upon him has already been determined.
- As we fight battles against evil, we remember that the war has already been won.

***And He said to them, "I saw Satan fall like lightning from heaven. Behold, I give you the authority to trample on serpents and scorpions, and over all the power of the enemy, and nothing shall by any means hurt you." —Luke 10:18-19***

- All believers face the constant struggle between good and evil as Satan tries to rule our lives.
- Jesus has already defeated Satan and has won this battle through His death and resurrection. Even though the battle continues, we can be assured that, with Jesus' help, the important victory—eternal life—is already ours.

***For we do not wrestle against flesh and blood, but against principalities, against powers, against the rulers of the darkness of this age, against spiritual hosts of wickedness in the heavenly places. —Ephesians 6:12***

- The spiritual realm has two sides—God's side and Satan's side. Those who have accepted Christ as Savior are on God's side, which automatically makes them enemies of Satan.
- Our battle is against forces that are real, powerful, and should not be underestimated. Their goal is to make believers ineffective for God's kingdom and to keep unbelievers away from God.
- The battle rages constantly, usually beyond our earthly vision. At times, however, we see it clearly when we face temptation, difficulty, and trials.
- Satan knows where to attack. Our strength for the battle is in God.

*No soldiers of Christ are ever lost, missing, or left dead on the battlefield.*
—John Charles Ryle

***Be sober, be vigilant; because your adversary the devil walks about like a roaring lion, seeking whom he may devour. —1 Peter 5:8***

- The moment a person becomes a Christian, Satan tries to make him ineffective through sin or through struggles with discouragement or suffering. Believers need to be sober and vigilant, resisting Satan by remaining "steadfast in the faith."
- Satan is a defeated enemy, so believers need not fear him. When we resist Satan, he will flee (James 4:7).
- We resist Satan through maintaining our steadfast faith in Christ, wearing the armor that God provides, and remembering that we are not alone in our suffering.

7

## PRAYER STARTER

Lord, we pray about the spiritual battle being faced today. The enemy wants to defeat our friend today, and we want to claim the promises that You make in Your Word of victory over Satan and all of his schemes . . .

## RECOMMENDED RESOURCES

*Reclaiming Spiritual Warfare*, American Association of Christian Counselors Courageous Counsel Tapes Series, by David Powlison

*Spiritual Renewal in Counseling*, American Association of Christian Counselors Courageous Living Counsel Tapes Series, by Steven Arterburn

*Spiritual Warfare for Every Christian*, by Dean Sherman

# Stress

## 1 PORTRAITS

40% of workers report that their jobs are "very or extremely stressful".[1]

- John sat on the side of the hospital bed and buttoned his shirt. Yesterday he was sure he was having a heart attack. His chest was tight, and he struggled to breathe. But today, after many tests, his doctor told him that his heart was fine. Nothing was physically wrong. "I think you're under a lot of stress," his doctor told him. He recommended seeing a counselor.
- Kailey has been through a lot lately. Her husband lost his job and the bill collectors are beginning to call. In addition, her mom has been sick, her kids have been having difficulty in school, and the water heater just died. Kailey doesn't think she can handle one more crisis. She feels exhausted all the time.
- Micah is trying to be a good student, but lately things have been tough. His mom and dad are getting a divorce, his grades are slipping, he lost his place on the basketball team for missing too many practices, and he has finals next week. Micah feels completely overwhelmed. He's having intense headaches every day.

## 2 DEFINITIONS AND KEY THOUGHTS

26% of workers report that they are "often or very often" burned out or stressed by their work.[2]

- Stress is a normal part of life and **can be positive**, alerting us to a problem or area needing attention and helping us to respond to it. This kind of stress stimulates creativity and productivity.
- Stress can also **be negative** when a person experiences pressure without relief or relaxation between challenges.
- Sometimes stress comes from a **difficult life situation**, but sometimes stress results from **perceptions about life situations**, such as worries about failure and perfectionistic tendencies.
- Stress without relief can lead to **physical symptoms** such as headaches, upset stomach, elevated blood pressure, chest pain, and problems sleeping.
- Some personalities more easily **cause stress** in themselves and in others. Some people may have extremely driven or perfectionistic personalities. Some live or work with a person who is driven, feeling the stress of the other person's drivenness.
- Stress can be harmful if it adversely **affects a person's relationships**.

- Stress can **affect the body, mind, and spirit.**
- Finances, children, in-laws, and sex are often causes of stress in couples' relationships.
- If we don't learn to control stress, it will eventually **control us.**
- We need not be overwhelmed by stress. Philippians 4:7 says, "The peace of God, which surpasses all understanding, will guard your hearts and minds through Christ Jesus."

## 3 ASSESSMENT INTERVIEW

Stress is a common corollary to many other problems addressed in this guide. In fact, any unresolved problem creates additional pressure in a person's life. If you discover another presenting problem, ask the questions in that section of the guide.

**Q1** What brings you here today?

**Q2** What would you say are the stressors in your life right now?

**Q3** Is someone in your life causing you stress (for example, a stressful spouse or boss)?

**Q4** Are you causing your own stress by being a perfectionist or trying to control situations over which you have no control?

**Q5** What percentage of your stress is being caused by each of these stressors?

**Q6** How long has each of those stressors been present?

**Q7** Tell me about each stressor. *(Get as many details as you can so you can begin to assess how the person views these stressors.)*

**Q8** How realistic is the possibility of the things you're worried about? *(For example, if the person is experiencing persistent fears of job loss, is this fear based in current reality?)*

**Q9** With whom do you talk about your stressors? *(The impact of stress is greater if an individual feels he is alone in handling it.)*

**Q10** Are those people helpful to you?

**Q11** Are you using other types of things to handle the stress? *(Sports? Drugs—either OTC or prescription? Alcohol? Excessive television or computer use?)*

**Q12** Where do you experience the least stress in your life?

**Q13** Is there any place where you do *not* experience stress?

**Q14** Is change possible? Is there any way that you can perceive to reduce your stress level?

> *Do not anticipate trouble, or worry about what may never happen. Keep in the sunlight.*
> —Benjamin Franklin

> *Health care expenditures are almost 50% higher for people who report having high levels of stress.*[3]

**Q15** What has helped?

**Q16** If not, what are some healthy ways you can think of to handle the stress you're currently under?

4

## WISE COUNSEL

If the person is experiencing physical effects of the stress and hasn't seen a physician, encourage him to **schedule a physical**.

*75–90% of all doctor's office visits are for stress related ailments and complaints.*

Are there **immediate situational stressors** that need attention, such as resolving a situation in the workplace or finding help needed for a problem with a child?

Assess ways to **provide a break** from the stress. Suggest:

Exercise

Take frequent breaks throughout the day

Pray and meditate on a Bible verse

Share your burdens with a trusted friend

Take a vacation, even short breaks for a day or two can help

Because stress affects the mind, body, and spirit, the person needs to protect all three:

To protect one's mind—think truthfully, refuse to make mountains out of molehills, and set priorities.

To protect one's body—get enough sleep, eat well, and breathe deeply.

To protect one's spirit—meditate on God and His Word, learn to trust God, and pray without ceasing.

5

## ACTION STEPS

### 1. Gain Perspective

- Gain some perspective on what is causing the stress.
- "Break apart" the stress overload into manageable pieces.
- Prioritize and begin to address each component.

### 2. Consider What God Is Doing

- One of the best antidotes to stress is seeing God's purposes in the difficulties.

- God may use certain situations to develop one of the fruits of the Spirit in you. Knowing that God uses every situation - even the petty, irritating situations of life - to teach you to become more like Jesus can help you to feel less stressed by things you can't control.

### 3. Get Alone with God

- Planned times of quiet and solitude are a good balance to a busy life. Cultivating a heart of prayer helps you see God's perspective and to more fully experience His presence throughout the day (Psalm 16:8 11).
- Many people expect prayer to change a stressful situation. Although this may happen, prayer often doesn't change the situation as much as it changes you.
- As you purposely quiet your heart each day, the Holy Spirit has a chance to change the way you see your stressful situation.

> *Stress not only dampens our spirits and frazzles our nerves, but the constant rush of adrenaline overstimulates the heart and can weaken the immune system, leaving us prone to more illnesses and stress-related problems.*
> —Leslie Vernick

### 4. Share Your Burden with Others

- Talking about your stressors can bring relief and prayer support.
- Perhaps some of the stress is because you're doing too much. Even Moses had to delegate when he got overwhelmed (Exodus 18:13-23). Maybe you can do the same.

### 5. Guard Your Heart

- Stress has a way of focusing our attention on the things that are wrong in our lives.
- Guard your heart and mind against negativity and pessimism. Take time each day to check your thinking and take every thought captive to the obedience of Christ (2 Corinthians 10:5).

> *When you're laughing, your attention is focused. You can't do anything else. Everything else, whether it's depressions or stress, stops.*
> —Robert Leone

### 6. Live Intentionally

- Stop majoring in minor things. At the end of life, many of us will realize that we spent most of our time on what mattered least, and the least time on what mattered most.
- Decide what is really important, choose your priorities, and live for them. Become more intentional about the way you spend your time and energy. Learn to say "no" to things that aren't as important.

### 7. Remember Your Limits

- Often, our lives become filled with stress because we refuse to accept our limits. We think we should be able to do it all!
- Feeling overwhelmed may be a reminder that you are not living within the limits and boundaries that God has created for you. It may be time to reevaluate, cut back, say no, or slow down.

### 8. Laugh a Little

Allow for some levity in your life: a comic strip, a favorite saying, a great story, or a joke. Find time to enjoy friends.

## 6 BIBLICAL INSIGHTS

***You will keep him in perfect peace, whose mind is stayed on You, because he trusts in You. —Isaiah 26:3***

- Jesus reminded His followers that "in the world you will have tribulation" (John 16:33). The prophet Isaiah wrote that God gives peace in spite of conflict and turmoil.
- Peace is basic to God's nature part of His name. God the Father is the "God of peace" (Philippians 4:9; Hebrews 13:20), and God the Son is "the Prince of Peace" (Isaiah 9:6).
- The Holy Spirit produces peace in our lives (Galatians 5:22). To have "perfect peace," wrote Isaiah, we need to focus our minds on God and trust in Him.

*Many of us crucify ourselves between two thieves—regret for the past and fear of the future.*
—Unknown

***Let not your heart be troubled; you believe in God, believe also in Me. —John 14:1***

- Jesus' words reassured the disciples who were bewildered and discouraged. Jesus had said He was going away, that He would die, that one of the disciples was a traitor, and that Peter would deny Him.
- "Let not your heart be troubled," Jesus told them. Believers can rest their troubled hearts, knowing that Jesus is in control regardless of the circumstances.

***Persecuted, but not forsaken; struck down, but not destroyed . . . —2 Corinthians 4:9***

- For us, each day is filled with different levels of stress. Regardless of occupation, age, social status, or lifestyle, we all experience stress.
- We bring some stress on ourselves—from poor planning, saying "yes" too often, or being disorganized. Hopefully, we learn our lesson so it won't happen again.
- Stress also arises from factors outside our control—the weather, a crashed computer, or an unexpected difficulty or sorrow. At those times, we can

control only our reactions to the stress. Our reactions reveal our character and our trust in God.

***Be anxious for nothing, but in everything by prayer and supplication, with thanksgiving, let your requests be made known to God; and the peace of God, which surpasses all understanding, will guard your hearts and minds through Christ Jesus. —Philippians 4:6-7***

- Stress and its companion, worry, do their best to immobilize believers. People are often anxious about the future—they are anxious about events that *haven't* happened but *could* happen.
- So what can believers do about their stresses? When we trust God with our stress, He replaces it with His peace that "surpasses all understanding."
- When we feel stress rising, we can turn to God in prayer. He will give us the peace He promised.

***My brethren, count it all joy when you fall into various trials, knowing that the testing of your faith produces patience. —James 1:2-3***

- Everyone faces trials in one form or another. We can't control what we will encounter, but we can control the stress level that situations cause. Instead of being stressed, we can remember to trust God's sovereignty and give thanks..
- The Holy Spirit will help us learn the lessons God teaches and the wisdom He provides. There's no better prescription for dealing with stress.

*Stress is linked to six of the leading causes of death: heart disease, cancer, lung ailments, accidents, cirrhosis of the liver, and suicide.*

## 7 PRAYER STARTER

Thank You, Lord, that my friend has come today for help in relieving this burden of stress. You never intended for Your children to live overwhelmed and unhealthy lives by carrying undue amounts of stress all by themselves. Give us wisdom to handle what we can, Lord, and we ask Your hand in the situations that are beyond our control . . .

## 8 RECOMMENDED RESOURCES

*Adrenaline and Stress: The Exciting New Breakthrough that Helps You Overcome Stress Damage*, by Archibald D. Hart

*Making the Best of Stress: How Life's Hassles Can Form the Fruit of the Spirit*, by Mark R. McMinn

*Stress and the Woman's Body*, by W. David Hager and Linda Carruth Hager

# Suffering

> *Never judge God by suffering, but judge suffering by the Cross.*
> —Father Andrew

## 1 PORTRAITS

- Janet bit the inside of her cheek to fight back tears. Her friend chatted blithely about their family going on a trip next week, but Janet nodded woodenly and smiled. Inside, she was in pain. No one could understand what it was like for her to continue to live in the marriage that she had committed to ten years ago. The day-to-day pain of trying to love and respect her husband when he didn't return her love was very difficult.
- Bob just couldn't get through the pain. The death of his eldest son in a car accident had caused a hole in his heart that no one could fill. He couldn't even relate to his other children or his wife because the pain was so fresh every morning and the suffering so intense. If only their last conversation hadn't been an argument . . .
- Mark and Jill lost everything in the recent floods on the Mississippi River. Their house was destroyed, and few of the objects inside were even salvageable. They have the clothes on their backs, a photo album, and two cots at the local Salvation Army.

## 2 DEFINITIONS AND KEY THOUGHTS

- Suffering occurs for **many reasons**:

  Suffering may be a result of **personal sin and failure**. For example, some people may suffer financially by being wasteful or not carefully budgeting their money. Some people may suffer the loss of friendship through their hurtful words or gossip.

  Suffering may also happen due to **other people's sin and failure**, such as the drunk driver who causes an accident.

  Suffering can also occur from **forces outside of our control.** For example, a tornado can devastate a family.

  Suffering can come as a **result of a person's faith**—standing for Jesus in some parts of the world is an invitation to persecution.

- The Bible contains many passages that describe suffering as a part of life:

  Deserved suffering occurs when we sin or act foolishly—1 Peter 4:15

Undeserved suffering is part of following in Jesus' footsteps—1 Peter 2:21

Suffering can be for growth—2 Corinthians 12:9-10

Suffering can be for testing and God's glory—John 9:1-3

Suffering can help us be able to help others—2 Corinthians 1:3-5

- Helping others in pain requires a **"theology" of suffering**. How do you see God using suffering in people's lives? How do you see God using suffering in your own life?
- Suffering is common to all people and isn't magically removed by the presence of the Holy Spirit. Being a Christian is not a "get out of suffering free" card. **Christians experience suffering** like everyone else.
- Sometimes **God sends suffering** into our lives and we don't know why. His promise to us is not to make our suffering understandable but to be present with us in it.
- Needless suffering, such as pain we experience when we refuse to take medication, is not taught in Scripture. There is **no merit to simply enduring pain for suffering's sake.**
- Suffering is easier to endure when it is **purposeful** (2 Timothy 4:6) and when there is an **end in sight**. Romans 8:22-23 says, "For we know that the whole creation groans and labors with birth pangs together until now. Not only that, but we also who have the firstfruits of the Spirit, even we ourselves groan within ourselves, eagerly waiting for the adoption, the redemption of our body."
- Suffering **produces character** in us. Our culture views suffering as evidence that we are failing in some way or that we are doing something wrong, but God uses it to produce strength, faith, and hope.
- When you talk to someone who is suffering, guard against wanting to "fix things" or give answers too quickly. It is much more important to **listen.**

*I consider that the sufferings of this present time are not worthy to be compared with the glory which shall be revealed in us.*
—Romans 8:18

## 3 ASSESSMENT INTERVIEW

### Rule Outs

**Q1** Are you suffering physically? Is there pain that needs to be handled? *(If the person is suffering physically, be sure that he has gotten adequate medical treatment, and if he hasn't, encourage him to do so.)*

**Q2** On a scale of 1 to 10, with 1 being "feeling terrific" and 10 being "feeling suicidal," where would you place yourself on most days? *(If you sense that the person is suicidal, deal with that issue first. See the section on Suicide and get outside help.)*

> *A Christian is someone who shares the sufferings of God in the world.*
> — Dietrich Bonhoeffer

### General Questions

**Q3** Tell me what is going on in your life right now. *(When someone is in pain, don't move too quickly to answers, but understand his situation and empathize with him in it.)*

**Q4** How can I be of the most help to you?

**Q5** How do you understand your situation?

**Q6** How long have you been facing this pain?

**Q7** Can you give it a definite starting point (a certain event) or is it more vague?

**Q8** Who is walking with you through the pain?

**Q9** What is your support system?

**Q10** With whom are you the most honest?

**Q11** How is this suffering affecting the other parts of your life?

**Q12** Do you see an end to the suffering, or of the intensity you're currently experiencing?

**Q13** How is your relationship with God right now?

**Q14** Do you see God's hand at work in any way in your suffering?

## 4 WISE COUNSEL

God promises that "a bruised reed He will not break" (Isaiah 42:3). As a friend, model your caring after **His loving care.**

If the person is suffering for the **consequences of his own sin,** he may also be dealing with guilt and shame. Help him confess sin, assess the lessons learned, and come up with an action plan to move forward.

If the person's suffering is because **of someone else's sin or failure**, listen to the story and gently guide the person to ways that he can walk through the pain and grieve the hurt and loss.

If the person's suffering is due to **circumstances beyond his control** (an illness or an "act of God" such as a fire or tornado), assess steps to take that will help him handle the situation. Taken in one big chunk, the situation is often too big to handle. But one step at a time, he can get through it.

Remind the person that suffering can do three things in his life:

Despite the pain, suffering can be very valuable. Suffering **clarifies what the heart truly worships**, especially when the pain is unexplained and unabated. Does he worship the hope of deliverance, or the Deliverer?

Suffering also **purifies the heart** by deepening our desire for the day when all tears will be wiped away. His growing discontent with the sin and evil in this world increases his hope for heaven.

Suffering not only clarifies and purifies, but it also **motivates the heart to action**. If we see a child cry, we offer tenderness. If we see the wounds of a victim, we offer solace. Human suffering arouses anger, invigorates action and, as a result, enables us to push back some of the darkness of the Fall. Suffering humanizes the heart and increases our hunger for God.

Offer **comfort** and **encouragement** and **name any strengths** that you see in the one who is suffering. Silently **pray for the discernment** to understand what God is doing in this person's life.

## 5 ACTION STEPS

### 1. Trust God

- Sometimes God allows suffering to come into believers' lives in order to strengthen their faith, or in the lives of unbelievers to show them their need for God.
- Rejoice because of what God will do in your life and what He promises for your future.
- Cast your cares on Christ (Psalm 55:22; 1 Peter 5:7).
- Strengthen your faith (1 Peter 4:12-13; 2 Timothy 2:11-13; Romans 8:18; 2 Corinthians 4:7-10).

### 2. Seek His Lessons

- What do you think God is teaching you in this situation?
- What would you like to learn? How would you like to come out of it at the other end?

### 3. Seek His Actions

- What could God possibly be doing in your situation? Where do you see His hand at work?
- Which of the lessons (how suffering clarifies, purifies, and motivates the heart) do you think God is teaching you right now?

### 4. Take Small Steps Forward

- What small step can you take today to move through the pain?
- What do you need to do in order to function effectively at home, at work, etc.?

> *Suffering doesn't happen just to people. The Bible teaches that creation itself is suffering until a day when it will be redeemed. God Himself suffers, and looks forward to the day when He will bring His people to be with Him.*
> —Dan Allender

- What small step can you take today to begin the process of rebuilding your life?

**5. Get Support**

- Join a small group to help walk you through the pain, follow up with you, and help you take some of the action steps that are needed.
- In addition, find a support group of people who have faced similar pain. They will have advice that has been tested "in the trenches."

## 6 BIBLICAL INSIGHTS

***Then Job arose, tore his robe, and shaved his head; and he fell to the ground and worshiped. And he said: "Naked I came from my mother's womb, and naked shall I return there. The Lord gave, and the Lord has taken away; blessed be the name of the Lord." —Job 1:20-21***

- God never explained Job's suffering or help him make sense of his loss. Instead, God underlined the reality of His sovereignty and the fact that He acts on His own without human advice or explanation. He expects people to trust Him and His goodness regardless of what happens.
- Although Job's health and wealth were eventually restored, that's not the central message of the story. The Book of Job shows us that our love for God should not be conditioned upon how we think He is treating us. Suffering well is an indication of unshakable trust in God.
- We need to trust in God through times of trial as well as times of blessing. This faith reflects the redeeming power of Christ and His unconditional love toward us.
- No matter what we face in life, we can trust that God is in control. We can rely on Him and His goodness.

*One sees great things from the valley; only small things from the peak.*
—G. K. Chesterton

***Now when Job's three friends heard of all this adversity that had come upon him, each one came from his own place. —Job 2:11***

- Job's friends attempted to help him with their advice. If they had listened more and talked less, they would have been more helpful. They were convinced that Job was being disciplined by God for his sins. They were sincere, but wrong.
- We should be very careful about making assumptions regarding others' circumstances. Things are not always what they seem. It's more helpful to empathize with a suffering friend than to try and rush in to explain his or her suffering.

***For You, O God, have tested us; You have refined us as silver is refined. —Psalm 66:10***

- Silver ore must be refined by fire in order to remove its impurities. Every time the silver is heated and the dross is removed, the metal becomes more and more purified.
- In like manner, the fire of trials purges sin, burning away the lusts and impurities that pollute people's lives. Although unpleasant, suffering often removes the impurities from our lives and helps us grow. God refines us "as silver is refined" so that we can reflect His glory.

> *We could never learn to be brave and patient, if there were only joy in the world.*
> —Helen Keller

***Beloved, do not think it strange concerning the fiery trial which is to try you, as though some strange thing happened to you; but rejoice to the extent that you partake of Christ's sufferings, that when His glory is revealed, you may also be glad with exceeding joy . . . Therefore let those who suffer according to the will of God commit their souls to Him in doing good, as to a faithful Creator. —1 Peter 4:12-13, 19***

- Nothing happens to believers that surprises God. He may allow suffering for a time, knowing that it will strengthen His people's faith.
- Suffering provides the opportunity to trust God.
- We can commit our lives to Him, knowing that He is completely faithful and trustworthy. He will remain with us through our suffering, and in the end bring us to glory.

## 7 PRAYER STARTER

Lord, my friend has come in today feeling overwhelmed with suffering. The pain is intense and is affecting his daily life. He needs Your presence in a powerful and personal way today. Put Your arms around him, and be a God of comfort and encouragement. Give us wisdom, Father, as we seek the best path forward. Our hope is in You, Lord, and the knowledge that You are always with us and always at work in our lives . . .

## 8 RECOMMENDED RESOURCES

*Broken-Children, Grown-Up Pain: Understanding the Effects of Your Wounded Past*, by Paul Hegstrom

*Man's Search for Meaning*, by Victor Frankl

*The Thorn in the Flesh: Hope for All Who Struggle with Impossible Conditions*, by R. T. Kendall

# Suicide

*The problem is not that such despairing people want to die; it is that they do not know how to live.*
—Gary P. Stewart

## 1 PORTRAITS

- Ida had diabetes and was facing amputation of her foot. The day before surgery, she wrote notes to her grandkids and overdosed on her pain medications.
- Aaron had been unable to work due to complications from the hazardous chemicals he used at his job. He was now running out of money. He'd been turned down for Medicaid, Medicare, and disability payments, despite his chronic illness. He didn't want to be a burden to his family, so the month that he ran out of money, he gave away his valuables and cleaned up his apartment. He found a home for his cat and put a gun to his head.
- Victor drove off a bridge the night before his graduation from college. Afterward his parents found out that he had been failing all his classes—because he wasn't attending them—and he had been told that he wouldn't be allowed to graduate.
- Raysha got drunk at a high school party and made a fool of herself. Humiliated, she left the party, obsessed with all the other stupid things she'd done lately. When she came to the railroad tracks, she decided to wait for a train.

## 2 DEFINITIONS AND KEY THOUGHTS

- Suicide is the tragic and lethal culmination of a psychological process that results from **unresolved stresses** that create **depression and hopelessness**.
- Someone who is considering suicide **can't see any hope** that the future will be different than the painful past or present.
- The risk of suicide is **greatest within the first year after a failed attempt**.
- **Males tend to use more violent means** for suicide (guns, cars) and are **more often successful** than women.
- **Females** attempt suicide **more often than men** but are **less often successful** at the attempt because they use **less lethal means** (pills, cutting).
- **Suicide and substance abuse** often go hand in hand. Substances are involved in 20–50 percent of suicides.
- Ironically, people are more at risk of suicide **after depression starts to abate**. A person who was inert with depression may become decisive with new energy—enough energy to commit suicide.

- Those who have **recently begun antidepressants** may be more at risk because their energy level may rise before their mood improves.
- Suicidal individuals suffer from **tunnel vision**. They don't see any option except death. To them, suicide is a "logical" thing to do. That's why suicidal people sometimes take the lives of others as they kill themselves—they are *not* seeing the big picture.
- Always **take seriously the threat** of suicide.

## ASSESSMENT INTERVIEW

3

If you think that the person you are interviewing is suicidal, **don't panic**. Stay calm and know that by coming to you, he has already taken a step away from the decision to harm himself.

**Don't contradict** the suicidal person. Empathy is more helpful. You won't argue him out of how he feels.

### For the Suicidal Person (adapt for the person who comes to you with a concern about someone)

**Q1** Are you feeling as if you want to harm yourself?

**Q2** If so, how would you do this?

**Q3** Do you ever wish you were dead?

**Q4** When was the last time you felt that way?

**Q5** Have you thought about how you would try to kill yourself?

**Q6** Do you have any weapons?

**Q7** If so, are they locked up? Who can get to them?

**Q8** Have you ever attempted to hurt yourself in the past? If so, when? *(A recent, nearly lethal attempt may indicate that this person is very serious in his desire to die. Numerous unsuccessful suicide attempts could indicate that the individual uses suicide attempts to gain attention. However, either way you must take the suicide talk seriously.)*

### General Questions for the Suicidal Person

**Q9** How old are you?

**Q10** Have you recently had a baby? *(This checks for post-partum depression.)*

**Q11** Have you suffered a recent loss?

- Suicide is the taking of your own life. Some 30,000 people in the U.S. die annually by their own hands.
- The rate of suicide in 15 to 24 year olds has tripled since 1960.
- People over 60 commit suicide more often than people of any other age group.

—WWW.NMHA.ORG

Q12 What has happened recently to make you feel so hopeless?

Q13 Do you ever abuse drugs or alcohol?

Q14 If so, when did you last use?

Q15 How often and how much do you use?

Q16 Has anyone in your family committed suicide or attempted suicide?

Q17 If so, who was it?

Q18 How old were you when it happened?

Q19 What happened?

Q20 Do you know why it occurred?

Q21 How did it make you feel?

Q22 Is there someone you'd like to get revenge on? Is there anyone you are very angry at? Have you ever thought of your death as the ultimate revenge?

Q23 What is most distressing to you when you think about the future?

Q24 Can you think of any reasons to go on living?

Q25 What would make life worth living for you? See if you can list ten things. Are any of them within reach?

Q26 Where are you spiritually?

Q27 Do you think that God cares if you live or die?

*Many suicides are preventable. Most suicidal people desperately want to live; they are just unable to see alternatives to their problems. Most suicidal people give definite warning signals of their suicidal intentions, but those in close contact are often unaware of the significance of these warnings or unsure what to do about them.*

—WWW.SUICIDOLOGY.ORG

**General Questions for the Friend or Family Member**

Q9 How old is your loved one?

Q10 Does he/she suffer from any painful or debilitating medical conditions?

Q11 Has this person suffered a recent loss or recently had a baby?

Q12 If not, are there any other recent distressing circumstances?

Q13 Is there a family history of suicide or attempted suicide?

Q14 Does this person abuse alcohol or drugs?

Q15 If so, has he/she ever tried to stop?

Q16 Has your loved one's behavior changed recently?

Q17 If so, in what ways?

Q18 Has this person been taking care of himself/herself physically?

**Q19** Is he/she sleeping regularly (i.e., not sleeping too much or too little)?

**Q20** Has your loved one been giving away important possessions?

**Q21** Has he/she seemed uninterested in plans for the future?

**Q22** Has he/she made jokes about death or disappearing?

**Q23** Is this person extremely angry?

**Q24** Would he/she like to get revenge on someone?

**Q25** Could suicide be a form of revenge for him/her?

*Four times more men than women complete suicide, but three times more women than men attempt suicide.*
—WWW.SUICIDOLOGY.ORG

## 4 WISE COUNSEL

**Protecting the suicidal person must take priority.** Don't worry about embarrassing the person by calling paramedics—better to be embarrassed than dead.

While some Christians resist suicide because they believe it is a sin, that standard is **meaningless to those with tunnel vision**.

Although it may comfort discouraged or sad people to know that God loves them, **suicidal people are often too depressed to believe it.** Avoid trite spiritual platitudes.

## 5 ACTION STEPS

### 1. Get Help Immediately

- Call police or paramedics if this person has a plan and the means to commit suicide. He or she must be protected.
- Inpatient psychiatric units are locked to keep people from harming themselves. Every attempt is made to remove the means of causing harm from the unit.
- Don't try to transport a suicidal person to the hospital by yourself. It's too dangerous.
- If the suicidal person is under the influence of drugs or alcohol, arrange for him or her to be supervised constantly while detoxing and becoming sober. At that time, the suicidal ideation should be re-assessed. If no longer suicidal, this person should be strongly encouraged to seek treatment for substance abuse.

In 2002 (the latest year for which we have national statistics), there were 31,655 suicides in the U.S. (87 suicides per day; 1 suicide every 17 minutes), with 11.0 of every 100,000 Americans killing themselves.
—WWW.SUICIDOLOGY.ORG

### 2. Follow Up

- See if the suicidal person will sign a contract stating that he/she will not attempt suicide for 24 hours. Of course, this contract is only as good as the suicidal person's word. It's not a legal document.
- If willing to sign a contract, send the person home with supervision.
- Reconnect with the suicidal person the next day (DON'T FORGET!), and see if the suicidal thoughts have subsided.
- If he/she has not improved, seek help.

### 3. Investigate the Tunnel Vision

- Sometimes the problem can actually be solved rather simply.
- Ask a person with tunnel vision to sign a contract to not harm himself/herself while you investigate the circumstances for three days. In that time, work to find some solutions.
- However, during those three days, the person should be supervised. If you can't make substantive progress in three days, then refer the person to a professional therapist or a hospital.

## 6 BIBLICAL INSIGHTS

***Then Saul said to his armorbearer, "Draw your sword, and thrust me through with it, lest these uncircumcised men come and thrust me through and abuse me." But his armorbearer would not, for he was greatly afraid. Therefore Saul took a sword and fell on it. —1 Samuel 31:4***

- Because Saul had turned away from God, he was left completely to his own devices. He had great potential in a high position as the chosen king of Israel, but he squandered it with jealousy, anger, and disobedience. In the end, when all was lost, he believed he had nowhere to turn but death.
- Suicide is attractive to a desperate person. These people need to be shown God's gracious love and forgiveness. There's always hope with God.

***Then he threw down the pieces of silver in the temple and departed, and went and hanged himself. —Matthew 27:5***

- Judas was a complex and deluded man, and his relationship to Christ was complicated. While he acknowledged that he had sinned, Judas didn't repent and seek reconciliation to Christ as Peter later did for his betrayal (John 21).

- Suicides aren't always impulsive decisions. For example, suicide often results from a prolonged, severe, deep depression. Because we can only guess at Judas' motivation for betraying Jesus, we need to be cautious in our conclusions about his life. Judas may have become angry and indignant, nursing his resentments when Christ failed to fulfill his expectations of what a Messiah should be and do.
- A genuine Christian doesn't lose his salvation by killing himself, but in the case of Judas, the Bible indicates that even though he regretted the consequences of his betrayal, he died lost and alienated from Christ (John 6:70; 17:12; Acts 1:25).
- Faced with the result of one horrible act that he couldn't undo, he made the mistake of committing another sin. We don't know what his final thoughts were, but by his self-destructive act, Judas eliminated the possibility of ever getting right with Christ.

*Suicide ranks third as a cause of death among young (15-24) Americans behind accidents and homicides.*

—WWW.SUICIDOLOGY.ORG

## 7 PRAYER STARTER

Dear Lord, my friend feels as if there is no reason to live. But You wouldn't agree with that statement. Please help my friend find true hope, peace, and purpose. Help him to know how much You love him. In Jesus' name, Amen.

## 8 RECOMMENDED RESOURCES

*Aftershock: Help, Hope, and Healing in the Wake of Suicide*, by David Cox and Candy Arrington

*Finding Your Way after the Suicide of Someone You Love*, by David B. Biebel and Suzanne L. Foster

*Grieving a Suicide: A Loved One's Search for Comfort, Answers, & Hope*, by Albert Y. Hsu

# Trauma

## 1 PORTRAITS

- Janet startled awake. Her heart was pounding and the sheets were tangled around her. For a few moments she wondered where she was. The nightmare had been so vivid and the screams had been real. "What is happening to me?" she wondered. The accident was three years ago, but lately the dreams were more frequent.
- Mindy has been in a cycle of bad relationships over the course of her college years—often with older men. She is only now beginning to understand that her desperate need comes from a time when her father walked out on her and her mom. That moment is forever etched in her brain and the pain is as fresh as ever.
- Rafe had been in a Bradley Fighting Vehicle when the roadside bomb went off. In the chaos and smoke inside, he could see body parts scattered around—one was his own leg. Now, three years later, Rafe is on medication to keep his rage from exploding at his wife and children.

## 2 DEFINITIONS AND KEY THOUGHTS

*After the terrorist attacks in the U.S. on September 11, 2001, thousands of Americans felt the threat of harm and a post traumatic stress disorder (PTSD) outbreak.*[1]

- Some events in life cause pain that **goes deeper and lasts a long time**. These are "traumas," and they include violent crimes, accidents, incidents in war, and any other shocking event.
- A trauma is a situation beyond control, one that shakes a person to the core. A trauma can lead to mental disorders or to suicide. Recovery is often slow, and flashbacks are common.
- Traumas may not even be remembered, but they can still **influence people** in certain unhealthy ways or cause them to make unhealthy decisions.
- Those with unreasolved traumas may **damage others**, including their own families.
- Traumatic events **overwhelm the person's ordinary adaptations or coping mechanisms** in life.
- With trauma, each component of the ordinary response to danger continues to persist in an altered state long after the actual danger is over. There are **profound and lasting changes** in psychological arousal, emotion, cognition, and memory.

- Symptoms of trauma include: anxiety and panic disorders; depression; intense fear; anger; loneliness; attachment disorders; flashbacks; helplessness; loss of control; threat of annihilation. The combination of panic, anxiety, flashbacks, and anger sometimes are labeled under the diagnosis of Post Traumatic Stress Disorder—PTSD.

- Traumatic reactions occur when the person is exposed to an intense emotional situation that threatens the life or well being of himself or others. When neither resistance nor escape is possible, the human system of self-defense becomes **overwhelmed and disorganized**. Traumatized people often act as if their nervous systems have been disconnected from the present. They become hypervigilant.

- Traumatic memory becomes encoded in an **abnormal form of memory** that breaks spontaneously into consciousness, both as flashbacks and as nightmares. The traumatic experience is not just remembered; it is relived.

- Traumatic memory is not a verbal, linear narrative, but can **have a frozen, wordless quality.** When high levels of adrenaline and other stress hormones circulate during the traumatic event, the memories are deeply imprinted.

- Traumatic memory may also **be suppressed**. The intrusion and suppression of the memory form a dynamic that doesn't provide a way to resolve the experience and achieve balance.

*Blessed be the God and Father of our Lord Jesus Christ, the Father of mercies and God of all comfort, who comforts us in all our tribulation, that we may be able to comfort those who are in any trouble, with the comfort with which we ourselves are comforted by God.*
—2 Corinthians 1:3-4

People may experience two distinct types of traumas: invasion and abandonment.

### Invasion Trauma

- **An event happened** and caused damage.

- **Emotional invasion** occurs when people feel criticized, shamed, or blamed, either verbally or nonverbally.

- **Physical invasion** occurs when a person is physically abused. This form of trauma may create permanent physical damage. The emotional effect of this can also be experienced if a person lives in a home where someone else is being physically harmed.

- **Sexual invasion** happens when a person is penetrated or touched in sexual areas in a manner that disrespects his personal boundaries and leaves him feeling confused and violated.

- **Spiritual invasion** takes place when people are led to believe that they are unworthy of God's love and grace. Often rigid, fear-based religious teaching, even if it is well-intended, can result in shame that people can't seem to shake.

### Abandonment Trauma

- **Something did *not* happen** to a person (such as not feeling loved, protected, or nurtured) that creates damage.
- Abandonment trauma can be **harder to recognize** because the person doesn't know what he is missing, never having had it.
- **Emotional abandonment** occurs when love, attention, care, nurture, and affirmation aren't given, resulting in profound loneliness.
- **Physical abandonment** happens when people's basic needs for food, shelter, and clothing aren't met. People who aren't touched enough—with hugs or cuddles—experience "touch deprivation." Another form occurs when people aren't getting enough information or modeling on physical self-care.
- **Sexual abandonment** occurs when parents and other responsible adults don't educate children about and model healthy sexuality. Lack of correct information can have devastating results.
- **Spiritual abandonment** happens when healthy spiritual teaching and modeling are not available.
- These two **categories can overlap.** Damage in one aspect of a person's life can have an effect in another. For example, a girl who is sexually abused may withdraw from people, even those who love her and could help heal the wounds from the abuse. Sexual invasion, then, led to emotional abandonment..

*The Lord gets his best soldiers out of the highlands of affliction.*
—C.H. Spurgeon

## 3 ASSESSMENT INTERVIEW

### General Questions

**Q1** Are you having physical symptoms? Are you able to eat and sleep? *(If the person is dealing with physical issues as a result of the trauma, encourage a medical checkup.)*

**Q2** On a scale of 1 to 10, with 1 being "feeling terrific" and 10 being "feeling suicidal," where would you place yourself on most days? *(If you sense that the person is suicidal, deal with that issue first. See the section on Suicide and get outside help.)*

**Q3** Describe the problems you are having.

**Q4** Do you recall a particular event in your life that was traumatic?

**Q5** If you don't recall anything in particular, what can you tell me about your childhood, other past relationships, and other situations in your life?

*Post traumatic stress disorder (PTSD) is the 5th most common psychiatric illness. In any given year, 5.6% of the U.S. population suffers from PTSD.*[7]

**Q6** Describe what you feel about that situation. *(Help the person express grief or anger.)*

**Q7** Have you ever sought help for this problem before?

**Q8** Did you receive help at that time?

**Q9** What is your daily life like for you currently?

**Q10** Do you feel safe?

**Q11** Who do you talk to about this?

**Q12** Do you have a support group or network with whom you feel safe?

## 4 WISE COUNSEL

If the person is exhibiting behavior that reveals past trauma that **can't be remembered** or attached directly to a specific event, refer the person to a Christian professional counselor.

While the traumatic event or events can be horrific and the resultant emotional damage overwhelming to the person who is traumatized, **healing from the effects of trauma is possible**.

Often, someone who is traumatized wonders if he is losing his mind. Reassure the person that **what he is experiencing is normal.**

The person needs **comfort, acceptance, and a nonjudgmental listening ear**. He wants to know that you can **give him hope**.

Losses need to be grieved and anger resolved in order to move forward. This can be **long-term work** and may involve individual or group counseling.

## 5 ACTION STEPS

### 1. Understand the Nature of the Trauma

- Discuss what happened, and try to remember as much as you can. There's no hurry, so take your time.
- You didn't deserve the hurts that happened to you, and you didn't cause them.
- Depending on the nature of the trauma, understand that you may need to erect some boundaries with particular people so that you won't be hurt again.

*The Lord is near to those who have a broken heart, and saves such as have a contrite spirit.*
—Psalm 34:18

> *The Lord does not measure out our afflictions according to our faults, but according to our strength, and looks not what we have deserved, but what we are able to bear.*
> —George Downame

**2. Express the Feelings**

- Express your real feelings. If you feel anger at the perpetrators of your trauma, express it.
- This doesn't necessarily mean you need to confront them. There are symbolic ways, such as writing letters that won't necessarily be sent, which can be just as powerful.
- If you're angry with God, express that as well. He can handle it.
- If you grieve over a loss experienced through the trauma, express that grief. (For help, see the section on Grief.)

**3. Know that You Will Heal**

- Healing will come with God's help.
- Find a counselor or support group that can help you take steps forward.

**4. Know that You Will Have Victory**

- Beyond just healing, you can have victory over the trauma. Begin to consider some of the strengths you will have in your life as a result of healing from this trauma.
- You will eventually be able to forgive those who hurt you—and possibly, yourself. And then, you'll be set free. (For more, see the section on Forgiveness.)
- Eventually, you will be able to comfort others who experience similar traumas.

## 6 BIBLICAL INSIGHTS

***Is it nothing to you, all you who pass by? Behold and see if there is any sorrow like my sorrow, which has been brought on me, which the Lord has inflicted in the day of His fierce anger. —Lamentations 1:12***

- God doesn't leave our side when we suffer.
- When we trust God, we can change our perspective on life's traumas from "Why me?" to "How can I grow from this?"

***And [Jonah] said to them, "Pick me up and throw me into the sea; then the sea will become calm for you. For I know that this great tempest is because of me." —Jonah 1:12***

- Trauma upon trauma eventually caused Jonah to turn to God. God rescued Jonah and gave him the opportunity to fulfill his promise.
- Traumatic experiences can drive people away from God or to Him. In both cases, a person may ask, "Why would God do this to me?" Those who turn *from* God ask the question in anger and accusation. Those who turn *toward* God ask the question to learn His lesson for their lives.
- When traumatic experiences come, turn to God, not away. As Jonah learned: "When my soul fainted within me, I remembered the LORD; and my prayer went up to You, into Your holy temple" (Jonah 2:7).

*God will never permit any troubles to come upon us unless he has a specific plan by which great blessing can come out of the difficulty.*
—PETER MARSHALL

***"Arise, go to Nineveh, that great city, and preach to it the message that I tell you." So Jonah arose and went to Nineveh, according to the word of the Lord. —Jonah 3:2-3***

- Trauma changes people. Jonah nearly died in the ocean—he couldn't help but be changed. Jonah recognized the hand of God in his circumstances, but when all hope was lost, God was there.
- When Jonah found himself alive on a beach, he praised God who had given him another chance. This time, when God called, Jonah obeyed. Trauma changes us—whether the change is good or bad often depends on how we respond. God uses our troubles as tools to shape our souls.

## 7 PRAYER STARTER

My friend is in a lot of pain today, Lord, remembering a situation of the past that still looms large across the landscape of his life. We don't yet understand why You allowed this to happen—what purpose it could possibly have—but we want to trust that You are forging a stronger person through this difficult time . . .

## 8 RECOMMENDED RESOURCES

*Coping with Trauma: Hope Through Understanding*, by Jon G. Allen

*Post Traumatic Stress Disorder*, Broadcast Cassette, by Focus on the Family

*Restoring Hope and Trust: An Illustrated Guide to Mastering Trauma*, by Lisa Lewis, Kay Kelly, and Jon G. Allen

# Workaholism

> *Don't let Satan let you overwork and then put you out of action for a long time.*
> —Charles Simeon

## 1 PORTRAITS

- "I can't remember the last time I really relaxed," explained Dave. "I think what seems to keep me going is fear—fear that if I do stop, I'll lose everything I've worked so hard to achieve." He continued, "My parents lived through the 50's and instilled in me the notion that what matters most is getting ahead in life. They raised me to never be in a position to depend on anyone for anything. Even when I'm with my wife and kids, I can't seem to stop thinking about work. Somehow, everything that isn't related to my work seems like a waste of time."
- Pam can't enjoy her home or her children. She constantly cleans, picks up after her kids, always attempting to maintain a spotless, "Better Homes and Gardens" house. The children aren't allowed to play anywhere but in their rooms.
- Bill is climbing the corporate ladder and faces expectations that he feels he must meet in order to make it to the next rung. The stress is affecting his family.

## 2 DEFINITIONS AND KEY THOUGHTS

### A Healthy Work Ethic

- Some Christians believe that work is a **form of worship**, a sacred extension of the ongoing creative process by which God still functions.
- Because of disobedience to God, man was cursed to eke out an existence from the earth, struggling to live by the sweat of his brow until death (Genesis 3:17-19). Yet **God has redeemed work** and looks upon people at work with dignity and protection.
- God wants us to work honestly, heartily, happily, and as though we are working for the Lord (Exodus 23:12; Ecclesiastes 5:19; Colossians 3:23).

### An Unhealthy Work Ethic

- Work life should be **managed** in the context of a healthy relation to God, marriage and family life, and commitments to church and community. When this **balance** is not found, work can become an idol, a terrible taskmaster.
- While God created work as a meaningful part of life, for some, for workaholics, work becomes the primary avenue by which they find **approval, respect, and success.**

## Workaholism

- Workaholism has become an **all-consuming obsession** for too many modern workers, a sleep-depriving, health-robbing, greed-festering monster that may be the most rewarded—and least challenged—addiction in America.
- This issue is **not limited to people in the workplace**. It can also include women at home who are striving to have the "perfect" home and family.
- Workaholism is an **addiction** and needs to be treated like one.

*You can always find reasons to work. There will always be one more thing to do. But when people don't take time out, they stop being productive. They stop being happy, and that affects the morale of everyone around."*
—Carisa Bianchi

## Symptoms of Workaholism

- Working **60-70 hours a week** or more.
- A **chronic sense of urgency** in every activity.
- An **inability to rest**.
- **"Hurry sickness,"** being time-conscious and rushed.
- An addictive **need for acceptance and significance** in the eyes of others as a result of one's work.
- **A workaholic ignores** the emotional and spiritual demands of **family,** under the guise that he is providing a better lifestyle.
- Workaholics are seen by one's children as **inattentive, irritable, lacking humor, and always in a hurry**.
- **They value performance** over showing love and grace.
- The family doesn't feel "safe." Aside from financial security, the family members know that their **feelings or concerns are generally not valued**. Playful times are replaced by **competition.**
- Workaholics struggle with a **poor self-image**, rigidity, and problems with intimacy in relationships.
- They view stress at work as **a challenge to overcome** and a way to find significance.

## 3 ASSESSMENT INTERVIEW

Like all addicts, workaholics need to admit their obsessive drivenness and confess its many costs. They neet to establish and maintain times for rest, play, family, and leisure. Work addicts need to realize that the deeper life with Christ comes only after they are able to be still and know God.

**Q1** Do you work more than 40 hours a week?

**Q2** Do you often feel fatigued and stressed?

> *I'm constantly amazed by the number of people who can't seem to control their own schedules. Over the years, I've had many executives come to me and say with pride: "Boy, last year I worked so hard that I didn't take any vacation." It's nothing to be proud of. I always feel like responding: "You dummy. You mean to tell me that you can take responsibility for an $80 million project and you can't plan two weeks out of the year to go off with your family and have some fun?"*
> —Lee Iacocca

**Q3** Do you have problems sleeping?

**Q4** Do you have stress-related physical issues such as back pain, headaches, indigestion, ulcers, or chronic fatigue?

**Q5** Do you take work home? on weekends? on vacation? on holidays?

**Q6** Do you feel guilty when you relax or have fun, especially when there is work to be done?

**Q7** Do you sometimes resent others for not working as hard as you do?

**Q8** Do you get impatient with coworkers who have other priorities besides work?

**Q9** Has your family given up expecting you on time?

**Q10** Do you find that it is difficult to schedule time for those you love?

**Q11** Are you able to have fun with your family?

**Q12** Do you suffer from "hurry sickness," and you're always in a rush?

**Q13** Do you feel that the more you work, the more pleasing you will be to God?

**Q14** Do you have difficulty saying "no?"

**Q15** Do you sometimes feel that people who have needs are weak?

**Q16** Do you feel better about yourself when you earn more money or realize achievements in your work?

**Q17** Do you feel that you do things rapidly to avoid wasting time?

**Q18** Do you often compare yourself to others?

**Q19** Do you find that free time bores you because you would rather be working?

**Q20** Tell me about your growing up years. What were your parents like?

**Q21** How did your parents assess your worth? Did you feel that you had to achieve at a certain level in order to be accepted or loved?

## 4 WISE COUNSEL

Generally, people who are addicted to work feel:

- highly self-critical
- a pervading sense of emptiness
- a compulsive need to do things perfectly and be better than others
- pain from the past—their worth can only be found in their achievements
- that unrelenting sacrificial service is honorable before God
- that they must measure up to their own impossible standards
- a constant struggle with pride

Communicate unconditional love and **avoid evaluative remarks.** Initially, affirm the person's inner qualities and the courage to address this issue.

**Express empathy about the stress** the person is experiencing. Give hope that you will help him find a way through the pressure.

The person may be completely unaware about what is fueling the stress and finds little value in self-reflection. You will need to gently encourage him to **explore the factors** that are fueling the addictive behavior.

Move the focus from himself and what he feels he must *do* to have God's unconditional acceptance. God is more concerned about who he is becoming than what he is doing.

God's invitation to the workaholic is to let Him take the burden of his life and give him rest in its place (Matthew 11:29).

## ACTION STEPS 5

### 1. Assess the Problem

- Ask: Why do you think you work so hard and so intensely? What do you think is behind your desire to succeed? *(Help the person perceive the problem and own it. )*
- Help him understand that workaholism is an addiction and needs to be treated as one.

### 2. Evaluate the Past

- Identify negative messages he received about self-worth from his parents, siblings, and/or peers.
- Point out that his significance is provided through Christ, not work.

### 3. Refocus on God

- Promote daily time for prayer, Scripture reading, and meditation.
- Tell the person that he needs to seek God for guidance as to the activities for the day.
- Encourage him to read and meditate on the Scriptures that demonstrate God's unconditional love and his identity as a follower of Jesus Christ. *(Be sure to place this activity in the context of a relationship and not just as another job or task.)*

### 4. Find Balance

- Evaluate the activities in his weekly schedule, and assess which involvements are unnecessary and are contributing to the addiction.

*The workaholic maintains a frantic schedule. He is consistently preoccupied with performance. He finds it difficult to refuse additional responsibilities. He is unable to relax. If someone you know exhibits these characteristics, he or she is probably a workaholic.*
—Bill Hybels

- Encourage a balance between time spent at work and time spent in meaningful relationships.
- Explain that work should be maintained in proper relation to God and to family. When this balance isn't in place, work can become an idol—a false god that is a terrible taskmaster.
- Have the person "schedule" times for leisure and play. Make sure that he treats these times as a priority.
- Encourage him to honor the Sabbath as a day of rest so his body and soul can be refreshed.

*There can be intemperance in work just as in drink.*
—C.S. Lewis

### 5. Slow Down

- Help the person establish a slower pace for each day and to seek rest.
- Remind him to honor the body that God has given him by getting sufficient rest, exercise, and eating a nutritionally-balanced diet.
- Explore ways that he can include enjoyable activities in his schedule—especially family time.
- Remind him that change takes time and that God will take care of the things that concern him (Matthew 6:25-34).

### 6. Get Support

Encourage him to seek help from a counselor, accountability partner, or group where the focus is on coming to terms with the underlying motivations for the addiction to work.

## 6 BIBLICAL INSIGHTS

***This is what the LORD has said: "Tomorrow is a Sabbath rest, a holy Sabbath to the Lord. Bake what you will bake today, and boil what you will boil; and lay up for yourselves all that remains, to be kept until morning." —Exodus 16:23***

- God gave His people a day of rest, a day when they were not supposed to work. But everyone had to work hard the day before to be able to rest completely on the Sabbath.
- To take full advantage of our day of rest and worship, we need to prepare ahead of time. That way, we won't need to run to the store or finish a work project. We need to be organized enough to be ready to rest and focus on God on Sundays.

***Then King Solomon raised up a labor force out of all Israel; and the labor force was thirty thousand men. And he sent them to Lebanon, ten thousand a month in shifts: they were one month in Lebanon and two months at home; Adoniram was in charge of the labor force. —1 Kings 5:13-14***

- God had given Solomon wisdom to rule the nation. There was peace in the land, so the nation devoted itself and its resources to building a glorious temple for God.

- As Solomon planned its construction, he used great wisdom. He drew upon the nation's labor force, divided it into three groups, and rotated the groups so they would work one month in Jerusalem and then two months at home.
- Solomon scheduled work without burning out his workers or hurting their families. No matter how important the work, the workers' families must not be neglected.

***Here is what I have seen: It is good and fitting for one to eat and drink, and to enjoy the good of all his labor in which he toils under the sun all the days of his life which God gives him; for it is his heritage. —Ecclesiastes 5:18***

- Work is a double-edged sword in Scripture. Transformed into "sweat" as part of the Curse after the Fall (Genesis 3:19), work is also an honored activity through which God gives many blessings.
- The Bible emphasizes the importance of work as a God-given activity in life. The ability to enjoy the fruits of our labor is also something God provides.
- The ability to work, enjoy work, make money, and share our income with others is a gift from God.

## 7 PRAYER STARTER

Lord, we know that it is good that we work honestly and diligently, and that work is part of Your plan for us. We know that You are honored through our sincere labor. As You help us with our tasks and occupations, help us also to honor You with our rest. Give us, God, the wisdom to achieve much needed balance so that we may be still and know that You are God. Free Your child here from the destructive pressures of workaholism . . .

## 8 RECOMMENDED RESOURCES

*Balance that Works When Life Doesn't,* Susie Larson

*Cleaning Up: One Man's Redemptive Journey Through the Seductive World of Corporate Crime,* by Barry Minkow

*Halftime,* by Bob Buford

*LifeKeys: Discovering Who You Are, Why You're Here, and What You Do Best,* by Jane Kise, David Stark, and Sandra Krebs Hersh

*Margin: Restoring Emotional, Physical, Financial, and Time Reserves to Overloaded Lives,* by Richard A. Swenson

*Your Work Matters to God,* by Doug Sherman

# Worry

## 1 PORTRAITS

- Amy just said "yes" to Don's proposal, and now they are engaged. Later that night as Don lies in bed, he wonders how in the world will he be able to support her when he can barely live alone on what he makes.
- Randy is two hours late getting home from being out with his buddies. His parents are angry with him for not calling, but all they can think of is that he must have had car trouble, or worse, an accident.
- Phil joined his department of five employees two years ago. Now they are down to three, and rumor has it that soon they will be down to two.
- Christine is pregnant again. After losing the last baby during the second trimester, she can't help but wonder if this new little child will ever have a chance to see this world.

## 2 DEFINITIONS AND KEY THOUGHTS

- Worry is defined by Webster as "mental distress or agitation resulting from concern usually for something impending or anticipated." In other words, worry is about **things that have not happened.** Worry is not an emotion—it is a mental obsession.
- It is natural to be worried or anxious when things are tough or unpredictable or when a solution to a particular problem is not clearly evident. This causes us to **replay possible outcomes** over and over again in our minds. Even when we can see a solution in our minds, we sometimes continue to worry, refusing to be satisfied until the solution becomes a reality.
- Being concerned can be positive when it propels us to action—such as seeing a doctor when we are ill or a mechanic when the car sounds strange. But **worry is rarely tied to constructive action and is usually unproductive**.
- Worry rises to an unhealthy level and **takes its toll** when:

  You're not sleeping

  You're not productive

  You're worried about two or more topics more days than not

  You're focusing on situations of worry more than the other business of life

  Your life feels out of control

*Worry is like a rocking chair; it'll give you something to do, but it won't get you anywhere.*
—Unknown

- Worrying about many things at once can contribute to the development of an **unhealthy level of stress**. This stress exhibits itself in an anxiety level that just won't go away.
- Worry is simply a symptom of fear, and **fear is the opposite of faith**. When we operate in fear or worry, we don't have the faith that God has a plan.

3

## ASSESSMENT INTERVIEW

Sometimes we ask questions not to solicit information, but to help the person see things differently. In dealing with worry and anxiety, this might be an appropriate time for such a strategy.

**Q1** What has worried you the most in the past that you no longer worry about?

**Q2** Did these previous situations work out the way you thought they would, or did they work out differently than expected?

**Q3** Did the pain of these previous situations help you to grow? If so, how?

**Q4** What do you currently worry about the most?

**Q5** How does your worry affect your mood, your performance, and your relationships?

**Q6** Do you think that these problems are too big for God?

**Q7** Do you believe that you are important to God?

**Q8** Will God take care of you in this current situation?

**Q9** Do you have control over whether you worry or not?

**Q10** What are some truths and promises in the Bible that help us trust God more so that our worry subsides?

**Q11** What is the worst thing that can happen in this current situation?

**Q12** How has worrying helped you in the past?

**Q13** Do you think that worrying will help you now?

**Q14** What difference will it make a hundred years from now?

> *Much that worries us beforehand can afterwards, quite unexpectedly, have a happy and simple solution. Worries just don't matter. Things really are in a better hand than ours.*
>
> —Dietrich Bonhoeffer

## 4 WISE COUNSEL

The worrier needs to understand that he really **does have control** over whether he worries or not. Some people are more inclined to worry than others. That isn't a character flaw, it's just a built-in reminder to pray and trust the Lord.

He **needs a plan** to help keep him from unnecessary worry. In the Action Steps, help him to devise that plan and pray through it. Let him allow his faith and actions coincide.

It's easy to simply say, "Don't worry," but it is difficult to change this pattern of thinking. One approach is to **set limits** so that the worry doesn't continue to rage out of control.

## 5 ACTION STEPS

The following plan is designed to help aid the person in changing the way he thinks about any issue that seems to stimulate worry.

### 1. Start Each Day with God

- Begin each day with time alone with God. Tell Him the concerns of the day (this is your time to pray about your problems—see Step 2).
- Anticipate your day. Pray about what's ahead, ask God to give you peace.

*To say that we are waiting on the Lord, and then to go around with a sense of worry, misery, and dread, is to contradict the truth.*
—Rosemarie Scotti Hughes

### 2. Pray about Your Worries

- Set up a specific time in which you can pray about your worries.
- Limit worrying to a "worry list," and take that list to the Lord in your daily Bible and prayer time.
- During the course of the day, when a worry strikes you, repeat the following sentence: "I will take care of that problem with God at my prayer time tomorrow morning."
- During the next prayer time, bring the worrisome situation to God, and ask for guidance and direction.

### 3. Keep a Journal

- Write down the prayer requests and the worries you bring to God.

- Write down the answers God gives. Go back and read these answers as constant encouragement that any new requests you bring to God will be answered one way or another.
- As you talk to God, write down anything you feel He is telling you about your course of action. Keep in mind that the course of action may be to purposefully do nothing until God gives you further direction.

### 4. Set Boundaries

- To prevent worrying unrealistically about a situation, get facts and expert advice.
- Set deadlines to make decisions rather than ruminating forever.
- Realize that you won't please everyone all the time.
- Learn to say "no."

### 5. Think Differently

- Delegate chores and other responsibilities.
- Give yourself permission to relax and to make mistakes.
- Eat, sleep, and exercise properly.
- Keep a sense of perspective and try to see the humor in a situation.
- De-clutter and organize, using calendars and to-do lists.
- Mentally put your worries in a box with a lid, and put them on the top shelf of your closet. No peeking!

### 6. Seek Balance

The goal is to walk in peace, calm, trust, and assurance by finding the balance of prayer action, and ultimately, freedom from worry.

*The next moment is as much beyond our grasp, and as much in God's care, as that a hundred years away. Care for the next minute is just as foolish as care for a day in the next thousand years. In neither can we do anything, in both God is doing everything.*
—C.S. Lewis

6

## BIBLICAL INSIGHTS

***And when Pharaoh drew near, the children of Israel lifted their eyes, and behold, the Egyptians marched after them. So they were very afraid, and the children of Israel cried out to the Lord. —Exodus 14:10***

- The Israelites found themselves trapped between Pharaoh's army and the waters of the Red Sea. In panic, they accused Moses of leading them to their deaths. By this time, Moses had seen enough of the power of God to respond in confidence.
- What unyielding obstacles are you facing? Don't panic. Instead, turn to God and trust in His power to do what seems impossible.

***Therefore do not worry about tomorrow, for tomorrow will worry about its own things. Sufficient for the day is its own trouble. —Matthew 6:34***

- Worry fills people's minds with useless clutter that leaves no room for God. Worry clouds perspective, causing people to focus on themselves rather than on God. Jesus said that God feeds the birds and clothes the flowers, so He will take care of His children.
- Trusting God involves trusting Him to care for us. Jesus tells us to "seek first the kingdom of God and His righteousness." As, believers we still must work to meet our needs. We don't sit back and expect God to do it all. We work, but we don't worry because we know that God will care for us.

***Then He said to His disciples, "Therefore I say to you, do not worry about your life, what you will eat; nor about the body, what you will put on. Life is more than food, and the body is more than clothing." —Luke 12:22-23***

- Worry can be a time-consuming, almost obsessive, behavior. After all, every day brings new things to worry about! Worrying about every situation in life—whether big or small—will only drive us to distraction.
- Not one problem is ever solved by worrying about it. In fact, many problems get worse because worry is immobilizing and no action is being taken to try to work through the dilemma.
- Jesus has the perfect solution for worry. Instead of worrying, He invites us to put our faith in God's provision and care. This can free us from the anxiety that is caused by worry.
- Trusting God doesn't mean that we shouldn't have goals, plans, investments, and so on. It does mean, however, that in everything, we should trust in God, putting Him first in our lives.

*Be anxious for nothing, but in everything by prayer and supplication, with thanksgiving, let your requests be made known to God; and the peace of God, which surpasses all understanding, will guard your hearts and minds through Christ Jesus.*

—PHILIPPIANS 4:6-7

***For God has not given us a spirit of fear, but of power and of love and of a sound mind. —2 Timothy 1:7***

- Those who worry aren't trusting God. Worry can be a natural first reaction to an uncertain situation, but persistent worry reveals a lack of trust that God is in charge.
- *Power* helps us have strength of character and confidence in any situation. *Love* helps us graciously deal with difficult people. A *sound mind* helps us remain self-controlled and self-disciplined no matter what happens.
- We can set aside our worry and replace it with these gifts from God.

## 7 PRAYER STARTER

Worry is immobilizing Your child today, Lord. We know that we don't know the future and You do. We know that we need to trust You, so we bring our worries to You today Lord, like a burden we can't carry, and we ask that You take them . . .

## 8 RECOMMENDED RESOURCES

*Certain Peace in Uncertain Times*, by Shirley Dobson

*How to Win over Worry*, by John Haggai

*Letting Go of Worry and Anxiety*, by Pam Vredevelt

*Living Above Worry and Stress*, Women of Faith Study Guide Series

*The Worry Workbook: Twelve Steps to Anxiety-Free Living*, by Les Carter and Frank Minirth

# Endnotes

## Abortion

1 David C. Reardon, *Aborted Women—Silent No More,* (Chicago: Loyola University Press, 1987) 11-21. See also, Mary K. Zimmerman, *Passage Through Abortion* (New York: Praeger Publishers, 1977) 62-70, and W. B. Miller, "An Empirical Study of the Psychological Antecedents and Consequences of Induced Abortion," J Social Issues 48(3):67-93 (1992).

2 Yvonne Florczak-Seeman, *A Time to Speak: A Healing Journal for Post-Abortive Women* (Clarendon Hills, Ill.: Love from Above, Inc., 2005). Used by permission. See www.lovefromaboveinc.com

3 Los Angeles Times Poll, March 19, 1989, question 76.

4 Lilo T. Strauss, Joy Herndon, Jeani Chang, Wilda Y. Parker, Sonya V. Bowens, Suzanne B. Zane, Cynthia J. Berg, Abortion Surveillance: United States, 2001, Division of Reproductive Health: National Center for Chronic Disease Prevention and Health Promotion.

## Addictions

1 National Center for Chronic Disease Prevention and Health Promotion, General Alcohol Information, September 2004, <http://www.cdc.gov/alcohol/factsheets/general_information.htm> (19 May 2005).

2 Pat Carnes, *Don't Call It Love* (New York: Bantam Books, 1991).

3 Mark Laaser.

4 National Center for Chronic Disease Prevention and Health Promotion, General Alcohol Information, September 2004.

5 National Center for Chronic Disease Prevention and Health Promotion, General Alcohol Information, September 2004.

6 National Center for Chronic Disease Prevention and Health Promotion, General Alcohol Information, September 2004.

7 www.stopaddiction.com; accessed July 2005.

8 National Center for Health Statistics. Health, United States, 2004: With Chartbook on Trends in the Health of Americans. (Hyattsville, Maryland: 2004).

9 Lynn F. Ranew and Daniel A. Serritella, *Handbook of Differential Treatments for Addictions* (Allyn and Bacon, 1992), 85.

10 Ranew and Serritella, *Handbook of Differential Treatments for Addictions,* 85.

## Adultery

1 Joyce Brothers, "Why Wives Have Affairs" in *Parade Magazine,* February 18, 1990, 4.

2 Andrew Greeley, "The Bad News is Not So Bad" in *Christianity Today,* March 1992, 42-43.

## Aging

1 Federal Interagency Forum on Aging Related Statistics, www.agingstats.gov/chartbook2004. November 18, 2004.

2 www.aoa.gov; accessed July 2005.

3 www.aoa.gov; accessed July 2005.

4 www.aoa.gov; accessed July 2005.

5 www.cdc.gov/nchs; accessed July 2005.

6 www.cdc.gov; accessed July 2005.

## Anger

1 NIMH Press Office (June 5, 2006). "Intermittent Explosive Disorder Affects Up to 16 Million Americans," www.nimh.nih.gov/press.

## Death

1 David K. Switzer.

## Depression

1 Archibald D. Hart and Catherine Hart Weber, *Unveiling Depression in Women: A Practical Guide to Understanding and Overcoming Depression.*

2 www.nimh.nih.gov/publicat/depression; accessed July 2005.

3 www.depression.com; accessed July 2005.

4 National Institutes of Health, 2003 statistics.

5 www.christianitytoday.com

## Divorce

1 Population Reference Bureau, "2000 Census Data—Living Arrangements Profile for United States," Analysis of Data from the U.S. Census Bureau, for The Annie E. Casey Foundation, (accessed May 2005 from www.aecf.org/cgi-bin/aeccensus.cgi?action=profileresults&area=00N: Annie E. Casey Foundation).

2 The Barna Group, "Born Again Christians Just as Likely to Divorce as Non-Christians," The Barna Update, 8 September 2004 [journal online]; available from http://www.barna.org/FlexPage.aspx?Page=BarnaUpdate&BarnaUpdateID=170; accessed May 2005.

3 The Barna Group, "Born Again Christians Just as Likely to Divorce as Non-Christians."

4 The Barna Group, "Born Again Christians Just as Likely to Divorce as Non-Christians."

5 Scott Stanley, *Personal Communication.*

6 Judith S. Wallerstein and Sandra Blakeslee, *The Good Marriage: How & Why Love Lasts* (New York, Houghton Mifflin Company, 1995), 6.

7 The Barna Group, "Born Again Christians Just as Likely to Divorce as Non-Christians."

8 The Barna Group, "Born Again Christians Just as Likely to Divorce as Non-Christians."

9 The Barna Group, "Born Again Christians Just as Likely to Divorce as Non-Christians."

## Fear and Anxiety

1 From The Anxiety Disorders Association of America at www.ADAA.org

2 From The Anxiety Disorders Association of America at www.ADAA.org

## Forgiveness

1 Everett L. Worthington, Jr., *Forgiveness and Reconciliation* (New York: Routledge, 2006), 66-67.

2 Everett L. Worthington Jr., "Forgiveness: Laying the Emotional Foundation," *Christian Counseling Today,* 12(3), (2004), 46.

3 Ibid.

4 Everett L. Worthington Jr., *The Soul Care Bible* (American Association of Christian Counselors: USA, 2001).

## Grief and Loss

1 Elisabeth Kubler-Ross, *On Death and Dying.*

## Love/Belonging

1 Gary Chapman, *The Five Love Languages* (Chicago: Northfield Publishing, 2004).

## Money Crisis

1 Margaret Mannix, "How to Bail Out of Debt," *US News and World Report,* 15 February 1993, 83.

## Pain/Chronic Pain

1 Corrie Ten Boom, *The Hiding Place* (Old Tappan, N.J.: Fleming H. Revell, 1971).

## Parenting

1 David Blackenhorn, *Fatherless America: Confronting Our Most Urgent Social Problem* (New York, BasicBooks, 1995).

2 Rebecca O'Neill, "Experiments in Living: The Fatherless Family" (Accessed June 2005 from http://www.civitas.org.uk: The Institute for the Study of Civil Society, September 2002).

3 Lawrence Bauman and Robert Riche, *The Ten Most Troublesome Teen-age Problems and How to Solve Them,* (Secaucus, NJ: Citadel Press, 1998), 8.

4 Archibald D. Hart, *Stress and Your Child: Know the Signs and Prevent the Harm,* (Dallas: Word, 1992).

5 Lawrence Bauman and Robert Riche, *The Ten Most Troublesome Teen-age Problems and How to Solve Them* (Secaucus, N.J.: Citadel Press, 1998), 7.

6 The National Center for Fathering, The Consequences of Fatherlessness (accessed June 2005 from http://www.fathers.com/research/consequences.html: Author).

## Sexual Abuse

1 National Center for Injury Prevention and Control, Sexual Violence: Fact Sheet (April 2005), http://www.cdc.gove/ncipc/factsheets/svfacts.htm (accessed 19 May 2005).

2 D. Finkelhor, G. Hotaling, I. A. Lewis, and C. Smith, "Sexual Abuse in a National Survey of Adult Men and Women: Prevalence, Characteristics, and Risk Factors," Child Abuse & Neglect, 14, 19–28 (1990); C. Bagley, "Development of a Measure of Unwanted Sexual Contact in Childhood, for Use in Community Mental Health Surveys," Psychological Reports, 66, 401-402 (1990).

## Stress

1 National Institute of Occupational Safety and Health (1999).

2 "Stress at Work," retrieved from www.cdc.gov.

3 "Stress at Work," retrieved from www.cdc.gov.

## Trauma

1 Nikki N. Jordan. C. W. Hoge, S. K. Tobler, J. Wells, G. J. Dydek, and W. E. Egerton, "Mental Health Impact of 9/11 Pentagon Attack: Validation of a Rapid Assessment Tool," American Journal of Preventive Medicine, 26 (4) (April 2004), 284-94.

2 National Institute of Mental Health, Reliving Trauma: Post-Traumatic Stress Disorder, A Brief Overview of the Symptoms, Treatments, and Research Findings (2001); O Frans, P.A. Rimmö, L. Aberg, and M. Fredrikson, "Trauma Exposure and Post-Traumatic Stress Disorder in the General Population," Acta Psychiatrica Scandinavica 111 (4) (April 2005), 291-93.